THE OTHER VOICE

Other books by Brent A. Haskell

JOURNEY BEYOND WORDS
A Companion to the Workbook of the Course

A **Miracles Studies** Book

THE
OTHER VOICE

A COMPANION
TO
THE TEXT
OF
THE COURSE
CHAPTERS 1-15

Received by
Brent A. Haskell, Ph.D., D.O.

DeVorss Publications
Camarillo, California

The Other Voice
Copyright © 1997
by Brent A. Haskell

ISBN: 978-087516-715-2
Library of Congress Card Catalog Number: 97-77527
Third Printing, 2011

DeVorss & Company, Publisher
P.O. Box 1389
Camarillo CA 93011-1389
www.devorss.com

Printed in the United States of America

MIRACLES STUDIES

is a term suggested

by the

Foundation for Inner Peace,

and which may be used

to designate materials

which provide information

about and/or interpretation of

A COURSE IN MIRACLES.

Such materials pertain to,

but should not

be confused with,

the original

Course.

TABLE OF CONTENTS

PREFACE

The Jeshua Tapes are a series of channeled auditory tapes whose reception by me began in November, 1989, and continues into the present. The source of these tapes refers to himself as Jeshua, also as Jesus, and therefore also as the author of *A Course in Miracles*. With the exception of the very first one, the first forty-nine of the tapes have become the book Journey Beyond Words, which was published in 1994. *Journey* was given as a companion to the Workbook of *A Course in Miracles*. The fifty-two tapes which comprise *The Other Voice* were given as companion material to the Text of the Course, Chapters 1-15. A subsequent volume will accompany Chapters 16-31.

One of the questions I needed to address during the reception and subsequent publication of this material was why the author felt that he needed to give us more material relating to the Course, especially since the Course seems so complete as it was originally given. The answer to that question has presented itself in the years since *Journey* was released and I have been afforded the opportunity to travel around the country and share Jeshua's message with fellow students of the Course.

There are many passages in the Course which relate to a very important theme, although a theme which seems to have escaped the attention of many, perhaps most, Course students and teachers. This theme relates to the Course's description of what our thoughts are, and how our thoughts and thinking function in our lives here in this world of space and time. An understanding of this theme and its importance is essential if we are to capture the real message that the author is attempting to bring to us. I have attempted to clarify and discuss this very important theme in the subsequent Prologue to this book.

Scattered throughout the Course are other statements which have great bearing on our ability to understand and experience its message, but which present themselves in a fashion subtle enough to be easily overlooked. Given the masterfulness with which the author has brought the Course to us, it is reasonable to assume that those statements are presented in that fashion for a very good reason. That reason, in my opinion, is that the emphases on these aspects of the Course were planned for a later time, when we were more ready to hear and accept them. That answers for me the question of why more material relating to the Course would eventually appear. And now, some twenty-odd years after the Course was initially published, many of its students are ready to give heed to these statements, and to take the next steps on the journey that must take us to the experience of the peace of God.

Thus it is that *Journey Beyond Words* and *The Other Voice* do not really contain anything new, nor information that cannot be gleaned from the Course itself. However, they do bring emphasis to important themes which many of us, including myself, had not noticed until Jeshua brought it to our attention through new material. An excellent example of such material is the lengthy discussion of values and valuing which is to be found in *Journey Beyond Words*.

Given as companion material to the Text of the Course, the chapters of *The Other Voice* exactly parallel the chapters and sections of the Text, Chapters 1-15. The words bring new meaning, fresh insights, and a clarity much desired by many Course students. But beyond that, the material allows us to hear the message of the Course from a different vantage point, from a perspective which lies beyond the ego. A great deal of the Course is written to the ego. That is to say that it speaks to us as if we actually were egos, and as if the ego actually existed. It is now time to let that notion go. For the truth remains that from within the framework of the ego, we cannot truly come to the experience of the peace of God. Thus the purpose of *The Other Voice* is to help us move to a clearer understanding of the message of the Course, so that from there we can proceed beyond the words, past the message itself, to the peace of God.

The section entitled The World of *A Course in Miracles* is designed to serve as an introduction to the principles of the Course for those readers who may be less familiar with the Course than others. The section also serves to introduce some of the significant concepts which appear in the Jeshua tapes, as well as in the Course itself. The reader may wish to be aware that the section was written by myself, and is not to be construed as coming directly from Jeshua. The reader may also wish to refer to the Preface of the Course itself, wherein is contained a synoptical discussion of what the Course says.

The Prologue is a discussion of what the Course says about our thoughts themselves, and about their domain, which is consciousness. When we allow the specified collection of seemingly isolated passages from the Course to come together to form a unified whole, we discover that the realm of thought is not at all what we had supposed it to be. The conclusions we arrive at are, in my opinion, of great importance if we are to truly understand our life here in space and time, and if we are to be at all successful in our attempts to hear the message of the Other Voice, which is really the same as the Voice of the Holy Spirit, the Voice of God, and the Voice of our inner Self.

All the material in the fifty-two chapters which comprise the body of the book came directly from Jeshua. Given in auditory form, it has been edited, under guidance, for the purpose of readability. It is my intent and belief that the basic content and meaning of the material has been unchanged.

Appendix I is an outline which lists the chapters of *The Other Voice* and specifies which chapter and sections of the Text are being discussed by Jeshua in each of those chapters. The student may wish to use the Course and this book together as he endeavors to experience the truth contained in the Course.

Appendix II is a list of the direct quotations from *A Course in Miracles*. I extend my gratitude to the Foundation for Inner Peace, which holds the copyright and trademark on the Course, for allowing those references.

Being a part of the reception and dissemination of the Jeshua material has been without question the most significant event of my life. A number of friends and colleagues, not all named here, have been instrumental in making the production of this book possible. My gratitude goes out to each of them.

I extend my heartfelt thanks to Carole Flaherty and Don Merrill, who devoted many hours to the transcription of the original tapes. In addition, Carole was one of our friends who spent significant time proofreading the manuscript and offering helpful suggestions.

The other friends who offered their skills and assistance with proofreading the manuscript are Bob Sandoe, Carol Fritz, and Lon and Meredi Hatfield. I extend my gratitude to them for their help.

I am grateful to Ed Mayer for his gifts of love and personal support of my work. I am most grateful, however, for the simple fact that he is my very dear friend.

The members of our Course in Miracles study group in Des Moines, Iowa, have remained, even across the miles, my friends and family. My gratitude goes out to them at this time.

I am extremely grateful to my beloved wife, Sydney (same wife, different name) for her willingness to support and be part of this work. Her sharing of the vision of this work has been invaluable. I extend to her my gratitude for being my wife, my colleague, and my best friend.

Lastly, I wish to express my deep appreciation to the kind, courteous, and very professional staff at DeVorss and Company. Arthur Vergara has been very helpful and cooperative with the editing of this book, as well as *Journey Beyond Words*. Gary Peattie has lent his creative energies to the design of the covers for both books, and with great success. Hedda Lark has always been willing to offer much appreciated good advice, advice based upon her many years of experience in the field. They have treated me very professionally as an author. But beyond that, they have treated me as a friend. To each of them, a heartfelt thank you.

Brent A. Haskell, Ph.D., D.O.

WHAT IS *A COURSE IN MIRACLES*?
And How Does The Other Voice Relate to It?

A Course in Miracles was first published in 1976. Since that time approximately one million copies have been printed. The Course, which states its own purpose to be that of a teaching device, is comprised of three sections, The Text, The Workbook, and The Manual for Teachers. The Text is primarily theoretical, and describes the thought system upon which the message of the Course is based. The Workbook consists of 365 Daily Lessons, which may be used on a daily basis over one full year. There is, however, no pressure on the student to strictly adhere to a one-a-day format, only the suggestion that the student not do more than one lesson in a given day. The Workbook emphasizes the experience of the Course through application, which applications are often suggested in the Lessons. The Manual for Teachers has a question and answer format, and appears designed to answer many of the common questions which may arise during the student's learning. It also includes a Clarification of Terms, which explains a number of terms from within the framework of the Course.

The story of how the Course came to be is both inspiring and fascinating. The story has been admirably told by Robert Skutch in a book entitled *Journey Without Distance*, which is available from bookstores, or from the Foundation for Inner Peace, holders of the copyright and trademark on the Course.

A Course in Miracles came into being as a collaborative venture between Helen Schucman, William Thetford, and a Voice which spoke through Helen. Helen's function was to receive the material from the Voice and write it down. Bill's function was, in part, to type the material from the "dictation" Helen had taken. There was no doubt on the part of Helen and Bill that this was a mutual project which they were involved in together.

The coming of the Course was preceded by an experience in which Bill, after one too many frustrating staff meetings, became overwhelmed with an inner realization that "there must be another way" for us to relate to each other. Helen, as if guided, agreed to help him find it. What *A Course in Miracles* became is "another way", another way of seeing and experiencing ourselves, our relationships, the world, and life itself.

The Course suggests that there does exist a universal experience (might we call it Truth?) which we all, of necessity, will one day share. It also states that a universal theology is not possible, which is to say that there must exist different, yet valid, pathways to that Truth. The Course is one of those pathways.

The universal experience described in the Course is one which includes the awareness that we all are One with God and with each other, and which also creates for us a life of peace, love, joy, and freedom. If there is within you, as there was within Bill Thetford, a quiet longing for "another way," rest assured that the pathway is there awaiting you. And it may be *A Course in Miracles*.

Insofar as Jeshua refers to himself as the author of the Course, we are wont to ask certain questions. Whence the name Jeshua? Why the need for more material from the same source? If it is the same author, should this material be treated as more of the original *A Course in Miracles*, or as it states itself to be, a discussion of the original Course?

Historically, one of the names used for Jesus has been Jeshua (sometimes Yeshua). Since the Course implies that Jesus is the Voice that Helen heard, the two names can be seen as compatible.

Over the years, I have met many persons who aspired to experience the message of the Course, but who, as one friend put it, "couldn't get past the language." This simply meant that the terminology, the wording, the metaphors of the Course were not conducive to their quest for peace. The Jeshua material comes to us in conversational tone, which makes it easier for many to relate to and understand. Such has definitely been the case for many of the thousands who have read *Journey Beyond Words*. Even though I personally have never had difficulty with the language of the Course, the Jeshua material has greatly clarified my understanding of the same Course. To that end, there may be many like myself who will benefit from its presence in their lives. Thus, the simplest reason for the appearance of the Jeshua material is the clarification of the meaning of the Course itself.

As mentioned in the Preface, I now believe that The Jeshua Tapes are, in part, designed to clarify and emphasize aspects of the Course which, within the imagined flow of time, needed to be emphasized now, rather than at the time of its initial release. It is only reasonable that more material would come to accompany the original Course as we have become ready to receive it. It is likewise reasonable that more shall be coming in the future, as we in turn become ready for it.

The Foundation for Inner Peace has a goal, with which I concur, which is to ensure that any reader not become confused about what is THE *A Course in Miracles* (meaning the original Course), and what is discussion of, or interpretation of it. As Jeshua states at the beginning of the book, and often throughout, this material is a discussion of *A Course in Miracles*. In that regard, this book, in my opinion, consists of material which is designed to accompany the Course and serve as an adjunct to it.

To that end, one point needs to be made. There are many references by Jeshua to "the Course" and also to "this Course." Those references should be understood as references to *A Course in Miracles*, and not as implying that this material is THE Course itself.

The Jeshua material uses language and metaphors different from the Course, which, I believe, is for reasons stated above. This does not change the fact that its goal, like the Course itself, is to guide us to the universal experience of truth, and to allow us to open to the awareness of God, which must, as always, lie deep within.

THE WORLD OF *A COURSE IN MIRACLES*

As you begin to experience *A Course in Miracles*, you will find yourself entering a new world. Contained within its pages are the tools which will allow you to see your life in a completely different light. What you will discover is a world of unchangeable love, a world of unshakable peace, a world of childlike joy, and a world of absolute freedom. This love, this peace, this joy, and this freedom are so great that they extend even beyond what we can comprehend with our thinking minds. This new world of *A Course in Miracles* already exists deep within you, where it has always been, and shall always remain. And all it takes to enter that world is your own willingness to reconsider, to challenge, every belief you now hold.

When your body dies, YOU do not die. The ultimate reality of what you are does not lie in your body, but in the Spirit that continues to exist after you die. Most of you reading these words already believe that to be true. The real You, which is created in the image of God, is Spirit. It is that Spirit which is part of God, and which shares with Him His creative power. One of the fundamental messages of *A Course in Miracles* is that this Spirit, which IS the reality of what you are, is alive and well right now, even though you seem to currently exist as your body. Your Spirit does not cease to exercise its creative power, it does not leave for distant parts of the universe, simply because you right now seem to be walking around in your body. Because Spirit is alive and well RIGHT NOW, and because it IS your source of creative power, your Spirit is active in this world, NOW. As such, it is your Spirit that determines what you experience, and what seems to happen to you. The physical world is controlled by the creative power of Spirit, and not the other way around. That awareness suddenly turns the world upside down, as you come to realize that everything in your life has its source in the creative power of your Spirit. That awareness shall become for you a source of great peace, and great joy.

In a word, the world of *A Course in Miracles* is a world of freedom. That is all. If you understood freedom in its entirety, freedom as it truly is, no further words would be necessary. You are free. That is all.

Your real nature is Spirit. And as Spirit you are free. Spirit lives without limitation. It is not limited by space or time. You could only say that Spirit exists everywhere, forever and ever, without beginning and without end. It is in this sense that we are created in the image of God, who likewise is Spirit. Soon, as the Course spells them out for you, you begin to realize the implications of being Spirit, and of being totally free.

Spirit is as free as an idea. In that sense It is completely safe and beyond attack. For what can harm an idea? Spirit is beyond being threatened by anything. It is completely safe in God's world. There is no external circumstance which can alter the nature of your Spirit. Or in the words of the Course, you are invulnerable.

Just as you are invulnerable, so is God Himself. A being who is invulnerable NEVER has any reason to fear the attack of another being. Indeed, a being who is truly invulnerable is incapable of even sensing that an attack is present. As a Being possessed of infinite strength, God is completely beyond being attacked, threatened, or offended by ANYTHING His Son might choose to experience. Because that is so, God naturally extends to His Son absolute freedom to be and to experience whatever he can imagine. The extension to another of such complete freedom is what you shall come to know as Love. Such Love is only possible when seen through the eyes of Spirit.

As a Being of Spirit, created by God in His own image, you possess other attributes which we find delineated in the Course. Your mind is part of God's Mind. This makes you holy, because you are part of God. This also means that the strength of God is within you, that the Love of God is part of your being, that the vision which can and does see the truth about Life is within your mind. It also means that you, as Spirit, and as part of God, are always sustained and protected by the Love of God. There is within each of us the desire to be cared for, protected, and loved. The God of *A Course in Miracles* blesses us with just those gifts, raised to perfection, and extended without exception of any kind.

As we struggle and toil through this earthly life, it is far from obvious that the preceding paragraphs are true. That is because we view this world through eyes which do not see the truth. We make our interpretations of what this world is based upon the thoughts within our brains. The Course refers to those thoughts as the "thoughts we think we think," but which are not our real thoughts.

In order to experience the world of *A Course in Miracles* we must be willing to consider the notion that the thoughts of the brain do not bring evidence of what is true. In fact, we must open to the awareness that it is not even possible to discover our true nature so long as we insist upon functioning within the thought system of this world.

The world of *A Course in Miracles* is to be found beyond your thoughts. The thoughts of this world, the thoughts of the brain, take the form of perception. Perceptions are always formed in response to an experience which is born in the creative part of your mind and then projected onto the screen of space and time. Your perceptions are thoughts formed after the fact, about an experience born in your mind. *A Course in Miracles* states this by saying that you see only the past, and that your earthly mind is occupied only with past thoughts. Perceptions, since they are after the fact, do not have creative power. As such, the Course states, they have no meaning.

The sum total of our perceptions forms what is basically a filter through which we see the physical world, including ourselves. Insofar as our perceptual framework has its basis IN this world, we are constrained to believe that this world is reality, and that our own reality exists within it (i.e. you believe that your body is what you really are). The message of *A Course in Miracles* is that our real nature is Spirit, that we are not bodies, and that the perceptual framework of this world does not, and cannot, tell us what we are. It is in that sense that the thoughts "we think we think" are meaningless, for they do not tell us the truth about our Selves.

There does exist, however, a perceptual framework which comes very close to informing us of what our real nature is. The Course refers to this framework as True Perception. True Perception is quite fascinating, for it is not something that you "figure out." It is not a reward that comes after years of studying and contemplating a complicated thought system. In fact, the Course states quite emphatically that there is nothing for you to DO that shall achieve for you the end result, which is the peace of God. The pathway to True Perception and the world of peace lies in your willingness to open to the simple truth that your true nature IS Spirit, and that it is not to be found within this world of bodies and space and time. And when once you open to the possibility that truth and peace lie beyond this world, you will find that they already exist within you, and have always been there.

Beyond the level of our bodies, beyond the level of our brain's thoughts, there is the level of mind. It is there that all creative activity takes place. If you desire to experience anything, or to change your current experience in any way, you must do so by functioning at the level of mind. You touch the level of mind by doing your best to silence the thoughts within your brain. You do not bring with you the interpretations and judgments which this world has taught you. You do not bring with you stigmas of guilt from the past. You do not bring with you fear of the future. Indeed, you already know through your own experience that you are the closest to being fully alive when you simply EXPERIENCE your life, when you lose yourself in what you are doing, so that there are no thoughts of past, future, or consequence. We all know that this is so, whether we refer to playing the piano, hitting a golf ball, or enjoying a sunset. The level of mind is akin to that state in which you are free of your thoughts, and are simply being alive. It is at that level that you encounter your creative reality. The Course has a goal of helping us learn to live our lives at that level of mind.

What we learn in *A Course in Miracles* is that when we leave the busyness of our thoughts behind, and choose to listen, we can hear the Voice of God. That Voice is always there in the silence of our minds, quietly awaiting the day when we open ourselves to Its presence. That Voice will teach you of a new world, a world in which there is nothing but love, a world of peace, and joy, and freedom beyond what your thoughts can comprehend.

What will you discover as you enter the world of *A Course in Miracles*? You will discover that your true nature exists as Spirit, as an idea in the Mind of God. As such, you are part of God and can never, under ANY circumstances, be separated from Him. As part of God, you have been endowed with the creative power of the universe. There is essentially nothing which you cannot do as you exercise that power. Furthermore, it is God's Will that you use that power without limit or restriction, for the purpose of creating joy, which automatically extends to all of Creation.

You will learn, however, that creation always extends itself in one direction (outward). The creation cannot turn tail and alter his creator. This means that you, the Son of God, cannot reverse the direction of creation, that you cannot change God or what He has created. The only limitation on your absolute freedom to create is that you cannot change God or what He has created, which includes your Self. You are as God created you, and MUST remain so. You are locked safe and secure in the arms of God, always to remain so, and there is no power in the universe that can do or imagine anything to change that fact.

I have already alluded to the fact that we are invulnerable. This, in application, means that there exists no power in creation which can do anything to us against our own will. Since our creative power lies within, it also follows directly that we must be the creators of whatever we experience. The Course states quite directly that no happenings can come to the Son of God (us) except by His own choice. As you come to experience this truth within the world of *A Course in Miracles,* it will be for you a doorway to rejoicing and to freedom.

As you realize that you are the creator of your own life, to the last detail, and that all experience arises within you, what disappears is all tendency or desire to blame your brothers for the circumstances of your life. What then disappears with that awareness is your anger. Without struggle and without effort, anger disappears from your life. And in its place appears peace.

Since every being, in his invulnerability, creates the circumstances of his own life, it follows just as surely that you can never do anything to hurt another. With this awareness, guilt dissolves into nothingness. And as the cause for guilt, sin has dissolved with it. The Course repeats over and over that the Son of God (you) is absolutely without sin. Your freedom and your invulnerability make sin impossible. Such is the Love, such is the wisdom of God.

Within the world of *A Course in Miracles,* you will also discover that God is One. God is All That Is, and nothing exists but what is part of God, and is God. This includes you and me, and every brother who walks this Earth with us. At the level of Spirit, at the level of mind, at the level of our reality, we are all One, created thusly by God, always to remain so. Within this world, you soon come to realize that all of Life is one grand, splendid harmony of existence, and which is an expression of our God-given creative power in action.

As you realize that you are truly One with your world, there will come a new vision of your brothers and this world we share. As you look upon each aspect of your life as but an aspect of yourself, you will automatically approach it with a compassion and a gentleness you had not known before. As the Course suggests, you will walk this world in quiet gratitude, and you will be peaceful as you recognize each experience in your life as a form of your own gift to yourself. You will find that same gratitude and gentleness caressing your eyelids while you sleep in quiet peace.

Always one must ask about the seeming tragedy in this earthly life. What about the violence, the killing, illness, death, the sadness and the tears? The Course helps us realize that all of it stems from fear. There is no man who strikes out at his world except that he be screaming at his own fear and his own pain. Fear has its source in the mistaken belief that this world IS what we are, and is our reality. Insofar as we believe that we are bodies, separate and alone in the presence of other bodies, constrained to be the victim of circumstance, and cursed with the inevitability of death, we must live in fear.

The process whereby we identify ourselves with this world is called valuing. The Course tells us directly not to value anything which will not last forever. This means, quite simply, for us not to become confused about our real nature. We are Spirit. Our reality is not our body. When we believe that our body, or this world, IS what we are, we are valuing it. Furthermore, our belief that we ARE our body, which we know will one day pass away, must lead to the fear of that day when we (our body) shall die. Thus we create the fear of death. The fear of death, indeed fear itself, could not have arisen if we had not valued this world by equating it with what we are.

The Course states that nothing in this world is worth valuing. Nothing in this world is or can be the reality of what you are. Therefore, the loss of nothing in this world is to be feared. In the Real World of *A Course in Miracles* there is no fear. You simply realize that what you are is the Son of God, eternal, incapable of dying, absolutely safe, absolutely loved, and absolutely free. You then realize, as the Course says, that there is NOTHING to fear.

The Course tells us not to value this world. It is important to realize that not to value does not mean not to love. In fact, just the opposite is true. It is not possible to truly love another being unless you do not value the relationship. The reason becomes clear when you realize that love is freedom, as we learn in the Course. If you value a relationship with someone else, then you have made that person part of who you are, and you NEED that person. Whenever you need someone, you automatically resist any changes in that person which affect your relationship. In essence, you desire to deny freedom to the person you claim to love. It is not possible to truly love another unless you grant that person complete freedom. God knows that, and created us totally free.

As you do not value, you do not need, and you are only then able to allow complete freedom to another. Only by allowing real freedom can you truly love. And because we are One, it is only by GIVING such freedom and love that you can RECEIVE that same freedom and love into your own life. The love of *A Course in Miracles* brings you freedom and joy, and without effort casts fear totally out of your life. In the absence of fear, you will see beyond what the world calls tragedy.

As you look at the seeming tragedies of the world with the vision of the Course, what you see is beings who have valued this world, and are acting out their fears as they try to experience the impossible dream that they could be what they are not, that they could be separate from God and from each other. Beyond the fears, what you see is beings created free by God, who are totally loved, absolutely safe, and who cannot separate themselves from the loving arms of God, even though they may try to imagine it otherwise. Nothing in this world is worth valuing because none of it can have any effect on the real beauty of what they are. For they are the Son of God, and shall always remain so.

As you begin to experience *A Course in Miracles*, you will find yourself entering a new world. It is a world of freedom, where all beings are so free that they literally choose and create every detail of their lives. In the invulnerability of that freedom, there cannot exist blame, or anger, or guilt, or sin. All that exists is the Love of God, which all beings share equally and fully.

It is a world of Oneness and harmony, in which all beings honor and rejoice in the creations of every other being. It is a world in which everything is in harmony with the Will of God, which is nothing more than the total freedom to create and to be. It is a world in which God's only plan for our lives is the joyful expression of that freedom with which he has endowed us.

Above all, it is a world of joy. God's Will is for you to be co-creator with Him in this grand adventure called Life. You have within you the power of God, which makes you invulnerable. Because you are invulnerable, you are totally safe in God's world. Because you are completely safe, you are free to experience whatever you will. Within the context of such freedom, joy becomes inevitable. And that joy IS the Will of God for us all.

The most beautiful aspect of the message of *A Course in Miracles* is its promise that every being in God's Creation will one day return to the full awareness of his true nature. It is not possible for anyone to remain in fear and darkness indefinitely. As you grow into the experience of love and freedom, never doubt that you are but taking the journey home. And home is the place where you shall dwell forever in peace, freedom, joy, and a love which is beyond the measure of anything you can comprehend.

PROLOGUE:
THE NATURE OF THE OTHER VOICE

It is essential, even critical, in our quest for the peace of God that we come to an accurate understanding of what the Course is actually saying about thought itself. Very early in the Workbook lessons, the Course begins to develop its theme that the thoughts of consciousness, the thoughts of which we are aware, are NOT our real thoughts, and furthermore, do not resemble our real thoughts in any way.

In Lesson #4, entitled "These thoughts do not mean anything . . ." (1), the Course tells us, while we are selecting the subjects for the day's lesson, not to be afraid to use "good" thoughts as well as "bad." For "None of them represents your real thoughts, which are being covered up by them. The 'good' ones are but shadows of what lies beyond . . . The 'bad' ones are blocks to sight . . . You do not want either. This is a major exercise . . ." (2) It is important that we hear that last sentence: "THIS IS A MAJOR EXERCISE."

In other lessons, the same important idea is repeated. Lesson #10 makes it clear that all the thoughts of which we are aware, or of which we become aware, are not our real thoughts. (3) Lesson #45 is even more specific as it informs us that there is no connection between our real thoughts and the thoughts we think we think (or the thoughts of which we are aware). It also is firm about stating that what we think are our real thoughts do not resemble our real thoughts in any respect. (4) Lesson #15 refers to the thoughts "we think we think," which are not thoughts, but which are simply images, and as such are actually nothing at all, since they are nothing but images that we have made. (5) This theme is mentioned a number of other times, all with the same intent, which is to help us realize that the thoughts of which we are aware, the thoughts of consciousness, are NOT our real thoughts. Furthermore, it is important that we remember that being aware of this fact is a MAJOR exercise within the teaching plan of the Course.

As it becomes clear that the thoughts of consciousness are not our real thoughts, it behooves us to explore what the Course says about consciousness itself. Although the Course mentions the word but a few times, it does tell us that "Consciousness, the level of perception, was the first split introduced into the mind after the separation, making the mind a perceiver, rather than a creator. Consciousness is correctly identified as the domain of the ego." (6) As we probe this passage, we hear it telling us that consciousness, or the thoughts we think we think, or the thoughts of which we are aware, is actually the domain of the ego. Therefore, as long as we function at the level of conscious thoughts, we are constrained to the level of the ego. Yet every Course student learns early on that going beyond the ego is one of the primary goals of the curriculum of the Course. This can perhaps seem to imply that we should function, here in this world, without conscious awareness, or without thinking. This would seem a great challenge, indeed.

Elsewhere in the Course, we find another important passage. "In this world the only remaining freedom is the freedom of choice, always between two choices or two voices. Consciousness is the receptive mechanism, receiving messages from above or below, from the Holy Spirit or the ego. Consciousness . . . cannot transcend the perceptual realm. At its highest it becomes aware of the real world, and can be trained to do so increasingly." (7)

There is one other quote from the Course which needs to be mentioned. In Lesson #131, as it describes for us how to reach the truth, we find these words, ". . . and we will ask to see the rising of the real world to replace the foolish images that we hold dear, with true ideas arising in place of thoughts that have no meaning, no effect, and neither source nor substance in the truth." (8) So subtle, so brief in its passing, but here is the Course stating that our thoughts (the ones we wish to let go in favor of truth) have no meaning, and NO EFFECT . . . This seems to state that our thoughts (the thoughts of consciousness), in having no effect, have no creative power at all. If this be true, and we want to change our lives or our world by changing our thoughts, we must realize that the level of conscious thought is not only NOT the level at which changes can be made, but that conscious thoughts actually have no power to change anything.

Based upon my own understanding of the message of the Course, and upon the Jeshua materials I have received, I now propose to explain how all of this makes sense, and how it fits into a unified whole which is fully compatible with the teachings of the Course. What follows has had a major impact on my own life. It has also led me to a better understanding of The Other Voice, which is the title I was given for this book. I offer it here in the hope that it may bless the reader's life as it has blessed my own.

The Course speaks often of our invulnerability, and how it is that nothing can happen to us by chance or accident. (9) This must even apply to the making of this world of illusion. It is important that we be able to embrace the fact that the production of this world was undertaken from within a state of full awareness, and that everything that seems to happen here is by careful design. No mistakes have been made, and no blunders have caused us to seem to be trapped here in space and time. Granted, it SEEMS otherwise. But that, too, must be part of the design. If it were not so, we would not be invulnerable, and the Course would be in error.

Thus it is that we desired to make a world which would have the APPEARANCE of accomplishing the impossibility of separation, all the while being fully aware that it was not possible to actually do so.

This demanded a scheme whereby we could design this world of separation, somehow forget that we had done so, and then look upon that same design and believe it to be reality. We must realize that this required creative genius at its best. And we have done a masterful job of making just such a world.

The manner in which we did this is essentially the same as the way we create our own sickness, and which the Course describes very well in the second through the fourth paragraphs of Lesson #136. This world was not an accident. It is a carefully laid plan of self-deception, whose purpose is to hide reality. We made it up, then devised a clever plan for forgetting that we had done so, and then proceeded to look upon that plan and seem to experience it as being real. The means by which we were able to do this is most clever indeed.

We first imagined that it was possible to actually BE what we cannot be, which is separate from God, and from Life Itself. In the next instant, in order for that imagined notion to survive, it was necessary for us to seem to split our mind. This simply means that there had to be a part of the mind that was not aware of the carefully laid plan of separation, while another part was fully aware of that same plan and its guaranteed outcome, which had to be the eventual return of the mind to wholeness, or the end of the dream of separation, if you will. ("This is a required Course." [10])

In order to do this, we devised projection and perception. We made up a screen onto which we could project whatever we wanted to seem to experience in this world of illusion. We then projected the chosen images onto that screen, and in an instant split our awareness so that part of our awareness could focus on the screen and pretend that the images were of reality, without remembering where the images came from in the first place. This was done by the selfsame mind that was now looking upon what it had projected.

We could not actually BE separate, but we could manage to look upon the set of projected images and pretend that they represented something real. However, the images are not real, and can never be so. Thus it is that, in reality, this world never happened.

The exciting and possibly alarming insights are the ones that follow. We must ask the nature of the screen onto which mind projected its dream of illusion, and the nature of the images which it chose to project there. And this is the answer. THE SCREEN WHICH MIND CREATED AND ONTO WHICH IT CHOSE TO PROJECT ITS ILLUSIONS IS CONSCIOUSNESS ITSELF. AND THE IMAGES WHICH IT PROJECTED ARE NONE OTHER THAN THE THOUGHTS WHICH DWELL IN THAT CONSCIOUSNESS. That is why the Course accurately states that consciousness is the RECEPTIVE mechanism. (7) For it is simply the screen onto which mind projects that which it would perceive. That is why consciousness was the first split introduced into the mind after the separation was imagined, making the mind a perceiver, rather than a creator. (6) And that is why our thoughts here are nothing but images we have made. (5) And that is also why the Course tells us that "perception involves an exchange, or translation, which knowledge does not need." (11) The exchange, or translation, is the process whereby an image is projected, the process is instantly forgotten, and the selfsame mind then views what it projected the moment before. And, finally, that is why the thoughts of which we are aware, the thoughts of consciousness, are not our real thoughts, and truly have nothing to do with the real thoughts (4), which do and must reflect the creative power of mind itself.

After we arrive at a point where we are able to open to the truth of the preceding paragraphs, we have arrived at the realization that the thoughts of which we are aware are not our real thoughts. We also realize that ALL of those thoughts must lie within the domain of the ego, and that to dwell upon those thoughts in our search for truth is to try to discover truth while looking through the mask which was designed to hide that same truth. We then realize that there must be a way to move beyond that mask, wherein we shall discover truth and the peace of God.

The way in which we shall move beyond the thought system of the ego, beyond the trappings of conscious thought, is to revisit an above-mentioned passage from the Course, the one which tells us that the ONLY freedom we have here is the freedom of choice, and that that choice is ONLY to which voice we shall choose to listen. (7) We then need to ask how it is that we do, or can, choose between the two voices. For it is only by listening to the "Other" Voice that we can discover the truth and peace of God.

We are told that the ego and the Holy Spirit suffer from a complete failure of communication (12). The reason for this is that the two operate within completely different thought systems, one whose fundamental premise is the possibility and existence of separation, and the other whose fundamental premise is that separation cannot, and never did, exist at all. If we harbor even an inkling that God is in any way separate from us, we are choosing the thought system of the ego, and we cannot truly hear the Voice of the Holy Spirit. As a simple example of this, if we would pray to God, and ask God to grant us the requests we make of Him, we are making the subtle assumption that God is SEPARATE from us. We are assuming that God's Will might be DIFFERENT from our own, making it necessary for us to somehow influence God so that He will hear and answer us. Thus, we are speaking with the voice of the ego, and the Holy Spirit cannot answer. For It cannot bridge the complete communication gap which exists between Its own thought system and the imagined thought system of the ego.

We also remember that the realm of conscious thought is the domain of the ego. (6) If we insist upon dwelling in that domain and trying to "figure out" the message of the Holy Spirit, we are doomed to failure. For all of our "figuring out," all of our analyzing, all of our hours of debating and discussing are, by definition, constrained to the realm of the ego. And it must be in an arena where these processes cease that we can at last hear the "Other" Voice, which is really the Voice of the Holy Spirit, the Voice of God.

Thus we come abreast of a most important question. How is it that we can truly listen, and therefore truly hear, the Other Voice? How can we, while we yet dwell in this world of space and time, hear the Voice of God? The answer is to be found in the Course itself, and in one of its most beautiful and moving paragraphs:

"Simply do this: Be still, and lay aside all thoughts of what you are and what God is; all concepts you have learned about the world; all images you hold about yourself. Empty your mind of everything it thinks is either true or false, or good or bad, of every thought it judges worthy, and all the ideas of which it is ashamed. Hold onto nothing. Do not bring with you one thought the past has taught, nor one belief you ever learned from anything. Forget this world, forget this course, and come with wholly empty hands unto your God.'' (13)

It is clear from this passage that the Course is advising us to let go of all our conscious thoughts, concepts, and judgments. For to do this is to divest ourselves of the ego and its thought system. And it is in doing just that, that we are able to truly listen.

The fact remains, however, that for most of us, so long steeped in the belief that our consciousness is a vital and integral part of what we are, taking this step can seem frightening indeed. That is because letting go of consciousness is the same as letting go of the ego. And we have designed this world so that it SEEMS as if the ego is what we are. Thus letting go of the ego SEEMS tantamount to choosing to die, a step which most of us do approach with fear. For we cherish being alive, and do not desire to cease to exist, above all by our own choice.

Listening to the Other Voice, however, is far from frightening. It is the most rewarding, the most meaningful, and the most beautiful experience we can afford ourselves here in this world. It is also the only way to understand and experience the peace of God.

When we make the choice to listen, we do it by allowing our minds to become still. In this place of silence, in the absence of our conscious thoughts, the ego is no longer present, and there is an immediate sense of increased peace. What then begins to appear is an awareness, a presence, which defies definition. But arising out of this awareness, we discover what might be called a knowing, or a certainty. It is this knowing that blesses us with an awareness of what to do, where to go, and what to say, as we live our lives here in this world. The awareness that arises from out of our silence can and does translate into our knowing how to live our lives here, even though this world of space and time is but a world of illusion. But this same awareness can and does cause us to see the world differently from the way we had seen it before.

What this literally means is that it is possible to live life here in this world, to be able to function within the realm of perception, and yet to see the world through the eyes of the Holy Spirit, rather than through the eyes of the ego. That is why the Course has stated that consciousness, although it cannot transcend the realm of perception, can become aware of the real world, and can be trained to do so increasingly. (7) This state is called true perception, and can only be reached by listening to the Other Voice.

If our only choice here is to which voice we shall listen, and we desire to hear the Voice of the Holy Spirit, we seem to come upon a significant dilemma. If the way to hear the Other Voice is by quieting our conscious minds, by ceasing to think these unreal thoughts, then what role does *A Course in Miracles* play? What role does this book play? Do not the books, the tapes, the lectures, the study groups, all demand that we read, study, and discuss in order to learn this Course? And is not all of that confined to the domain of the ego, as the Course tells us? Is it not contradictory for Jeshua to have given us the Course in the first place? In short, is there a place for the study of this material? And how does such study relate to being able to hear the Other Voice?

Insofar as consciousness CAN be trained to see the real world, there must exist avenues whereby that training can be accomplished. All of those avenues relate to our willingness to open our conscious awareness to the truth. This is the same as willingly opening our minds to a different way of looking at the world. Unless we are willing to entertain a different vision of life as we know it, AND A DIFFERENT VISION OF WHAT WE OURSELVES ARE, we cannot escape the thought system of the ego, and we cannot discover the peace of God.

First, there must exist within us the awareness of the truth of God. We could not separate ourselves from that truth, even though we might vainly imagine that it be possible. When we open to new ideas, such as we meet when we read the Course or books like this one, we experience a quiet resonance within which affirms the presence of truth. Every one of the old (ego) thoughts which we desire to preserve can only serve as a block to this process. But as we truly open, WITH A WILLING ANTICIPATION OF A NEW WAY OF SEEING, ideas such as we meet in the Course and this book will, because of the feeling they generate within us, tell us that we are approaching the center of truth. Then when we enter the silence and return, the awareness we bring back will be magnified by the presence of those ideas we had encountered and had chosen to admit into our consciousness.

Secondly, we are not bodies. Rather we are mind exercising its creative power. It is mind which projects onto the screen of consciousness that which it would perceive. And since this is a required Course, part of the design MUST BE the eventual projection onto consciousness of the truth. Therefore, part of the original design of this world included the planned introduction into consciousness, over the span of time, of the awareness of the truth.

Jesus established the Atonement by being the first person to bring into human consciousness a life which was fully in tune with the truth of God. And he asked those who had ears to hear to listen. The Course, and for those who choose to believe so, *Journey Beyond Words* and this book, are some of the many other vehicles through which mind introduces the truth into consciousness, all for the purpose of bringing mind back to its original state of wholeness.

As we read, as we listen, as we study *A Course in Miracles,* or *Journey Beyond Words,* or this book, or any of the many other sources available, we are choosing to make fertile the ground upon which the Other Voice will plant the seeds of truth. Therefore, such endeavors are appropriate indeed for those whose guidance is to follow that path. However, it is most important that we not lose sight of the fact that we shall not understand the truth of God, nor experience His peace, until we choose to quiet our minds and listen to the message of the Other Voice.

We hear that Voice by entering the silence, by choosing to listen with openness of heart, with the anticipation of remembering, and with a willingness to accept a new vision of who and what we are. And out of the silence shall come the pathway to the peace of God, which truly does pass all understanding.

But the other [voice] was given you by God,
    Who only asks that you listen to it.

A Course in Miracles

INTRODUCTION

Greetings. I am Jeshua.
I have come to discuss with you,
A Course in Miracles.
But more importantly, I have come
That you might become free
In the knowledge of what you are.

I am Jeshua. Though names as such do not matter.
But indeed, I am Jeshua.
I am the one you call Jesus.
But, hear me well. I am you.
I am each one of you.
Which means, I am your brother.
I am, like you, the Son of God.
And nothing more.

I will speak with you of many things.
I will speak of things which are real.
And I will speak of many things,
Including this world of space and time,
Which, indeed, are not real.
And of those things which are not real,
They are but the blocks you have created
To keep you from knowing
The reality of what you are.

This whole world you see is not real.
Many times you have listened to words
Which speak of this life, of your body, of this world,
As being illusion.
That is exactly so in this sense—
An illusion is something which you perceive,
And therefore which your mind thinks is real,
While in reality, you are but exercising
The creative power given you by God
In order to seem to see

That which is not there at all.
It is because you harbor within your being
The creative power of the universe
That you are able to see, to perceive, your world
Exactly as you desire it to be.

And because it is perception,
What seems to be reality
Can change in the twinkling of an eye.
That which is real, that which is of God,
Does not change.
It is not subject to your perception and your beliefs.
It is not subject to your space and your time.
For it is far beyond any, and all, of those.

I speak to you as your brother.
For that is what I am.
In reality, in essence, I am no different from you in any way.
I am the Son of God, just as you are the Son of God,
Just as every friend, and every enemy, that you perceive
Is likewise the Son of God.
I come to you as a brother,
In your sense of time perhaps older,
And definitely wiser.
And I come to you from the vantage point
Of being free of the illusion that is this world.

Those who are free of the illusion of this world
Can seem, to you, to do miracles.
But what you experience, rather than miracles,
Is the contrast between what it is like to be free of the illusion,
And on the other hand, to still be bound by the belief
That in some measure, the world is real.

It is appropriate for you to respect me.
'Tis appropriate for you to look up to me.
Indeed, I come in order that you might do that.
When I walked this earth,
I told your brothers, and therefore you as well,
That there is nothing that you see me do
Which you cannot do also.
In truth, you have within you,
As I have within me,

The power to do works so much greater
Than what you have seen,
That you could not comprehend
If I tried to tell you.

Important is this. Hear me well.
THERE IS NO DIFFERENCE,
IN REALITY, IN ESSENCE,
BETWEEN YOU AND ME.

I am absolutely free, as are you.
I have the ability to do what your world calls miracles.
And that same ability is possessed by you,
Although blocked by your fear.
I have no talent that does not lie within you,
Albeit perhaps hidden at this time.
I am free of space and time.
I am free to go and to come anywhere I choose,
Within any aspect of space, and any aspect of time.
And indeed, so are you,
Even though that ability lies hidden
Beneath the mask of your fear.

Do not be frightened by these statements I have made.
Rather, think of life, if you wish, as a great learning, a school.
Think of me as a much older brother
Who has advanced through the entire curriculum,
And who has a full mastery of all the material
That you, too, shall be learning.
And the fact that you are at a seemingly
Less advanced level of learning
Means nothing more than that.
It does not make you good, or bad.
It does not make you less.
It does not make me better.
For we are, indeed, the same.
It merely means that you are where you are.
Nothing more.

There is that about you, and about me,
Which makes us the Son of God.
And that, truly, can not change.
We are free.

And that freedom includes our ability
To imagine, to perceive, whatever we choose.
This entire world is an example of just that.
But none of us, not you, nor me,
Can change that which is real,
That which was created, and given us, by God.

There are many things which shall become clear
As we move through this Text, and these pages.
Among them are the things which are not real,
And which, because they are not real,
Do not exist.
Among those things are sin and guilt.
For there is no cause for sin.
And without sin, there is no cause for guilt.
They are of the imagination.
Nothing more.

Another thing which does not exist is your body.
By that I simply mean this—
Your body is not what you are. That is all.
You are Spirit. You are free.
You are created by God.
And nothing can change that.
Your imaginings that you are a body,
Or that you are, in time, confined within a body
Which shall somehow age and decay and die—
Those imaginings, as real as they may seem,
Do not, in any sense, change what you are.
And thus it is that the body is not real.
'Tis a suit you have donned.
'Tis a plaything you have chosen.
Its purpose is for learning, for experience.
And its ultimate goal is to be set aside without a second thought
When the learning is done.
For it is not you,
And has no effect on the reality of what you are.

My resurrection was the expression, in this world,
Of that truth.
What I AM, as the Son of God, was not affected
By nails, by a cross, or by death.
And likewise, what you are, as the Son of God,

Is not affected by the illusion of your body,
And whatever it may be that seems to happen to it,
Including its death.

So the truth is that this world is not real.
That does not mean that this world
Should be disdained, or scorned.
You will come to realize that this world is, in its reality,
A creation of the Son of God.
It is but an expression of His creative power.
All of you who walk here, in your Oneness,
Have created this world.
And as such, it is, and must be, beautiful.
For indeed, you, in your reality, are beautiful.
It is your perception of this world
That has seemed to turn your life upside down.
And what we shall help you to change is just that—
Your perception of this world.

We will speak of perception, and of true perception.
It shall be your true perception,
Which is as close as you can come on this earth
To the experience of God,
Which shall change entirely
Your experience of this world.
You shall learn to rejoice in your freedom,
Which allows you to experience this world
For as long as you like,
And when you are done,
To let it go in that selfsame freedom,
And to move on.
For as the Son of God, what is given you to experience
Is the infinity of creation itself.

I come not to bring you fear,
But to bring you peace.
I come not asking that you give up something
Which is cherished, which you value.
I come merely to show you a better way.

I do not come asking you to struggle.
I do not come asking you to fight within yourself.
For the true expression of your freedom

Follows without effort.
I come merely to show you what you are.
And as you come to realize, as you experience,
Beyond your thoughts, beyond your fears,
What you truly are,
Then that which you value now
Shall simply pass away,
To be replaced by something richer and fuller,
And more beautiful than you can imagine.

For when you trade one toy, if you will, for another
Which is far more beautiful, far more delightful,
Than the old one,
It does not represent a loss at all,
Merely a transition.
And so I have come with the greatest of love,
To assist you, and to guide you,
Toward that transition which you can make
From one world to another.

What you shall move FROM
Is your current perception of this world,
Which may include the belief that your body is real,
That it can do things over which you have no control;
Which may include the belief
That such things as sin and guilt and illness
And misery and death actually exist.
What you shall move TO
Is the true perception of this same world,
In which you realize that you are, in fact,
Like me, the Son of God,
In which you realize that you are absolutely free,
And that nothing in your life can happen to you
Without that it be your choice.

I come to guide you to that awareness.
And as you reach that awareness,
As you move beyond the beliefs
Which bind you to this world,
It shall not be a loss at all.
It shall be a growth unto a new freedom
In which you seem to lift your wings
And rise above all that was,

To a new life, and to a joy
Which you had not previously imagined.

I come as your friend.
I come to tell you that you are absolutely loved.
I come to tell you that there is nothing you can do
Which can possibly change how much you are loved—
That there is nothing you can do which, in reality,
Can separate you from God,
And thus from each other.

I come to tell you that you are free.
I come to tell you that you are One with me,
One with all of your brothers.

I come to bring you peace, and joy—
For that is your right, and your inheritance,
As the Son of God.

Blessings upon you all. That is all.

THE MEANING OF MIRACLES

Greetings again. I am Jeshua.
I have come this day to discuss with you,
The meaning of miracles.

In Heaven miracles do not exist.
In Heaven miracles are not necessary.
Therefore, miracles can not be known.
Miracles can only be perceived.

You will become much more aware, as we progress,
Of the meaning of perception,
Of the meaning of knowledge,
Which, in fact, cannot be obtained in this world.
But suffice it for you, this day,
To realize that miracles are only necessary here
In this world of space and time,
In this world of thoughts,
And therefore, of perception.

What, then, do miracles reflect?
Very simply, miracles reflect that which you already are,
And that which you already have.
What keeps you from experiencing miracles
Is your belief, your perception,
That they are not part of you,
And that you, as you perceive yourself,
Are somehow not entitled to them.

What do miracles reflect?
Miracles reflect the simple truth that you HAVE everything.
But beyond that, miracles reflect the simple truth
That you ARE everything.
There is nothing that you do not already possess.
There is nothing that is, or that can be,
Outside of, or apart from, you.
And that which cannot be outside of, or apart from, you

Must actually BE you.
Thusly were you created by God.
And that cannot be changed.
For what God created IS,
And does not change.

When you chose to come here to space and time,
It was not without full knowledge
Of the conditions that you would find here.
All of Creation is One Mind.
And your sojourn here was designed by you,
But in conjunction with God, your Creator,
With all other beings,
And in harmony with All That Is.

How could that be?
Because of the simple truth that all of Life is One.
And in reality nothing exists separate from, or isolated from,
Any other aspect of reality.
Thus it is not possible that this world
Could have been imagined
Without the agreement of all of Creation.
How again, then, could that be?
How would God allow such a world to come into existence?
There is a two-fold answer,
Which you must come to understand.

God made you free, free in every sense,
Except to change your Self.
God made you so free
That you can imagine yourself
To be anything you wish,
Even to imagine yourself
To be something you are not.
Indeed, you cannot make yourself
Into something you are not.
But you are free to imagine
That you are different from what you are.

And thus it is that this world of perception,
Of egos and separation,
Of isolation, pain, misery, and fear,
Is nothing more than that—

A figment of your creative imagination.
It arose, if you will, as you wondered
What it might be like to be separate
From other aspects of Creation.
It arose as you wondered what it might be like
To be different from what you are,
Albeit that BEING different from what you are
Is impossible.
And therefore, this world,
As I suggested in the beginning,
Is not real.

That which is real can not be threatened.
And that includes your true nature,
What you ARE, which is the Son of God.
That which is not real does not even exist.
And that which is not real
Includes all of this world of perception.

The miracles you do, then,
Will arise from your deep inner realization
That what I have just said is true.
The reality of what you ARE as the Son of God
Cannot, in or out of time, be changed.
It simply IS.
YOU simply ARE—
Safe, unchangeable, and incapable of dying.
In your sense of time,
You already exist forever.

And your miracles will come from the deep inner realization
That, truly, this world is not real,
And not to be valued.
It is, indeed, a figment of your imagination,
A reflection of your exploration
Within your creative mind
Of what it might be like to be separate,
And to be something which you are not.

In a moment, you imagined it all—
Including space and time and bodies.
And in a moment, it was experienced and dismissed.
But in your imagining, you created it so that

You could SEEM to come and live here in space and time,
To play it out, if you will,
For the purpose of imagining
That you truly have experienced it all.
And the nature of God is such
That you are always free
To imagine whatever you will.

When you realize that truth, deep within,
Beyond ideas, beyond thoughts,
Beyond rationalizing, beyond discussing,
At the level of experience,
Then you shall, at that same level,
Realize that you DO create every circumstance
In your life.
And you will realize in that selfsame moment
That you are not separate,
And can never be so.

Imagine, for a moment, that you knew
That all beings were One with You—
That all beings ACTUALLY WERE YOU.
Let yourself open to the truth
That everything you imagine or experience
Is experienced right along with you
By all of Creation.
Suppose you knew that EVERYTHING
Which you did or imagined,
To or about any aspect of Creation,
Was automatically done, or imagined, to or about you.
It would be a different world, would it not?

When that happens within your awareness,
Beyond your thinking,
When you EXPERIENCE the truth
That you are actually ARE One with All That Is,
What you shall experience is joy,
And a fullness within which you cannot yet imagine.
What you shall experience
Is a freedom beyond your comprehension.
And your life shall be filled
With what you, at this time,
Would call miracles.

The absence of miracles is based upon level confusion.
I would like to make that less confusing, if I may.
The horizontal axis of which I have spoken
Is the one on which you seem to live—
This world of space and time and bodies.
And the things you see from that perspective
Seem to take time to happen.
What you call joining seems to demand
The physical action of coming together.
You find all of this frustrating,
For you inherently know that two bodies
Can never be one, as spirits are.
You have chosen to believe that time
Must follow in its own footsteps,
Second upon second upon second.
But, indeed, that is not so.
But as long as your perception,
Your choice of what you would perceive,
Dwells on this horizontal level of space and time,
Thus it shall seem to be for you.

You may understand the shift to a vertical axis in this way.
At this lowest level, you have this earth,
Space and time and bodies,
And the belief that they are real.
At the level above that you have
What you call your thoughts.
And you intuitively know that your thoughts
Are not confined to space and time.
You can think yourself to be anywhere in the cosmos.
Although you do not believe yourself to physically be there,
You are aware that your thoughts can travel there.
You can think yourself into the future,
Or the past.
So even at this simple level of your thoughts,
One step above the level of space and time and bodies,
Already you can sense the limitations diminishing.
However, the thoughts that you think you think
Have been projected onto your brain,
Which is a part of your body.
And in that sense they too
Seem to be confined to the belief in space and time.

Above the level of thoughts, there is the world of experience.
I say experience, because experience simply IS.
One does not anticipate experience.
One does not fear experience.
One does not look back upon experience after it is over,
And decide if it was pleasing or bad, happy or sad.
Experience simply IS.

Experience is open and shared.
There are no secrets in the world of experience.
True experience is your first step
Into the world of Oneness,
Although at that level you still seem to think of yourself
As an individual.
Indeed, there is an aspect of individuality within Creation,
Albeit beyond the understanding of this world.
But the level of experience still carries with it
Some of the perceptions of separation.

Above the level of experience
Is the level of Oneness, and true perception.
At that level, which is as close
As you can come to knowledge in this plane,
You are aware of all other beings as One with your Self.
You are aware that time and space and bodies ARE illusion.
You are aware that there is nothing outside of your Self,
Nor anything outside of any Self.
And all of that is experienced and understood
In terms of a great peace, and a great joy,
And a harmony that lies beyond
The thoughts of this world.

Lastly, above this level is the realm of knowledge.
Knowledge involves direct communication
Between God and His creations.
Knowledge is yours and cannot be taken from you.
But it shall not fully be yours in awareness,
As long as you seem to walk this earth.

So when I admonish you not to be caught in level confusion,
I am simply saying this—
Realize that the lower levels of existence here are not real—
That the level of thought is still confined to this world,

Although it is in many ways free of space and time—
That the level of experience is freer yet,
While still being somewhat involved
With the imaginings of the world—
And that the level of true perception allows you
To walk this world in Oneness, and in harmony,
In the full realization that it is not real,
And not to be valued.

This is by the way of introduction.
If it seems that I have given you too much for one sitting,
Do not be dismayed.
As we progress through this Course,
All things shall be expressed, reexpressed,
Defined and redefined.
For our goal is not that you learn
A philosophy, or a set of ideas.
Our goal is that you EXPERIENCE the peace of God.
And the reason for using these words,
For repeating, for defining and redefining,
Is to allow each of you, as you hear these words,
To experience a reality which lies, and goes,
Beyond them.

I have come, as I have said, as an older brother,
Not different from you,
But as one who does understand the reality of what you are.
I have come in love,
Never to chastise,
Only to guide and to assist.
Remember that you are always free here to be,
And to imagine, whatever you will.

It is not wrong. It is not right. It is not bad.
And always, if you can see the truth, it is good.
Because you are a creation of God.
In the biblical sense, when God created the world,
He said, ''It is good.''
And that includes, indeed, every aspect of Creation,
Even the imaginings of this world.

Blessings upon you all. That is all.

THE SEPARATION AND
THE ATONEMENT

Greetings again. I am Jeshua.
I have come this day to discuss, with you,
The separation and the Atonement.

Hear me well. The separation never happened.
Hear me well. The separation is not real.
The separation is but a figment of imagination,
And nothing more.
This entire world, which you seem to experience as physical,
Through space and time and bodies, and yes, thoughts,
Is not real.
Hear me very well.
This entire world never happened.

Certainly, it seems to you that your body is somehow real.
Even if you believe that your fundamental nature is spirit,
It still seems to you that there is some measure of reality
Which must be attached to your body,
To its thoughts, and to space and time.
But I tell you, that is not so.
And when we speak of the separation,
We refer exactly, and only, to that belief
That your body and space and time are real.
That belief, which is harbored deep within you,
Was created by you, is cherished by you,
And valued by you.
Were that not so, you would not, and could not,
Be able to imagine it real.

The separation arose out of a desire.
Since you think of things in terms of your time,
I shall use the words "before" and "after",
Merely for the purpose of helping you to understand,
And therefore to experience, the truth I bring.
Do not forget that "before" and "after"
Are terms which have no meaning.

For they are products of your thoughts.
And I have told you many times,
Your thoughts have no meaning.

In the terms of your time,
You must realize that before the separation occurred,
There was only Spirit.
There was God.
There was God's extension of Himself.
And that extension of God Itself was the creation of All That Is.
Thus it was also the creation of You who, in your Oneness,
Were made to be co-creator with God.
Before the separation, You, all of You,
Were total and complete, lacking nothing.
And that remains the truth of what you are.
For that truth you cannot change.

What arose, then, was a fleeting desire,
A fleeting thought, if you will.
That fleeting thought was a simple expression
Of the infinite creative ability
Given you by God when He created you.
What arose with that thought,
Out of the awareness of being,
Was an imagining,
The imagining of what it might be like
Not to be complete,
To be limited by one's individuality.
(I have told you that within Creation
There does exist what you would call individuality,
Albeit totally unknown to separation or division of any kind.)
And the imagining took form as the belief
That it be possible for You, within your Oneness,
To somehow exist as isolated and separate.
The imagining was like this:
What would it be like to be
The sole possessor of my own thoughts,
The sole creator of my world?
What would it be like if I could experience life,
Not as co-creator,
But as independent of all other beings?

In order for such a fantasy to occur
It required that You seem to be incomplete,
That You seem to exist apart from Creation Itself,
The existence of which You cannot deny.

Now, the property of God is extension.
Love is extension. And Love is freedom.
And that is what You are.
Extension, because it is the property of God,
HAS everything, IS everything, gives everything,
And therefore receives everything,
Without restriction or limit.
Extension leaves no room for secrets, or isolation.
Truly, God could not imagine a secret.

Within the freedom that is God,
It is possible to misuse extension, to miscreate.
The misuse of extension is projection,
Of which I speak so often.
I have told you that projection makes perception,
That ultimately projection and the perception that follows
Is what has created this entire world of illusion.

Projection happens like this—
Out of the completeness and wholeness
Which you HAVE and ARE, and which you cannot change,
You design to experience what it might be like
To be isolated and separate.

Extension is the offering to all of Creation of everything.
Projection is the offering to Creation
Of only PART OF everything.
When you project, you choose.
When you project, you select certain aspects of everything,
Which you then extend in a miscreated fashion.
But what must happen is that when you attempt to extend
But A PART of everything,
You limit yourself to what you can receive,
And therefore experience.
Within the Oneness giving and receiving must be the same.
So when you attempt to give IN PART,
It is not possible to receive other than IN PART.

As you receive, and thus experience,
PART OF the wholeness,
What you must sense within is absence of the whole,
Which you must experience as lack.
It is your projection, your choice
To send out to the world but part of everything,
That ultimately limits your perception,
Which makes it so that
You can only experience part of everything.
This demands that you experience the sense of lack.
When you feel lack, you believe yourself to be incomplete.
And what follows without recourse is fear.

Fear is the feeling you have, which arises from your perception,
That you are lacking in something.
Fear, therefore, is the feeling you have
When you anticipate the loss of something
You seem to have, but which could be taken from you.
Your proof that it could be taken from you
Is your sense of lack.
And recall, lack is an imagined state
Which is born out of your projection.

In the awareness that you have everything,
It is not possible to experience fear.
In the belief that there are some things
Which you do not have,
Or which could be taken from you,
There must follow— fear.

You literally choose everything that you experience.
You choose it by projecting.
You choose what it is you wish to experience,
And then send out, if you will,
The vibrations that contain that experience.
And when you interact with Creation,
Which must be the source of all experience,
All that comes back to you is what you have sent out.
You must perceive what you have projected.
Thus it is that projection makes perception.
For you must perceive what you have chosen to project.

There is nothing uniform, nothing absolute or true,
About what you perceive.
Indeed, there are some projections (and therefore perceptions)
Upon which you all seem to agree.
And thus your world seems to you, in many ways, to be stable.
If this were not so, you could not share in your belief
That this world is real, even though it is not.
But within that framework,
You find a myriad of individual variations,
As each of you projects, and perceives,
Whatever it is you wish.

It is absolutely certain in the world as God created it
That everything in your experience, in your existence,
Must be of your choosing.
For everything is contained within you,
And yet contains you.
You choose to project out parts of that everything,
And experience those parts in return.
Since you ARE everything,
There is nothing that is not you.
There is nothing which you do not have.
And there is nothing which you cannot experience,
If it be your choice to do so.
Your projection only makes it seem
As if there is lack in your life.
And from the belief in lack,
Fear is born.

The Atonement was designed BEFORE the separation.
(Remember the words of time—"before" and "after".)
You are the creation of God—
Eternal, complete, whole, and free.
And you have no power to change that fact.
You can imagine yourself to be otherwise.
And, as I have said, that is what this entire world is about,
Just such imaginings.

But there are limits.
You cannot change what God has created.
And if you would attempt to be different
From what God has created,
Then it must be only in your imaginings.

The Atonement is the design, the plan,
Whereby all beings who choose
To imagine themselves to be what they are not
Can, AND MUST, return to the awareness
Of what they truly are, which is the Son of God.

I have spoken of the Atonement as a single-edged sword.
What do I mean by that?
Within your imaginings which characterize your sojourn
In this world of space and time,
You will occasionally, often seemingly randomly,
But inevitably, think thoughts which speak to you
Of the truth of what you are.
When that happens, those thoughts,
Because they touch upon the essence of miracles,
Automatically extend to all of Creation,
Including yourself.

Your thoughts which are not in harmony with truth
Remain at the lower level of which I have spoken,
And serve to keep you, as it were,
Imprisoned here in this world of illusion.
But when you have opened to that first thought
That sings to you of the truth of what you are,
After you have allowed yourself to receive
Into your awareness its vibration, and its energy,
Then that thought remains within your awareness,
Making it easier for others to follow.
And so, do you see, the process feeds on itself.
Every thought you think which is compatible with the truth
Automatically extends to all of Creation,
And therefore back to you again.
Thus it is inevitable,
As you progress through your space and time,
That your thoughts shall, AND MUST,
Bring you back to the full awareness of who you are.
And then you shall be free to move out of
This world of space and time.
It must be so.

That is why I have told you that the journey back to truth
Is a required course.
You MUST return to the full awareness of what you are,

Which is the Son of God.
The nature of the single-edged sword is this, then—
When you think thoughts and imagine things
Which are not compatible with truth,
That is all you have done,
Imagined that which is not compatible with truth.
'Tis an error, and not compatible with truth itself.
It serves to keep you separate from your awareness
Of the truth about your Self.
But it does no harm. It is not sin.
And it is of no consequence.

As you think thoughts and imagine things
Which ARE compatible with truth,
Then they become an irremovable part
Of your experience here.
They bless you and benefit you,
And benefit all of Creation.
And they remain with you,
To assist you and all of your brothers
Along this pathway, this course,
That takes you back to the awareness of what you are.

Were the process like a double-edged sword,
Then if you thought a thought not compatible
With the truth of what you are,
The act of so doing would somehow harm you,
Would effect upon your life a negative consequence,
And could even be viewed by you as punishment.
But truly, there is no double edge on the sword
Of the Atonement.
It cannot harm. It can only bless.

A good example of the belief in a double-edged sword
Is the belief in sin.
For you believe that sin has the power
To separate you further from God,
And to require restitution,
Perhaps even your punishment at the hand of God.
I tell you this notion is absolutely false.
There is no sin. There is no double edge to the Atonement.
And guilt is totally of your own imagining.
Every time you think a thought compatible with the truth,

It flies unto the heavens, unto all of Creation.
And the heavens rejoice.
That selfsame thought inevitably comes back to you.
And whether you know it or not,
A part of you rejoices.
And that process MUST grow and grow,
And feed upon itself,
Until you are at last
Fully in harmony with your true nature.

The simple fact that you are reading these words
Should tell you that you are much farther
Along the path to knowing who you are
Than you perhaps realize.
You are well on your way to your freedom.
Too far indeed to be able to turn back.
Rejoice that this is so.

The pathway you are upon, this course you are following,
Will, AND MUST, bring you to the understanding,
To the experience, of true love, and true freedom.
This path shall lead you to freedom from projection,
To freedom from lack, freedom from valuing,
And freedom from the fear that must arise from them.
And each step you take brings you closer and closer
To the knowledge of what you are,
To the awareness that you truly are the Son of God.

Rejoice. You cannot fail.
Rejoice. You are not alone.
Rejoice. Life is truly wonderful.
Rejoice. You are absolutely free.
And even if you know it not yet,
The time is coming, and soon,
When you shall become aware of how free you truly are.

Blessings upon you all. That is all.

THE ATONEMENT AND
THE INNER LIGHT

Greetings, again. I am Jeshua.
I have come this day to further, with you,
My discussion of *A Course in Miracles*.

I have told you that the Atonement is a total commitment.
Be aware that this does not mean
That YOU must make a total commitment
In order to receive the Atonement.
The Atonement IS yours.
It MUST BE yours.
Nothing can change that truth, or take it away.
You can choose, if you wish, in your time,
To delay the moment in which you become aware
That the Atonement truly is yours.
But that is all that you can change.
You cannot change the fact that the Atonement
IS, AND MUST BE, yours.

The Atonement is a total commitment.
But that total commitment is on behalf of God.
That is another way of stating
That the Atonement truly is a single-edged sword.
The Atonement is yours, and always to remain so,
Independent of your time.
As you release the blocks that keep you from that awareness,
It shall become more and more clear to you
That what I have just said is true.
You can do this, if you wish, moment by moment,
Year by year, lifetime by lifetime.
But you WILL one day arrive at the awareness of your freedom.
You can do it, if you wish, in an instant.
Or you may spread it out across the pages of your time.
In the reality of God's Kingdom, both are the same.
The Atonement is a total commitment on behalf of God,
In the sense that nothing, hear me well—
Nothing you can do, or think, or imagine, or experience,
Or falsely believe you are experiencing—
NOTHING can keep you from the Atonement.

There is nothing you can do which,
In any real sense whatsoever,
Can separate you from God,
Or from the reality of what you are as His Son.
Likewise, there is nothing you can do, whatsoever,
That shall, in reality, detract even in the slightest measure
From what you are as the Son of God.
Ah, yes, you can imagine yourself not to be free.
And in your imagining can believe you are not free.
And in your believing can seem to experience all manner
Of pain and misery, and fear and death.
But in the reality of God's Kingdom, none of that changes,
In the slightest fraction, or measure, what you are.

There is nothing you can do to separate yourself
From the Love of God.
That is God's commitment to you.
You are absolutely free.
But you are not free to BE, to actually BE,
Something different from what you are.

However, what you ARE is everything.
What you HAVE is everything.
And when once you realize that,
There shall be cause only to rejoice in your freedom,
And in your realization that you have, and are, everything.
When there is nothing which you can need, or want,
When there is nothing that you lack,
Then it is not an imposition on your freedom
For God to have created you His Son,
And to demand that you remain as He created you.

I have told you that in order to reach the Atonement,
You must do so by releasing the inner light.
The key word here is "inner".
For "light" is simply another word that tells you what you are.
Truly, you are not a body.
And this body is not a measure of what you are.
You are a being of light,
Just as all of the Son of God are beings of light.
That you cannot change.

Release the inner light.
As you begin to release the inner light,
It is imperative that you come to a realization,
To a measure of certainty, WITHIN—
Ah, hear the word "within."
You accepted the word as I said it, without a flinch.
For even now, in your awareness,
You realize full well that the reality of life is to be found within.
Repeat those words, and be aware of your experience of them.
That will help you realize that all of you do realize,
Even now, that your true life is to be found within.
When I walked this earth one time,
I said that the Kingdom of God is within you.
No truer words were ever spoken.

So to release the inner light
You must begin by realizing that, truly, it is within you.
The inner light is not produced, or created, by your body.
It is not produced, or created, by this physical world.
It is not something produced, or created,
By anything outside of you.
For that which is within you comprises All That Is.

I refer again to level confusion.
Do not be confused about the level of space-time,
The level of thought, and the level of mind.
In reality, there exists but one level.
That is the level of mind.
The level of mind is far beyond the level
At which you seem to think.
I remind you again that the thoughts you think you think
Indeed have no meaning.
For they do not dwell at the level of mind.
The level of mind is closest to the level of your inner experience.
And your real thoughts are closest to that level.
The level of your inner experience
Is what touches the true creative level of All That Is.
You know intuitively, without argument,
That you are free to think whatever,
And whenever, and wherever you wish,
That nothing can restrict what you would choose to do
With your thoughts.

Even more free than that, if you can comprehend it,
Are your real thoughts, and your mind.

All things are products of the creative level of mind.
All of this world is a product of the creative level
And power of your mind.
Your body is a product of your creative mind.
All that you seem to experience in that body
Is a product of the creative power of your mind.
All experiences that seem to come to you
Through your body, and through its senses,
Are but products of the creative power of your mind.

This is a most important point,
And one which can easily lead to level confusion.
It does seem to most of you that your body
Is the source of your experience.
However, it is not so.
Everything that your body sees with its eyes,
Hears with its ears, feels with its touch,
Is a product and a reflection
Of what your mind chooses to create.

I told you that the body cannot miscreate in the mind.
This means that it is NOT POSSIBLE
For any physical or bodily experience
To have any influence upon, to affect, in any sense,
Your mind.
It is always, always, the other way around.
Your creative mind chooses what it shall see,
What it shall hear, what it shall sense.
And then the body, faithful servant that it is,
Proceeds to deliver to you exactly
What you have chosen to experience.

I also told you that the mind cannot miscreate in the body.
This means that everything which the body experiences,
Be it physical pleasure or physical pain,
Be it physical joy, or the worst illness,
Is an active choice at the creative level of mind.
EVERY physical experience is produced
At the creative level of mind,
And then projected outward in such a manner

That you do not believe
That your mind is actually the source of the experience.
But, indeed, it is.

Your mind CAN NOT err in its freedom.
Every seeming bodily experience is, and must be,
The product of your will in action.
Mind is ALWAYS the source.
And the body is helpless to affect its source.
Bodily experiences can have no effect whatsoever
On the purposeful beingness of mind.

Furthermore, it is not true that sickness of your body
Must reflect dis-ease in your mind,
Although that is usually the case.
Everything that your body seems to experience
Is the result of your active choice
At the level of mind.
The body cannot affect the mind.
The mind cannot mis-create in the body
And thus produce a different source of experience.
For there is only the level of mind.
And that level is the same as the level
Of the Kingdom within you.

If you would learn these truths,
If you would find the freedom, and the joy,
And the peace which you seek,
Then you find it by releasing the inner light.
And you start by always being vigilant with your thoughts.
You do that by allowing yourself to realize as best you can
That everything IS at the level of mind.
If you are ill, do not say "This happened to me."
Rather realize within that it is a full and conscious choice.
Indeed, you may not seem to understand why you chose it.
But realize full well that you did.
This applies to every aspect of your life,
Including every aspect of every relationship you experience.

In your vigilance, you must realize that,
At the level of mind, there exists no separation.
At the true level of what you are,
You are not separate one from another.

For all of you are One.
At the level of mind, every experience, every thought,
Is extended, shared fully without restriction or reservation.
This is so whether or not a being seems to possess
Conscious awareness of that fact.
It is true of every person, every tree, every rock.
At the level of mind, all of that which you are,
All of that which you perceive,
All of that which you experience,
Is shared with, and open to, all other beings.

And at that same level, because you ARE One,
The entire Oneness rejoices
In whatever you have chosen to create.
The Oneness rejoices that you ARE, indeed, the Son of God.
And within that same Oneness,
Nothing is ever done to you, or happens to you.
For within the Oneness, every experience
Is shared uniformly with all beings.

Indeed, there is true rejoicing,
Even when you are using your creative ability
To miscreate in this world of perception,
And to imagine yourself to be something which you are not.
For even that is to exercise the freedom which God gave you.
And with all other beings, it is the same.
Anything they experience or imagine is extended to all beings,
Including yourself.
Because truly you ARE One.
And so it is that in your space and time,
When two beings, or three, or four, or ten thousand,
Seem to interact together,
It is always with the mutual choosing, the mutual blessing,
And the mutual rejoicing of all those beings—
Even though it may seem that one or more of them are tyrant,
And one or more of them are victim.

The Kingdom of God is within you.
Begin there.
And as you realize that,
You will have released, in large measure,
The inner light.
And you will know that all creation,

In your life, in space and time, and in eternity,
Is at the level of mind.

Imagine for a moment, realize for a moment,
How free you know yourself to be with your thoughts.
And then, if you will, attempt to realize,
At a level of feeling,
That everything you see or experience
With your physical senses
Is truly nothing more than a creation of mind,
And that everything you see or experience
With your physical senses
Is as free as your thought.
And I tell you, truly,
That IS the way your life is.

In your freedom, as you become, as you grow,
As you learn this, if you will—
In your freedom,
You shall only find peace, and joy, and light, and happiness.
For the Atonement is a total commitment given you by God.
Always it is blessing.
Always it leads you to freedom and joy.
And nothing that you do
Can take it away from you,
Ever in space and time,
Or ever in eternity.
My blessed brothers, you are so free,
And so loved.

Blessings upon you all. That is all.

THE FUNCTION OF MIRACLE WORKERS

Greetings again. I am Jeshua.
I have come, this day, to help you to understand
What it means to be a miracle worker.

Therefore, today I shall be speaking about YOU.
For YOU are the miracle workers.
Because YOU are the Son of God.

If you are, indeed, a miracle worker, as I have said,
What do you do?
How do you DO these miracles?
Hear me well. The answer is, you do not.
But hear me well, once again.
The Son of God, which you ARE, does, indeed,
Perform what you, on this earth, would call miracles.

In order to perform miracles, you must extend them
Unto all beings, which includes extending them unto yourself.
To extend is what God does.
Extension is complete.
It gives everything, and receives everything,
With no exceptions, and with no restrictions.
Personalities, beings who somehow have imagined themselves
To be separate and isolated from God,
And especially from their brothers,
Are not capable of extending.
They are constrained to perceive, rather than to know.
And their perception arises out of their projection,
Which arises from their belief that they are alone.

I have also told you that if you would do miracles,
You need not be concerned about
Your own readiness to do them.
Rather be concerned about my readiness.
But more so, be concerned about your willingness
To let me control the miracles you would do.

When I tell you to let me perform the miracles,
When I tell you not to be concerned about your readiness,
But rather with my readiness, which is always there,
It is easy for you to become confused by those words.
For you tend to think of me in the same way
That you still think of yourself.
In your world of personality, and therefore ego,
It is difficult yet, for most of you, to see yourself as One,
As being beyond isolation and separation.
But, indeed, you are One.

When I say "I," referring to myself,
I use that word for the purpose of communicating with you.
For it is easier for you to imagine that a being like yourself
Is communicating with you.
But the "I" of whom I speak is beyond personality,
Beyond isolation, and beyond separation.
I do use the word "I."
However, the "I" of which I speak is not similar to the "I"
Of which you speak when you use that same word.

I stand in union with the Holy Spirit,
In full awareness of All That Is,
In perfect communication with all beings, without exception.
And just as the Holy Spirit knows all, and is aware of all,
In that same sense, so am I.

I do not bring values. I do not bring fears.
I do not bring restrictions.
I do not bring exclusion of any kind
To you, or to our relationship.

So when I tell you to let me do the miracles,
What I really mean is this—
In order for you to function as a miracle worker,
It is necessary that you release, if but for a moment,
(And a moment is enough)
The bonds of personality and ego,
And fear and doubt and restriction.
In that moment in which you release those bonds,
That which I AM, and that which in reality YOU ARE,
Will perform the miracles through you.

You will find a new awareness within your consciousness.
And you will know to the last detail
What you are to do, where you are to go,
What you are to say, what you are to be.
And that new awareness will flow through your being
Without effort.

But I have also told you
That the only function of the miracle worker,
YOUR only function as a miracle worker,
Is to accept the Atonement FOR YOURSELF.
That is fully sufficient.
For if you accept the Atonement for yourself,
It follows automatically
That you accept it for all of your brothers, without exception.
Hear me well.
If there is one brother whom you would exclude from miracles,
You must, in that desire, have excluded yourself
From the self-same miracles.

What does it mean to accept the Atonement for yourself?
I have already told you that the Kingdom of God is within you.
I spoke to you of the inner altar.
I spoke of level confusion, and the fact that
The only creative level is the level of mind.
TO ACCEPT THE ATONEMENT FOR YOURSELF
IS TO COME TO THAT REALIZATION
THAT THE ONLY CREATIVE LEVEL
IS THE LEVEL OF MIND.
When that happens, level confusion will have disappeared.
You will not view space, time, and this world,
As something which is real.
You will see it only as an effect
Of the creative power of your mind.
You will realize that anything
You would want to experience in space and time
Must be experienced at the level of mind.

Suppose for a moment that you knew that—
That the only level of creation was the level of mind,
That everything you perceived
Was but an effect of the great creative cause called Mind.
Then what would you realize

In conjunction with that awareness?
You already know that your mind is as free as,
No, freer than, the wind.
You already know that all minds are free,
And that you cannot control another's thoughts.
Thus you know that, in your own freedom,
No other mind can do anything to you.
Thus you know that you can not do anything
To any other mind.
So you would come to realize that all minds
MUST BE in constant sharing and Oneness,
That all of existence is but a splendid symphony of Oneness
Which exists ONLY at the level of mind,
At the level of true thought,
At the level of Spirit.

TO ACCEPT THE ATONEMENT FOR YOURSELF
IS TO BECOME AWARE OF THAT TRUTH
AND THAT REALITY.
When once you experience that truth,
You will realize, without effort,
That all beings are of the same nature as yourself.
You will recognize, without effort,
That all beings are nothing but mind.
And then you will have become a miracle worker.
For you will have looked within and seen the inner altar.
And you will know that the Kingdom within
Truly IS the source of All That Is.

There is nothing external to yourself.
The inner altar is to be found at the level of mind,
The level of freedom, the level of total sharing.
And when you experience that for yourself,
The gift of that experience will automatically
Flow outward to all of your brothers.

You will then see them in a light
Different from anything you have ever imagined.
As you SEE your brother,
Not with your eyes, not with your physical sight,
But as a being of light,
You shall see beyond all appearances and form.
For those are illusion.

You will see all beings as beings of light,
As beings of love and freedom,
Who are graciously honoring for you
Whatever it is you have requested at the level of mind.
Thus you shall know, for yourself,
That whatever you experience,
Be it alone or in interaction with anyone or anything,
It is always of your own creation, and your own choosing.

What you shall know then cannot be but gratitude.
Hear me well.
This applies to whatever may seem to befall you,
WITH NO EXCEPTION,
Be it a blessed love and a splendid relationship,
Be it crime that seems to be forced upon you,
Be it any manner of what you might call evil,
Or that which you do not seem to prefer to experience.
When once you have accepted the Atonement for yourself,
You will approach all things from the level of mind.
You will realize that your every experience
Is but the response to your own request.
And how can you then be less than grateful?

And so it is for all other beings as well.
What you then discover for your brothers and yourself
Is freedom—
Freedom to be whatever you wish,
To experience whatever you can imagine,
Always, always in cooperation with All That Is.

There are some principles that apply to miracle workers.
The first follows directly from what I have been saying this day.
Miracles abolish the concern for levels.
They abolish level confusion.
For miracles always occur at one level, the level of mind.
I will adjust space and time and their levels
To fit the miracles you extend.
Miracles are beyond your personality and its preferences.
They must occur at the level of mind,
Wherein it is clear that all beings are free,
And all beings are One.

It is not possible, when performing miracles,
To impose any experience upon another being.
If you believe that such could happen,
You are subjecting yourself to level confusion,
And you need return to the level of mind.
Miracles, as I have told you,
Must transcend personality and its projections.
Miracles involve your One Self, the light that you are,
The inner light, and the Great Rays.
And miracles must extend from you to All That Is,
Including to your self.

Because miracles do not involve personality,
They do not function under conscious control.
You cannot plan a miracle at the level of personality.
As you let go of personality and its belief in separation,
Miracles will simply flow out of you,
And out of the Oneness.

Miracles do not involve judgment.
Judgment is of personality.
Judgment is of time.
Judgment is of thoughts.
None of those are appropriate for miracles.
Miracles always accept what is, with complete forgiveness.
Since miracles do not arise out of judgment,
They can not arise out of your awareness,
At the personality level,
That someone is in need of a miracle.

The state of mind that shall bring you to miracles,
To your ultimate freedom,
To your ultimate peace,
To your ultimate joy,
Arises out of the realization that you are here to help.
You are, indeed, One with All That Is.
And whatever you do that transcends
Your imagined separation
Is always a blessing, and is always helpful.

Miracles arise out of your willingness
Not to impose your own personality and its desires
Upon your life,

But rather to open to my presence,
To the presence of the Oneness, and the Holy Spirit.
For when you do that you open your life to miracles.
And with that you will know what to do,
Where to go, what to say, and what to be.

Truly, you ARE a creative being.
Truly you ARE free.
And the exercise of that creativity and that freedom,
Beyond personality, beyond your imagined separation,
Is the level of miracles,
And the level of peace, and joy, and freedom,
Which at this moment are beyond your comprehension,
But are beautiful beyond what you can imagine.

Blessings upon you all. That is all.

FEAR AND CONFLICT

Greetings again. I am Jeshua.
This day I would speak with you
About fear and conflict.
How appropriate that we speak of those words together.
For always, when you are in conflict,
When you experience the absence of peace,
No matter how subtle,
It is due to your fear.
And always, fear is your own creation, your own choice.

It is true that fear is your own creation.
For everything in your life is your own creation.
And that includes your fear.
Therefore fear is, and must be, self-controlled.
Indeed, it seems to you that you BECOME afraid,
That circumstances have the power to frighten you.
All of you can remember times in which you felt truly afraid.
And even though someone might suggest to you
That a situation is not even real,
And that you should simply decide not to be fearful,
Still you seem helpless to let go of your fear.
But then you hear me tell you that
The mastery of fear must be up to you,
And that I cannot help you to overcome your fear.
And indeed, that is true.

Your fear is the cornerstone upon which
This entire world is built.
You created fear for the purpose of experiencing
This imagined world of separation.
And in the moment, in the instant,
Even though it be but for an instant,
That you totally let go of your fear,
Never again shall the world seem the same to you.

Ultimately, your fear relates to your answers to two questions—
"Who am I?" and
"What do I value, and why?"

In order to seem to experience this world of illusion,
You have deigned yourself to be separate.
And thus you made an "I,"
Which is but your definition of yourself as a separate being.
And that is what I call the ego.
But this ego, born out of fear itself,
Which is your creation, carefully designed by you,
Is exactly that which you fear to let go of.
And ultimately everything you value is that which,
In one form or another,
Provides and maintains your definition of what you are,
All of which is but your ego.

So it seems to you, hear me well,
It SEEMS to you that if you give up
Part of this definition of what and who you are,
That part of you must die.
It seems to you that if you cease to value
That which furnishes your beliefs about who you are,
That indeed, in some measure, you shall surely die.
Nothing could be further from the truth.

This is a perfect example of
What I have referred to as level confusion.
In this world of space and time and bodies, and the ego,
All of that seems so real,
And seems to be of great consequence.
When, indeed, nothing could be further from the truth.

And within that context, I have told you not to ask me,
Not to ask the Holy Spirit, to help you get rid of your fear.
For when you ask another to help you get rid of your fear,
You are implying and believing
That it is NOT your responsibility to get rid of it yourself.

Hear me well. If I, or any other being,
Were able to take your fear away from you,
It would destroy, in great measure, your freedom.
Hear me well. God is but Love.
And Love is but freedom.
And your freedom must entail your right
To imagine yourself afraid
For as long, and as often, as you wish.

If I, or another, took that fear from you,
If we COULD do anything to you against your will,
Even the extraction of your fear,
You would not be free.
And if you were not free, you would not be loved.
And if you were not loved, God would not be God.

'Tis absolutely true that you choose what you would experience.
You choose it at the level of mind.
And all that seems to follow is always a product of that level.
And so it is that if you desire to conquer your fear,
You MUST deal with your fear at the level of mind,
Where it does not exist.

And that is how I can help you.
That is how the Holy Spirit can help you.
That is how this Course can help you find
Freedom from your fear,
And freedom from its imagined consequences.
We can help you by guiding you—
First with your thinking here,
Then through your experience,
And then through your real thoughts
Which function at the level of mind.
We can help you move vertically
From the level of space-time to the level of mind.
And when you experience anything in its true fullness
At the level of mind, even for an instant,
Your fear shall pass away.

Whenever you are afraid,
It always means you have attempted to raise body thoughts,
The belief in space and time,
To the level of mind.
And that means that you are attempting
To assign some measure of reality
To bodies and space and time,
Which, indeed, they do not have.
Nothing is real but Spirit, Mind, and its creative ability.
That is your gift from God,
Your inheritance as His Son.
And from that creative level of mind follows All That Is,
Even though some of it seems to take the form of illusion.

To control your fear, to control your thoughts,
To release yourself from that which binds you to this earth,
Which is ultimately your answers to those questions—
Who am I? What do I value, and why?—
To release yourself from that prison,
You must direct your own thoughts to the level of mind.

And this is how it shall be for you.
As you sit in your silence,
As you read this Course, as you read other sources,
As you talk with other persons,
Whenever you experience something that is of truth,
Then that experience, that thought
Automatically flies to the level of mind.
And once there, it blesses all of Creation, including yourself.

It shall then seem as if I or the Holy Spirit
Brings back to you the truth of what you have thought.
And that happens without any effort on your part.
It is possible for you to totally let go of fear in one instant.
It is possible for you to let go of fear
As a longer, slower, process,
Which you shall imagine to take time.
Both are your choices.
For such is your freedom.

If you choose to take time, and, indeed, most of you do,
Then your goal is this—
To hear as best you can, the truth,
To try always to listen within,
In a stillness uncluttered by the thoughts and worries
Of your day to day existence,
To try as best you can to only allow those thoughts
Which are compatible with love.
And to the extent that your thoughts ARE compatible with love,
They shall cast out fear.
They shall fly to the level of mind,
And return to you as blessing upon blessing.

So whenever you would do anything, pause
And ask me if it is in harmony with our will as the Son of God.
If it is, you will have no fear.
That, indeed, requires some vigilance.

But truly it is not difficult.
The vigilance simply means that whenever you start to feel
Any discontent, any fear, any unrest,
Pause, and as best you can, be still, and ask—
Is this which I would do in harmony
With the Voice of God, and the Holy Spirit?
And you truly will find a feeling, an awareness,
An answer that shall come to you.
And as you follow that, you are taking the steps required
To banish fear from your life.

It seems rather simple, what I have just suggested to you.
And that is exactly right. It is.
And you do not know the measure of the power and strength
That shall come into your life as you choose
To take this simple step each and every time
You feel unrest and disharmony.
The change, the transformation, in your life,
When once you choose to do this with diligence and vigilance,
Will astound you.

Over and over again I have told you—
But listen for the Voice for God,
And It shall always be there.
And that is true.
You must, however, choose to face your own fear,
As I have suggested,
In order to hear that Voice for God.
But, indeed, you shall.

And then the Voice for God shall lead you,
Gently and directly, upon the road,
No, upon the highway,
To freedom, to peace, and to joy,
Where all is love.

Blessings upon you all. That is all.

LOVE AND FEAR

Greetings again. I am Jeshua.
I have come this day to speak to you
About fear, and about love.

Love is real. Love exists.
Fear is not real. Fear does not exist.

If you have fear, if you are afraid,
It is because you have chosen not to love.
I am aware that that can seem frustrating to you.
I am aware that that can seem difficult for you.
It seems as if I am saying, almost glibly—
If you are afraid, simply love perfectly, and you will be fine,
You will be free of your fear.
That is, indeed, exactly what I am saying.

The Bible says you cannot love two masters.
For you will hate the one and love the other,
Or love the one and hate the other.
The same is true of love and fear.
You either are afraid, or you love.
Love is freedom.
And likewise, you are either free, or you are not free.
It is not possible to be partly free.

I have described for you a sequence
In *A Course in Miracles*. (15)
The sequence describes for you
How to free yourself from fear.
And it goes like this—
Whenever you are in conflict,
Whenever you are not at peace,
Know first that it is because you are afraid.
Secondly, if you have fear,
It is because you have chosen not to love.
Thirdly, the only correction for the lack of love is perfect love.

And finally, perfect love is the Atonement,
As if to say that perfect love
Is the ultimate answer to whatever would destroy your peace.

Perfect Love IS all that matters.
Perfect Love IS the solution to all your problems.
And that is true.
Perfect Love, the Love of God, is extension.
And there is a reason for that.
Imperfect love, or fear, is projection,
Which always leads to perception.
And there is a reason for that.

Perfect Love arises out of a state of being invulnerable.
It follows from the awareness that
There is nothing that can harm you,
Nothing that can take away your freedom.
And above all, it follows from the awareness that
There is nothing that you do not have,
And that there is nothing that you, indeed, ARE not.
God, in a word, could be described as everything—
No lack, no absence, no incompleteness—
Simply everything—All That Is.

And you, as the Son of God, are the same.
You have everything.
And as Spirit, you ARE everything.
Thus you were created by God.
And nothing can change that,
Least of all your vain imaginings that create
The illusion of this world.

Love, then, very simply, is the awareness of that fact.
Love is the awareness that you HAVE everything,
And that you ARE everything.
When you have everything, then, of course,
There is nothing that you can lack.
Because you are Spirit,
Sharing the everything that you are
Expands you, and does not diminish you in any form.
So it follows, since you ARE Spirit,
That the awareness that you have everything
Automatically prompts you

To want to GIVE that same everything.
For it is in the giving that you become fulfilled,
And would become more than you already are,
Were it possible for there to be
Something greater than everything.
But, of course, it is not possible.
Your completeness, the everything that you are,
Expands without becoming greater.
Paradoxical? No, indeed.

Love is the giving that extends Itself outward,
And yet returns unto Itself.
Love is the inexorable sharing of the awareness of everything,
Moment upon moment upon moment, upon forever,
Upon the absence of time.
And that is the true nature of God.
And, hear me well, that is the true nature of you.
For you are the Son of God.

There is only Spirit.
Spirit is All That Is.
You could think of it this way, if you find it helpful.
There is only Spirit. There is only energy.
And even this world, within the density of its matter,
Is nothing but a dense form of energy,
Which in an instant could, and one day will,
Be transformed back into the sheer energy of Spirit.
Spirit is All That Is.
And you likewise, being Spirit,
Are All That Is.

There is nothing outside of you.
There is nothing, when you see it with true vision,
That shall seem to be apart from you in any way.
For in the awareness of truth
You shall recognize all of Creation and all of experience
As but your Self,
Albeit shared perfectly and completely with all of Creation.
There is no paradox here.
You are One.
And you are You.
And both are the same.

Fear always arises from the absence
Of the inner awareness that you have, and are, everything.
In the absence of that awareness, you perceive a lack.
You perceive scarcity.
You perceive that it is possible for something to exist
Which you do not have.
And therefore, you perceive that it is possible
That there be something which you need.
The counterpart of that is that you perceive
That there is something which you have,
But which could be taken away.
Both of those conditions represent fear.

Fear is the feeling you have
When you contemplate losing something
Which you perceive that you have,
And which you believe you need.
Likewise, fear is the feeling you have
When you contemplate not receiving something
Which you perceive you do not have,
And which you believe you need.

It is so simple.
Whenever you experience fear,
It is because you have not loved.
Ultimately, it is because you have not loved your self.
You have been created by God.
You have everything. You are everything.
And when you choose not to love your self,
You simply believe that not to be true.
You choose rather to believe
That there is scarcity, or lack, in your life.

The Atonement, which IS Perfect Love, is simply the realization
That everything is of Spirit, that everything is of mind,
And that everything IS yours.
Therefore, we say that this is a Course in mind training.

Since you have chosen to believe in time, and space,
I understand fully that most of you seem unable, in an instant,
To depart from your belief in lack and scarcity.
Therefore, as you undertake the training of your mind,
As you follow this Course that shall lead you

To the Atonement, to Perfect Love, and to perfect peace,
Begin with just this idea.
And eventually the idea shall move past your thoughts,
To experience, to real thoughts, and to knowing.
And then you shall be free.

Do your best, as you discipline your mind,
To realize that ALL THINGS are of mind,
That having anything, truly, is only as far away
As the thought that you have it,
Although the thought of which I speak
Lies within your experience,
Beyond the thoughts you believe you are thinking.

Certainly, you are aware of having had thoughts
Of possessing many things—riches, relationships, health—
And have been frustrated
When they have not appeared in your life.
True thought, which lies at the level of mind,
And which houses your creative power, is more.
You shall come to experience, and to know, that truth.

So hear me well as I speak to you this day.
All is Spirit. All is One. And all is Love.
And all of that is You.
For that is what you are, as the Son of God.
All fear arises from the belief
That you have less than everything.
And miracle-mindedness, right-mindedness,
Arises from the realization that you are, indeed, everything,
And that every brother also is everything.

The only function of the miracle worker
Is to accept the Atonement for himself.
The rest will follow.
So I commission you to do this—
Discipline your mind, your thoughts,
In every way you can.
And know that I shall always be present to help you,
At the level of mind, and of Spirit.

Discipline your mind to always realize
That you have everything, that you are everything.
And then you automatically will desire
To extend that everything,
To share that everything with all beings.
Indeed, when you once realize, if even for a moment,
That you have everything,
Then you will automatically realize the same of your brother.

If you do not yet realize that,
Then you are still choosing fear.
And it simply means that you are not yet ready
To perform miracles under my guidance.
For I cannot conquer your fear.
If I did, you would not be free.
'Tis more important for you to be free—
Even though it be free to be afraid—
Than it is for some external source,
Even though it might be God,
To take away your fear against your will.

Fear not. Your fear cannot harm you.
The Atonement is a single-edged sword.
The thoughts you think that are free of fear
Bless you, and all the world.
The thoughts you think that are based on fear
Are simply based on fear.
That is all.
They do not harm you.
They do not, in any sense, change or destroy
What you truly are in spirit,
Which is the Son of God.

Whenever you are not at peace,
Know first that it is fear.
Then realize that if you are afraid you have chosen not to love.
The remedy for lack of love is Perfect Love.
And Perfect Love is the simple realization
That you have everything,
And that you are, indeed, that same everything.

When once you realize that, the Atonement will be yours.
And you will be free.
And automatically, without effort,
You will extend that Love which you are
To every brother, and to all of Creation.
And your reward shall be a joy
Beyond anything you can possibly imagine.

Blessings upon you all. That is all.

INNOCENCE

Greetings again. I am Jeshua.
I have come this day, as always,
To speak with you about your Self.

YOU are a miracle.
Truly, *A Course in Miracles*, this pathway to miracles,
Is about you.
You ARE the Son of God.
All of you are the single Son of God.
All of you are One, one Being, One Self, one Mind—
And yet, with attributes that allow for creation.

Do not worry yourself if perhaps
You cannot seem to academically understand that which I say.
The truth lies, always, in that which you experience,
Beyond the level of your words,
And beyond the level of your conscious understanding.
When you cease to worry about whether you understand,
Thereby allowing yourself to be free,
To simply exult in being,
Then you begin to move far closer
To the awareness of your reality as the Son of God.

An attribute of God—
And it follows, then, that it is an attribute of you—
An attribute of God, which I will discuss with you this day,
Is innocence.

In simplest terms, to be innocent means NOT TO KNOW.
Well, if to be innocent is not to know,
Then how can God, who knows everything,
And is everything,
Be innocent?
How can you have, and be, everything,
And yet be innocent?
Are you innocent simply because
There is that which you do not know?

Hear me well.
THE INNOCENCE OF GOD
REFERS TO THAT WHICH DOES NOT EXIST.
Truly, God IS everything,
And in being everything, God HAS everything.
And the same is true of you,
As the Spirit which you are.

Everything and nothing cannot coexist.
Just as light and darkness cannot coexist.
When once you realize that you are everything,
Then it is not possible to be aware of lack,
Or absence, or nothing,
In any form.

And this world, which we so often refer to as illusion,
Is comprised of nothing.
It is comprised of, and formed out of,
Imagined thoughts, based on projection,
Which are based on the belief in scarcity and lack,
On the belief in nothingness.
And God, in his innocence, cannot know of nothing.

God has created you so free
That you can imagine yourself to be something you are not.
And as I have told you, seemingly countless times,
This world is but an exercise in imagining
That you are what you are not.
And within innocence, it is not possible to BE something,
And to NOT BE something, simultaneously,
As I refer to your time.
It is not possible to be something, and not be something,
Even outside of your time.

So within the innocence of God, within the strength that is God,
There lies the simple awareness that God, Spirit, IS everything.
And anything, albeit imagined,
Which would suggest that there can be less than everything,
That there can be lack, that there can be scarcity,
That there can be, in some small fashion, nothing—
All suggestion that those things might be
Is but illusion.

The illusions of this world are the blocks
That keep you from your own innocence.
I told you that I can correctly be identified as a lamb.
But you need realize that my meekness and gentleness
Do not decry strength.
Innocence does not, in any sense, imply weakness or absence.
Innocence implies, and represents, a strength so great
That nothing can threaten the awareness of its own being.

To be innocent, as God is innocent,
Is to know that you have, and are, everything.
And what you cannot know, then, in your innocence,
Is any lack, any scarcity,
Or anything which you might tend to refer to as evil,
Or the absence of good.

In my resurrection, I verified for all of you
That nothing could change, in any way,
The reality of what I am as the Son of God, as Spirit.
And that is the lesson for you—
That nothing can alter, in any way,
That which you are as the Son of God.
No circumstance that would seem to arise
Within your space and time,
Albeit of your own choice,
Can modify in any way, what you truly are, as Spirit.

Nails and a sword could not modify, in any way,
That which I was, and remain.
And that is the message of the resurrection.
If you but knew that message within your being, without doubt,
Then you would have within you a great, great, measure
Of the innocence of God.

In your innocence, you would know that you,
Always, moment upon moment,
ARE ABSOLUTELY SAFE.
You would know that there is no circumstance
That can effect, or change, that which you are—
Even if your body seems to die, as mine did.
No circumstance whatsoever changes you in any way
From what you truly are.

The innocence of God belongs to you.
It is your inheritance.
And when you learn to perceive from within your innocence,
You will find that you look upon all of your brothers with trust.
And indeed, your trust, your faithfulness,
Is what each brother deserves from you.

For, truly, you are Spirit.
And, truly, all of us are One.
And in the strength of your innocence,
There is nothing you can experience
That is not by your own reckoning,
And your own choice.

So as you attempt to grow, within your time,
Into your understanding of what you are,
Try as often as you can to focus on the awareness
That each brother with whom you interact in any way
Is honoring, for you, the trust that you have placed in him.
Were it not for your Oneness,
Were it not for the love which you are and which you share,
The world would BE as it so often SEEMS to you—
A world of separation and of competition,
A world of scarcity,
A world in which as you give
You are diminished.

And yet I tell you,
The reality of what you are
Negates entirely that vision of this world.
Your strength is so great,
Your freedom is so great,
That nothing except that which you request, and create,
Can become your experience.

And in your innocence,
As you come to understand and experience it,
You shall trust each brother.
For what each brother is doing, in interaction with you,
Is fulfilling the role which you have asked him to play.
THERE ARE NO EXCEPTIONS OF ANY KIND
TO THAT WHICH I HAVE JUST SPOKEN.
And it is your innocence, your completeness,

The fact that you are everything,
Which makes that true.

In your innocence, which you share with our Creator God,
You HAVE everything, and you ARE everything.
In your innocence lies strength.
In your strength lies the power to overcome
Anything that you would call evil.
This happens in the same sense that light eradicates darkness,
Without resistance of any kind from the darkness itself,
Which does not even exist.

Your innocence, and the awareness within
That you are only truth, and only love,
Erases that which you would call evil
In the same manner in which light eradicates darkness.
And it happens in an instant.

And your innocence, as it grows upon you,
Will bring you the certainty that you are safe, always,
That you are loved, always,
That you are free, always,
And that nothing can take away from you
The fact that you are everything—
And that nothing can change, in any way,
The fact that you are, have been, and shall always be,
The Son of God.

Blessings upon you all. That is all.

PERCEPTION

Greetings again. I am Jeshua.
I spoke to you last time of the innocence of God.
I did so to help you realize that you, as the Son of God,
Share His natural state of innocence.
For innocence is the realization that you have everything.
And in that state, there cannot be fear.
In that state, there cannot be lack.
And there cannot be anticipated fear.
For never can you be, or become, less than everything.

In that sense, then, you are absolutely safe.
Indeed, nothing truer could be said about you as the Son of God
Than to say that you, as the Son of God, as Spirit,
Are absolutely safe.
If you wish, you may think of yourself
As cradled in the arms of God.
You may think of yourself as a vibrant, free, roving spirit,
Released by his loving parent to explore anything that is.
And both would be true, or anything in between.
But in every case, in every scenario,
YOU ARE ABSOLUTELY SAFE.

In your world you think of the opposite of innocence as guilt.
And many times I have told you that guilt is the cause
Of all this world of illusion.
And if guilt is the opposite of innocence,
Then indeed, the antithesis of your innocence
IS the cause of all of your fears, all of your miseries,
And this entire world of illusion.

What also is the cause of this entire world is your perception.
And it is of perception that I would speak with you this day.
Perception arose after the separation.
Consciousness, that split-off part of your mind
With which you think you think—
Consciousness arose after the separation.

The separation was, is, remains,
Totally a thing of imagination.
And as such, it is not real.

Nevertheless, your power as the Son of God
Allows you to deem it real,
And to live out, with great intensity,
All your illusions, all your fears,
Even your death.
But again, I tell you, you are absolutely safe.

Perception arose from guilt,
Which is the opposite of your innocence.
And therefore, perception arises from the belief
That you do not have everything,
That you are not everything,
That there is something which you can, and do, lack.

Perception demands selection.
But as Spirit, existing in the state of innocence,
There is only everything.
Nothing can be excluded. Nothing can be included.
For there is only everything.
In your perception, in your imagined separation,
You must always, of necessity, and by design,
Choose that which you would be aware of,
And that which you would not be aware of.
It is the ability to NOT BE AWARE OF
That allows you to feel separate,
That allows you to imagine yourself alone.
And you all know that the thought
Of being totally alone seems to generate fear.

How is it that you become aware of lack,
That you become able to select
That which you would experience in this world?
Hear me well. In order to come here at all,
And yet believe this world of illusion to be real,
It was necessary, by your own design,
To create a part of your mind
Which could seem to be isolated
From another part of your mind,
A part which is aware of your true nature.

And thus arose the ability to project.
When you project, it is not simply taking thoughts,
Or interpretations, if you will,

And assigning them to another.
Projecting really means taking awareness
And putting it outside of your awareness.
To do this and remain in a state of innocence
Is not only absurd, but impossible.

For the purpose of playing with your creative abilities,
You then designed this world.
You designed the human beings you seem to be
With split minds.
Everything is within you.
And likewise, the separation comes from within.
The separation merely refers to the way in which
Your mind SEEMS to be split.

This imagined split is the basis for your perception.
That split is what allows you to even imagine
That illusion is real.
Illusion is formed by taking fragments of the whole,
Perceiving them as if they were separate wholes,
And then constructing images out of those isolated aspects,
Which you then think form a complete entity.

So in order to experience illusion at all,
You must begin by fragmenting,
By splitting off from your awareness,
Parts of that which is real.
And it is your projection that allows you to do just that.
A choice is made and placed within your consciousness—
Which as I have told you is the home of your ego—
A choice is made by you as to what it is
That you will project outside of your mind.
You choose what it is that you will maintain for a moment
Within the framework of consciousness.
And that which you retain
Within the framework of consciousness
Is what you use to build your illusions.

And that is what you project outside of your mind,
Based upon those aspects of the whole
Which you have selected.
And that is what makes your perception.
For your perception MUST be based

Upon that which has been projected outside of your mind.
And thus it is that projection makes perception.
And none of it could have arisen if you had not chosen
To seem to split your mind in the first place.

What then is true perception?
I have spoken of knowledge, and told you
That as long as you cling in any sense
To the illusion of space and time,
You cannot know.
Within this world of space and time, however,
You CAN perceive truly.
And that, of course, is true perception.
Your true perception will lead you to the Atonement.
And when once you leave the illusion of space and time,
The illusion of this body and all of its constraints,
Then you will begin to know.
Then you will understand true freedom.

True perception arises within your conscious awareness
When, from within that level,
You allow into your mind only, and nothing but,
That which is real, that which is true.
Now, hear me well.
You, ego, as I speak with you this moment,
HAVE NO IDEA OF WHAT IS REAL AND WHAT IS NOT,
OF WHAT IS TRUE AND WHAT IS NOT.
And as long as you choose to think,
To select from within your own consciousness
Your belief in what is real and what is not,
You will be wrong.
And you will fail to discover your One Self.

And that is why I request of you
That you place your conscious mind under my guidance.
If you wish, think of me as the being
Who is speaking to you this moment.
Think of me as the Holy Spirit.
Think of me as the higher part of your mind
Which is in touch with the Holy Spirit,
And is therefore capable of true perception.
But realize that you MUST be in contact with that Source
In order to perceive truly.

How do you start? Where do you begin?
I have told you many times
That the change can happen in an instant, if you wish.
And yet it never seems to happen like that, does it?
For as long as you harbor the hidden desire
To experience illusion,
As long as you project out of your conscious awareness
That which is true instead of that which is false,
You block the pathway to your true perception.

I remind you once again
That salvation is a single-edged sword.
For this is an important key to your true perception.
When you choose to see a brother, or yourself, truly,
Then what happens, without effort,
Is that that truth extends to the higher aspect of your Self.
It also extends to me, to the Holy Spirit, to all beings.
And it then returns to your consciousness
To reinforce for you
The truth which you have just invited into your awareness.

And here is another most important key—
If you quiet your mind, if you are still,
You will ALWAYS become aware of,
You will always experience,
The blessing which returns to your consciousness
From the higher aspect of your Self,
But which had its birth
Within the truth of your initial thought.

And so, if you would grow towards true perception,
Hear these words I speak this day.
And then be still.
For as you, within your consciousness,
Think truly of yourself or of your brother,
Then all the world shall be blessed.
And you, in your silence,
Will feel that blessing come back to you.
And this experience can, and will, grow upon itself,
And magnify at a rate which will truly astound you.
And what is required of you is your diligence,
And your willingness to be still and listen.

And if you choose not to be diligent in this way,
I, and the whole universe, shall not, in one iota,
Love you any less than we do right now.
You are absolutely free. You are absolutely loved.
And you are absolutely safe.

So I do not admonish you.
I am here only to offer you a pathway unto your freedom.
So if I suggest to you, as I have done,
How you can grow in the direction of true perception
And your ultimate peace and joy,
And if you seem not to do it as much as you might desire,
Or as much as you might intend,
Do not make yourself wrong.
Do not think less of yourself.
And above all, do not love yourself less.
For you are upon a pathway, a course,
Which cannot fail.

So as you, in your thinking,
Become aware of new ideas, new values,
As you hear the words of Oneness,
And of Love, and of freedom,
And as you allow yourself
To think of yourself and your brothers
In the light of that truth,
Then the higher part of your mind
Will bless all the world, including yourself.

And as you allow your mind to be still,
You shall hear and experience that blessing.
And that experience shall grow upon itself,
And grow, and grow, and magnify
Until one day you shall spread your wings,
And realize this truth within your being—
"Truly I AM the Son of God.
And truly I AM free."

Blessings upon you all. That is all.

BEYOND PERCEPTION

Greetings again. I am Jeshua.
I have come once again to further, with you,
My discussion of *A Course in Miracles*.

I have recently been discussing with you
Your innocence, and also your perception.
You will recall that your innocence is based on the realization
That you HAVE, and that you ARE, everything.
Just as God Itself has, and is, everything.
And you have, and are, everything
Because you are the Son of God,
Because you are One with God.

There is but one sense in which
You are not completely the same as God.
God is the Creator.
You, I, we, are the Son of God.
And as God's Son we do not have the power
To change what God has created.
In our Oneness with God,
In our completeness as the Son of God,
We are absolutely free,
Free to CO-CREATE anything that is.

The word "co-create" is very easy to understand.
It simply means that we are absolutely free
To be, and to create, anything that we desire,
Except for the fact that we cannot BE God,
Who is, and must remain,
The First Cause of All That Is.
Our creative power extends outward,
But cannot reverse direction and alter our Source.
We cannot alter our Source,
Or that which initially arose from that Source.
In other words, we cannot create, of ourselves,
Something which we are not.

For that would be to be able to change God,
Which is, and shall always be, impossible.
To co-create, then, is to participate freely
In the outward flow of creation,
But to be unable to alter the Source,
And what the Source has created.
And what the Source has created
Must include our Self.

Hear me well. Perception ALWAYS arises from the belief
That you ARE something which you ARE NOT.
Indeed, the summation of this Course
Could lie in the next sentence or two.
Your belief that you ARE something which you ARE NOT
Is always the belief that somehow you do not have everything,
And that somehow you are not everything.
Your perception also stems from the belief,
Which is synonymous with it,
That somehow you are separate from God Itself,
From your Source, and from all of Creation.

When you, within your being, beyond your thoughts,
Truly perceive, and experience,
To the fullness that space-time will allow,
The realization that you have everything, and are everything,
And are not separate, and cannot be otherwise—
When you truly perceive that truth,
You will be free of this Course,
Free to move beyond this world of illusion,
Any time you wish, including in the next instant,
And in the twinkling of an eye.

I would speak with you this day of how it is
That you can go beyond perception unto your freedom.
As I do that, we will clarify some terms,
Among them judgment, authority, and self-image.

Perception always arises from your projection.
And projection, as we have said, always arises
From your choice to select a PART of everything,
Which you then send out to Creation.
(For to send out is all that you can do in your role as co-creator.)
You project thusly in order that what you receive back

Shall be limited by that which you sent out, or projected.
In projecting you select a part of everything,
Send it out to Creation,
And then find yourself unable to experience
Anything more than you have sent out.

Projection, therefore, makes it impossible for you
To experience everything,
To experience the wholeness that is God.
Projection MAKES perception.
And yet projection cannot exist WITHOUT perception,
Which is based on the belief in lack, and in separation.
And if you would succeed in freeing yourself
From the limitations that projection imposes,
You will do so by going BEYOND perception.
It is certain that you will do that, in your time.
'Tis only a matter of when.
And "when" is nothing but an illusion.
For in reality there is no separation at all.

That which seems to make you less than everything,
That which seems to separate you
From the truth of what you are,
Is your judgment.
Judgment and perception are bedfellows.
In fact, it is important to ask
What would become of perception
If your judgment ceased to exist.
And the answer is that your perception would pass away.
Your judgment is always based on selection.
Selection involves preferring, choosing, and rejecting.
Judgment always involves some aspect of Creation
Which you would reject.
Judgment always involves some aspect of Creation
Which you would push away,
Which you would desire to put out of your mind,
Which you would select to be apart from you.
And that truly is the source of all of the misery of this world.

If your judgment creates all of your misery,
Why would you bother to judge at all?
And the answer is this—

You believe (a belief is a form of perception),
That you exist as a separate, isolated, being.

That is the nature of this world of illusion.
But more fundamental than that,
You believe that the "you" which exists,
Separate from your brothers,
Is somehow a creation of your own.
First, you believe that you are separate, which is not true.
But more fundamentally you believe
That the "you" which seems to be separate is furthermore
Created by an aspect of that same separate "you."
If anything in Creation could be labeled absurd,
That is it.

The authority problem is based on these questions:
Who is the author of Creation?
Who is the author of myself?
Who is the author of my brothers?
The questions are actually one. And the answer is one.
The answer is simple. The answer is without conflict.
'Tis perfectly clear.
The author of All That Is, without exception,
Is God.

Any belief, any perception, that anything which exists
Can be authored by ANY different source is false.
And what is false is not real, and does not exist.

In this world you struggle with your self-image.
Your psychologists would desire for you a healthy self-image,
One which seems to function well
In this world of illusion and conflict.
And all that self-image means is that
You have chosen a selection of beliefs about who you are.
And those beliefs form your self-image which, in each moment,
Seems to be compatible with the other beliefs you hold
About what life is.

Now, hear me well.
A major problem for you here in space-time
Is the fact that belief,
Although a thing of illusion,

And although a thing of perception,
Is not a thing of weakness.
That which you believe seems as real to you,
And has as much power over you,
As does the Will of God.
Your ability, as co-creator with God,
Allows you to believe yourself, to imagine yourself,
To be something you are not,
And to have that belief seem as real to you
As anything which God Itself might have created.

Rejoice! That is a statement about who you are.
You are Spirit. You are free.
You are a creation of God,
With such power that, as I said thousands of years ago,
Your belief can heal the blind,
Allow you to walk on water, or move mountains.
And it is true that this entire world of space-time
Stands waiting at your beck and call.
For such is the power of your beliefs.

Your self-image is your belief about who you are.
And the purpose of this Course is to help you
To realize, to experience,
That who you ARE is the Son of God,
Co-creator with All That Is,
That who you are is not a separate being, isolated and alone,
Not victim to circumstances which you believe
Are beyond your control.

Your freedom, then, lies beyond perception.
Your freedom lies in knowledge.
And truly knowledge is not a thing of this world.
But true perception is close enough.
So as you move to true perception do not feel incomplete.
Rather rejoice. For knowledge is not far behind.

To go beyond perception you simply need to evolve
To a true perception of what you are.
And what you are NOT is a separate being of your own making.
That is illusion. That is belief. That is false.
And in your time that notion must crumble and pass away.

What you ARE is Spirit, free, unchangeable.
What you are is the eternal Son of God.

And the reason that I say to you, and say to you again,
And repeat once more, that you ARE the Son of God,
That you ARE free, that you ARE co-creator,
That you ARE NOT separate, that you ARE indeed One,
That your life is truly a life
Of peace and joy and freedom—
The reason I say those words,
And say them again, and again, and again,
Is so that in your hearing them
You will be able to move toward the true perception
That they are indeed true.

And then you will find yourself, very quickly, in your time,
Moving to an awareness of your completeness,
Moving to an awareness that there is no lack,
That everything you are deserves to be shared,
To be extended, without exception.
For that is your joy.
That is your peace.
And that is Love.

Rejoice!
That which you believe about yourself—
That you are weak, separated,
A victim of the ravages of space and time—
Is not true.
And since it is not true,
There is nothing that any of it can do
To change you in any way whatsoever.

And therein lies your freedom,
And your peace, and your joy.
You are the Son of God.
You are complete.
You have everything. You are everything.
And THAT shall become your true perception.
That shall be your giant stride beyond perception,
Beyond the belief that you are the author of what you are,
Beyond all conflict, beyond all misery.

Once again, you are the Son of God.
You cannot fail.
Your inheritance, your gift ordained by God,
Which is unchangeable, and undeniably yours,
Is your complete freedom, your total peace,
And your full understanding of Love.

Blessings upon you all. That is all.

ILLUSIONS AND THE EGO

Greetings again. I am Jeshua.
I have come this day to discuss with you,
Illusions and the ego.

In so much of your literature,
And especially in *A Course in Miracles*,
You hear about the ego.
The authors, and even I, speak of the ego
As if it were an entity, a being,
Which has an existence of its own.
Nothing could be further from the truth.

As I address for you the illusions of the ego,
I will speak about illusions, and will speak about the ego.
However, never lose sight of the fact
That the ego itself is one of your greatest illusions.
The ego, that which you believe yourself to be,
Is an illusion.
And therefore it is not real.
YOU are absolutely real.
YOU are the Son of God.
YOU are possessed of knowledge, and truth, and freedom,
And the joy that accompanies those.
YOU are unchangeable.

The "YOU" of which I have just spoken is the "You" of Spirit.
The "you" of the ego is the opposite of all of those.
The ego has no creative ability of its own,
And in fact, does not even exist of itself.
And anything which does not exist of itself
Can hardly be real. Do you see?

How did the ego come to exist in the first place?
Such an important question to ask.
But, how the ego came to exist, in your time, in your past,
Is not important, or even relevant.

All that matters is NOW.
However, that which you call the ego,
Even though it be illusion, still seems to exist now,
For almost all of you.

To understand the nature of the ego will help to clarify
How it was that the ego came to be.
In order for the ego to seem to exist
You had to throw knowledge away.
In order for the ego to have existed in the past,
In order for the ego to have come into existence at all,
You had to choose to throw knowledge away.

Why would you want to do that?
The answer lies in the simple truth that you can't.
You are the Son of God. You are complete.
You are possessed of knowledge.
And knowledge is complete.
Knowledge is unchangeable. Knowledge is certain.
And you cannot change that.

The nature of God, however, is freedom.
God's freedom entails movement, ecstasy, joy,
The playfulness of a small child.
And it is natural that in your playfulness it would occur to you
That there might exist a state without knowledge.
And as a child wonders in his playing,
You might wonder what that state would be like.

In reality, you CAN NOT separate yourself from knowledge.
In reality, you cannot separate yourself
From the fact that you are the Son of God.
To the ego that could seem like a restriction.
It could appear to be a lack of freedom.
If I am totally free, you might say,
Why am I not free even to separate myself from God?
Indeed, at your level of understanding here,
You might imagine it logical that just that sort of playfulness,
Went on, goes on, this moment, within your creative mind.
And thus it is that there was the fleeting desire
To be free of completeness and knowledge,
In a sense to be free of God—
Just to imagine what it might be like.

Why is it that you cannot separate yourself from God?
The answer is very clear.
Everything exists at the level of mind.
At the true level of mind there is only thought.
(But remember that the thoughts of which I speak
Are not the thoughts of which you are aware,
Are not the thoughts of consciousness.)
Everything exists at the level of mind.
And you, and I, and all of Creation,
Exist only as an idea in the Mind of God.
And a truth which I have stated for you many times
Is that ideas cannot leave their source. (16)

In your belief in separation,
It can seem to you that this is not true.
However, the truth is that ideas,
Which are all that exist at the level of mind,
At the level of reality,
Cannot leave their source.
You are an idea in the Mind of God.
I am an idea in the Mind of God.
That truth is unchangeable.
For the idea that you are cannot leave its source.

This is not a lack of freedom. This is simply a fact.
You are the Son of God, created by God,
An idea in the Mind of God.
And that is so.
If, in your playfulness, you might wish to wonder
Whether it would be possible to be separate
From the Mind of God,
Then you would need to somehow throw knowledge away.
But knowledge is complete, as I have said.
And being possessed of knowledge,
It is not possible that you could actually do so,
That you could actually separate yourself from God.

To imagine that you COULD throw knowledge away
Would allow you, in your joy and exploration,
To IMAGINE that you actually were separate.
And so with the creative power of your own being
You devised a magnificent tool
That you could use to SEEM to throw knowledge away,

Albeit in your imagination,
And yet not to change, in any sense,
The reality of what you are.

This magnificent tool which you created is called "time."
And time is the basis for all of this world of illusion.
Time is what allows you to take an idea
And project it out of your mind,
To become unaware of it.

Think about that for a moment.
If there is an idea, part of knowledge,
Which you wish not to be aware of, and to have no access to,
Then you can call it "tomorrow."
If there is an idea
Which you would like to have out of your mind,
And yet be able to have access to if you desire,
You can call it "yesterday."
And that which you choose to be aware of this moment,
You can call "now."

And as soon as, in your creativity,
You seemed to have thrown knowledge away,
Then there seemed to be incompleteness, and uncertainty.
And what arose, for the first time, was a question.
The question was, "What am I?"
AND THUS THE EGO WAS BORN.
The ego is nothing more than the collection of thoughts
You have formed in answer to the questions
"What am I?" and "Who am I?"

And as fast as you change the answers to those questions,
The ego changes.
That which is of knowledge does not change.
And thus it is that I speak of learning.
Learning, always, is change.
The level of the ego, the level of perception,
Both came into being when you
Seemed to throw knowledge away.
And learning must involve changes in your system of answers
To the question, "Who am I?"
Learning MUST, therefore, involve change.
Those of you who do not want things to change

Are simply saying,
"I do not want to learn."
And when I speak of learning and teaching,
I simply speak of a state in which your mind
Is open to the possibility of, and ready for, change.

And the change that I wish for you,
And bring to you through these missives,
Is the change, the learning,
That shall bring you back to the point
At which your ego passes away,
At which your imagined belief in separation passes away,
And you return to the awareness of knowledge.

I would address somewhat more at this time the ego itself.
An analogy that may help you to understand the ego
Is related to your current world of computers.
Computers function not of themselves, but only via programs.
Some external consciousness, the programmer,
Must give the computer instructions,
Tell it, if you will, what to do.
(And in the case of the ego, tell it what it IS.)
And the computer follows its program explicitly,
And always does exactly what it is told.

As the programs become more sophisticated,
It often seems as if the computer has a life of its own.
And common language in your world may go like this—
"The computer couldn't find this."
"The computer says it isn't so."
"The computer says you don't even exist."
"The computer made a mistake."
"The computer will tell us."
All of it sounds as if the computer is a being
With an existence of its own.
And you know, novice or otherwise in computers,
That that is not so.

Likewise is the ego.
In the instant in which you seemed to throw knowledge away,
You left a vacuum,
A space created by the absence of completeness.

And what goes into that space
Is the whole system of beliefs about who you are.

And the list is extremely extensive.
Much of it relates to your belief in bodies—
You believe that you ARE a body,
This height, and this weight, this hair color, this eye color,
This particular form, these particular characteristics of operation,
These particular biological processes.

Beliefs about who you are also involve attitudes.
"This is my favorite. I like that. I do not like this.
I do not enjoy this. I can't stand him. I can't stand her.
I love this one. I do not love that one."
All of those, whether you know it or not,
Are part of the program YOU have written
In order to define who you are.
And the ego, like a computer, operates based upon its program.
It operates exactly, faithfully, without mistake,
Until such time as the program is changed.

And when I say this is a Course in mind training,
We are really talking about a Course
That shall help you to learn—
And to learn means to change—
A Course that shall help you to learn to change the program
Which you call and believe to be yourself,
And which is nothing more than your ego.

Ultimately, the program shall pass away completely.
For when you again open yourself to knowledge,
The ego is no longer necessary,
And indeed, must cease to exist.

And so it is that this ego of which I speak,
Which, in your meanderings through space and time,
You believe to be yourself—
This ego has no existence of its own,
Is only a program, if you will,
Which fills the vacuum created by the absence of knowledge.

All things are of mind. All things are but ideas.
Everything must exist ONLY at the level of ideas.

And so your ego is nothing but a collection of ideas.
It seems to take the form of space and time
And density, and bodies.
But all of it is simply a collection of ideas.
And, here, at the level of space-time, as the ideas change,
The form shall change instantly to follow the ideas.

That is why I tell you that things like healing
Can happen in an instant.
Those of you who may have thought about,
Or read about, enlightenment
Have usually read about persons
Who seem to become enlightened in a moment.
Instant enlightenment.
Some people, most of you, take decades, or years, or lifetimes.
But for some it seems to happen cataclysmically.
'Tis entirely possible.

To return to the analogy of the computer—
You have an entire system of beliefs about who you are.
It is like a computer program.
The program can be changed slowly, one instruction at a time.
The program can be removed in its entirety,
And replaced with another.
Or the program can simply be erased
And taken out of the machine.
If the latter should happen to your ego, then you would be free.
And knowledge would return.
There would be certainty, and peace, and freedom, and joy.
Most of you choose to change your programs
One instruction at a time.
And that is OK.
Do not make yourself wrong.
But realize always, that it can change, or be changed,
In an instant.

One last point— who is the programmer?
As I have spoken to you, often I have said
"Tell yourself . . ."
It seems, does it not, that I am telling YOU
To speak to YOUR SELF,
As if YOU and YOUR SELF are somehow different beings.
Ultimately I am telling "you," the creative aspect of your mind,

To address "your self," your ego,
And to write a new instruction into the program
That is your ego.
So when I say "Tell yourself, . . ."
That is what I mean.

The "you" of which I speak is a measure of the creative aspect
That you ARE as the Son of God.
That "you," at a level, is aware of Spirit,
Of the Holy Spirit, of your Oneness with all of life.
Yet, by your design, you cannot be completely aware of those
Until the ego has passed away,
Until you have ceased to throw knowledge away.

In brief summary,
You, creative child of God, in your playfulness,
Have chosen to explore throwing knowledge away.
In the seeming absence of knowledge,
You fill the space with a belief system of who you are.
That is your ego, your child, your creation.
It is not real.
It does not exist of itself.
Always it is the product of what you have chosen.

You are free as the Son of God.
But rejoice that you are not free
To be something you are not.
It is preordained, pre-chosen, by you,
Indeed, has already happened,
That you SHALL return to knowledge, to your right mind,
To the awareness of your Oneness with God,
And with All That Is.

As I close, I remind you that all of this,
The throwing away of knowledge,
The creation of the ego,
All that the ego seems to do, at your own instruction,
All of the yesterdays, all of the tomorrows,
All of the world of space and time,
Was conceived, experienced, and released
In less than an instant.
'Tis over and done.
In honor of the creative ability

Which you have as the Son of God,
You but seem to play it out in your mind.
But that, indeed, was the purpose of it all anyway—
The simple wondering, the experience of it all,
And its release.

You are complete. You are whole.
You are the Son of God, unchangeable,
Possessed of knowledge.
You are an idea in the Mind of God, never to leave.
You are absolutely safe.
And nothing that you do here can in any way
Alter that truth.

Be at peace and rejoice.
And while you play out your imaginings in space and time,
Play them out with as much joy as you can muster.
And if your program of your ego does not call for joy,
Then rewrite it.
For joy CAN be yours.
None of it can change what you really are.
Would you not rather play out joy than sadness?
And when, in your imaginings,
This illusion of time has passed away,
Then you shall have played it all out,
Simply in honor of your creative ability.
And that which took less than an instant,
And now but seems to take longer,
Shall be gone.

You shall then realize, from within this tiny aspect
Of the infinity of what you are,
That you are but One,
That you are but Spirit,
And that you are now, and forever,
Absolutely free.

My blessings upon you all. That is all.

THE EGO AND CONFLICT

Greetings again. I am Jeshua.
Today I wish to speak with you
About the hallmark of the ego.
Today I will discuss with you
The measure of what the ego is,
And what the ego represents.
Therefore, I will be giving you an absolutely reliable way
For you to know when the ego is dominating your life.

I will be giving you a very simple way
For you to know if you are truly pursuing
A course to peace, the pathway to your joy.
And that really is all I will be saying in this entire chapter.
I will be speaking of joy and peace.
The hallmark of the ego is the absence of joy.
The hallmark of the ego is the absence of peace.
THE HALLMARK OF THE EGO
IS THE PRESENCE OF CONFLICT.

Now, conflict is not as simple as war.
All of you know when you are at war.
When two of your egos seem to be in opposition,
There may be words, and anger, even yelling and screaming.
There may even be what you call physical confrontation.
And clearly you can tell that this is conflict.
However, conflict can be much more subtle.
In fact, when you experience
The slightest absence of joy and peace,
You may be absolutely certain that you are in conflict.

In all of Creation nothing really exists
Except the Will of God.
And in the Mind of God, in the Kingdom of God,
Conflict does not exist.
Therefore, in reality, conflict cannot exist at all.
Therefore, in reality, there is no conflict within you.
This means that conflict is always, always, illusion.

And the goal of this Course
Is to help you free yourself of illusion.
For as you do that, you will automatically claim
Your inheritance of joy and peace.

How does this conflict of which I speak arise?
Alas, 'tis by your own choice.
Recall I have spoken to you of the ego.
The ego is ultimately not real.
It is but a collection of thoughts which,
As you have certainly heard or read by now,
Do not mean anything.
The ego is but a collection of meaningless thoughts
About who you are.

As we have said, it was necessary to throw knowledge away
In order to believe yourself to be separate,
In order to believe yourself less than complete, less than whole.
And after your belief in lack and scarcity arose,
'Twas necessary to attempt to complete yourself.
And thus arose the thought system of the ego.

When I speak of the thought system
On which the ego is based, 'tis simply that—
The thought system of lack, and scarcity, and incompleteness.
So whenever you, for any reason of any kind,
Perceive yourself to be less than complete, less than whole,
Whenever you, for any reason of any kind,
Believe that you have less than everything,
You may be CERTAIN that you are listening to the ego,
And that what you are hearing is not real.

In your cleverness, in your playfulness,
In your desire to experience space and time and separation,
In your desire to experience all of this world of illusion,
You threw knowledge away.
Ah, in truth you but TRIED to throw knowledge away.

As I have said many times before,
You are the Son of God.
God is the creator.
We are co-creators with God.
We share the Will of God.

But we cannot change what God has ordained.
Therefore, you are One with God, always, in your time,
Or always, in the absence of your time.
It does not matter.
Your will is One with God's.

Is it not now clear?
In your desire, in your playfulness—
Really nothing more than that,
And of no more consequence than that—
In your desire to experience this
Which we shall call space and time,
You TRIED to throw knowledge away.
And it seems as if you have done so.
Such is the strength of your own will,
Given you, of course, by God.
It seems as if you HAVE thrown knowledge away.
And yet it is not possible to do so.

The thought system of the ego believes in lack and scarcity.
However, lack and scarcity do not, and cannot, exist.
And not you, nor I, nor anyone, can change that fact.
Is it not clear that there MUST BE conflict in this world?
Nevertheless, it is the choice you have made.

And I have told you all of it took less than an instant.
Do you not now see why?
Even in your time, suppose that you were
Certain of what I have already said—
That conflict proves to you that you are not aware of truth.
Suppose you already knew
That in the Kingdom of God there is no conflict.
Suppose you were already certain
That the absence of joy and peace proves to you
That you are entertaining something not real.

And suppose that you felt confident
About the slightest spark of intelligence
Being within yourself.
How long would it take to dismiss the conflict?
Of course, less than an instant.
And that is exactly what happened in reality.
It happened so briefly in your time

That 'twas hardly noticed in the scheme of creation.
But hear me once again.
You seem to play out your belief in space,
And above all your belief in time,
Merely in honor of what you are as co-creator with God,
As the Son of God with powers that seem very much like God's.
Indeed your creative power is exactly like God's—
With the exception that you cannot depart from His Will.

So you created this split mind.
Now, the word "split" is important here.
You created an imagined split in your mind
So that you could seem to have thrown knowledge away,
And could seem to harbor the collection of thoughts
That is your ego.
However, there is, and must be, by your own design,
A part of your mind which is always aware
Of your Oneness with God,
Which is always aware of your higher mind,
As I have spoken of it.
There MUST BE a part of your mind
Which is aware of the Holy Spirit.

But in your creative power, you designed it all in such a way
That the false beliefs, the collection of illusionary thoughts,
Could seem to supersede your awareness of your reality.
If that had not happened,
All of this could not have been experienced,
Even for less than an instant.

But, hear me well.
Because you are unable to separate yourself from God,
There is that part of your mind wherein lies the Holy Spirit,
And which you can become aware of at any time.
The design is so simple and so beautiful,
That all you have to do to open to that awareness
Is think your thoughts with God.
For when you do that, nothing can prevail
Against the Kingdom of God.

If you think a thought with God,
It extends to all of Creation,
And automatically blesses you and every brother,

Blesses me, and even God Itself.
And the goal of this Course is for you
To think ALL of your thoughts with God,
Just as I do, and just as you shall, in your time,
And which you already do in reality.

The rest of which I have to say today is extremely simple.
If you wish to learn, to experience, this Course,
All you need do is discipline your mind
So that all of your thoughts you think with God.
And that is all.
And all you have to do to accomplish that
Is give up the thoughts of the ego,
Not to think them anymore.
That is all.

Ah, but the ego is your seeming creation.
And just as God loves His creations, so do you love yours.
And so by your own design, you do not wish to give up
This child of your own godliness.
And therein lies the struggle.

However, to return to the beginning of this chapter,
The hallmark of the ego is conflict.
The hallmark of the ego is the absence of joy,
And the absence of peace.
And in your thinking with God,
Or in your thinking without God—
It does not matter—
How long should it take you to realize
That you DO NOT WANT conflict,
And that you DO want joy and peace?

Think upon that for a moment.
If that is true, what I have just said—
And I assure you that it is true,
Whether you believe it or not—
There is no one who would prefer conflict
To joy and peace.
Even if you think you might,
I promise you, you do not.

Given that your preference IS joy and peace,
Then you DO HAVE within you the deep desire
To train your mind to think only thoughts with God.
And all you have to do to achieve that
Is be vigilant and diligent with your thinking,
And to this extent—
Remember the signs of conflict.
From physical violence, to anger,
To the exchange of angry words,
To the experience of sickness, and death, and fear,
To the slightest fatigue, to the slightest sign of tiredness,
To the slightest distress, the slightest question that might ask,
"How do I decide about this, or about that?"
All of those are the signs of conflict.
And they are simple for you to recognize,
If only you choose to be vigilant in watching your mind.
Then when you experience the slightest conflict,
Simply realize within your being that it is not real,
And does not need to be part of your life.
Then be still.
And that is all.

I will repeat that.
It is so simple that perhaps you cannot hear it.
All you have to do when you experience
The slightest sign of conflict is to say
"This does not need to be. This is not real."
And then be still.

For when you are still,
You do not try to solve the problem on your terms.
And it is then that you will find
That you become aware of what to do,
Where to go, what to say, and what to be.
That is the promise of God.
That is the promise I make to you.
And that is the presence of the Holy Spirit within your life.

That presence is always there.
The split mind guarantees that in part of it
The Holy Spirit, the presence of Love, IS always there.
And as you are still, you will feel that presence.

So if you would learn this Course, start thusly:
Watch diligently, vigilantly,
For every sign of the slightest conflict.
And then say, to yourself, or to your world,
"This is conflict. This is of the ego. This is not real.
And this does not need to be in my life."
And you will have taken thousands of years
Off your search for your return to God.

And then say "I will be still
And listen to the Voice for God."
And in your listening,
You will have taken thousands more years
Off your search for the reality of what you are
As the Son of God.

Blessings upon you all. That is all.

ILLUSIONS AND COMMUNICATION

Greetings again. I am Jeshua.
I have been speaking with you of late
About the illusions of the ego.
One can almost chuckle at those words.
For there is no greater illusion at all than the ego itself.
This I have said to you many times
Your ego is the collection of thoughts, in your space and time,
About who you are.
Those thoughts are of perception, and therefore ultimately
Do not have meaning, and are not real.
Then it follows, of course, that the ego itself is not real.

That statement so often causes fear,
Which is a characteristic of the ego itself, and ONLY of the ego.
It causes a reaction of fear because, indeed,
It is a threat to the ego itself.
There is not much greater threat to the ego
Than for me to say it is not real,
And ultimately does not even exist.
For insofar as you believe yourself to BE your ego,
Then you can hear me say, in a sense, that YOU don't exist.
While nothing is further from the truth.
For YOU are the Son of God.
And YOU are the reality of All That Is.

If you did not exist, nothing would exist.
Truly, you are so much a part of God
That if you did not exist, God Itself would cease to be.
And since God IS, without qualification,
It must be that You ARE, without qualification.
And nothing shall change that, ever, in your time,
Or ever, outside of your time.

So the grandest illusion of the ego is that it exists.
Beyond that, however, recall that
The ego is a collection of thoughts about who you are.
The ego is based on perception,
Which is found within consciousness,
Therefore also within the framework of thought
Upon which the ego is based.

And in essence the thought framework
Upon which the ego is based
Is separation.
The whole purpose for creating an ego in the first place
Was to attempt to gain some measure of experience
Of what it would be like to be separate.

And so as long as you believe in the ego, which is to believe
That your thoughts about who you are are real,
Of that those thoughts have any consequence whatsoever—
As long as you believe either of those—
You are substantiating and supporting
The thought system of separation.

Separation, above all, cannot exist.
For the reality of God is Oneness.
And nothing exists except that which God has created,
And fully extended Himself into.
So there is not only nothing which is not OF GOD,
There is nothing which IS NOT God Itself.

So the ego is based on the thought system of separation.
And this brings us to the last major illusion of the ego,
Which is communication.
You think, as you walk this world of space and time,
That you communicate with one another.
And I tell you, you do not.
Now, it is not possible for you to be fully separate.
So there is a level at which, below your egos,
You are in fact in constant communication.
This is the level at which you, together in your Oneness,
Have created all of this world and its universes.

It is at that level of communication that you create the trees,
And the mountains, the rain, the snow, and the sun.
And it is at that level that all of you in a given location
See it rain at the same time,
See the sun rise at the same time,
That you all perceive laws of this world and of physics,
Which seem to be uniform for all of you.
So indeed, there is, and must be,
A level of communication in your world of space and time.

However, at the level of your personalities,
The level of your egos,
True communication does not, and cannot, exist.
Perception itself denies communication.
Even conscious thought itself denies communication.
For when you experience anything in your world,
You are experiencing what you, from within,
Have chosen to experience.
And that is true for all other beings as well.

However, the remarkable design
Of this world that you have made
Has caused you to deem yourselves separate.
And thus, by definition, no two perceptions
Of even what seems to be the same experience
Can be the same.

And furthermore, when you look outside yourself at another
You are only seeing, perceiving, what you wish to be there,
And what you have chosen to be there.
And your perception has nothing to do
With the reality of that which you think you are seeing.

Your perception sees only the past.
It sees only images you have made.
In your perception, you see only what you choose to see,
And experience only what you choose to experience,
With, hear me well, no concern whatsoever
For what you deem to be your outside world.
'Tis always what you would choose for yourself.

And then when, in your space and time,
Your outside world does not act according to
What you believe to be your desires,
You feel what is commonly known as anger.
And all you are doing is coming abreast of a measure
Of the truth of what I have just said.

True communication must occur in silence.
In silence, you discover your existence,
Without the busy-ness of the ego,
Without the constant drumming of the thoughts
Which your brain seems to produce.

If you would truly perceive another being,
And better yet, if you would truly perceive yourself,
Then it must be in silence.

For therein you shall find communication.
In silence there is total openness to what is.
There is total freedom within each moment,
Unbound and unfettered by the past,
And with no fear of consequence, or thought of the future.

So a grand illusion of the ego
Is the belief that it actually can communicate.
It is important that you not forget
That at the level of your thoughts, and of your brain,
True communication is impossible.

I am aware that while you are here in this world
You do process with words and thoughts.
And you will perhaps discuss this chapter with friends.
All of that is a chosen part of the human condition.
Do not make yourself wrong.
But above all, do not delude yourself into thinking that it is real.
The purpose of such attempted communication, however frail,
Is to guide yourself to the point,
Beyond your thoughts and beyond your words,
Where you shall touch the level of real communication,
Which is the silence within.

In your false attempt to believe
That you actually do communicate,
You have formed the body.
The body at superficial level
Is simply your vehicle for experiencing space and time.
And that is all.
You can think of it as a denseness of energy,
A consolidation that allows you to resonate
With the frequencies of space and time.

But really the purpose of the body is to validate for you
Your belief in separation.
And all the things that the body does
Are designed to convince you that you are alone.
This relates to your feelings and your experience,

Which you know full well
You cannot accurately communicate to another.
This relates to your unshakable desire to be One,
Which it is not possible for you to experience
Through your body, or bodies.
No matter the form in which you try,
The attempts must lead to frustration,
And the belief that you remain alone.

And the myriad of body experiences serve that simple purpose,
To cause you to believe in your separation.
The experience may be talking in words,
Which another does not perceive correctly.
It may be illness, which is a most efficient way
To validate your isolation.
It may be found in, perhaps, your ultimate concern,
That of your death.
For when your body dies that truly seems to isolate you
From all those beings who have not yet died.
All of this, the product of your own careful design,
Was made in order to substantiate for you
The belief that you are, and remain, totally alone.

It IS possible to walk this earth with true perception,
To experience space and time with joy, and without fear.
'Tis possible to experience joy with, and through,
This bodily illusion you have created.
But you cannot do that, hear me well,
Until you have reached the point,
Within your mind, within your thinking,
In your certainty, and in your experience,
Where you realize that this body IS an illusion, a facade,
Where you realize that it is not real
And truly is of no consequence whatsoever.
That was the message of the crucifixion and the resurrection.
That was my validation for all of you, my brothers,
That the body is indeed an illusion,
And of no consequence at all.
Therefore, be vigilant about your conflict, as I said last time.
And be vigilant further about your attempts
To experience what you call communication.
Remember that it is all right for you
To honor your space and time,

And to talk and share and discuss.
But in your vigilance, always be sure
To incorporate into that your silence.

You can practice silence in listening to one another.
You do so by being careful not to bring preordained thoughts,
But to listen with an openness to what it is
That is coming to you from your brother.
You can practice your silence
As you try to communicate with another.
You can do that, as a suggestion,
By trying not to rehearse or formulate ahead of time
What YOU will say or do.
Simply let your message flow
Out of the innermost depths of your being.
For then it will be in touch with your silence.

And all that I have spoken of
In these last few sentences, of course,
Is the Holy Instant.

So remain aware of the illusions of the ego—
The ego itself, the grand illusion;
The hallmarks of the ego, conflict, misery, and fear;
The illusion of communication
And the belief that you can indeed communicate
Through your perceptions and your body;
And the illusion which is perhaps hardest for you to release,
The illusion of your body—
For it is not what you are.

All of this is a message of peace and of love.
Tis not made to frighten,
But only to encourage you in your growth and your becoming,
As you learn this Course.

And as you learn it,
Your learning shall take you beyond illusion in every sense.
And on the other side of the veil of illusion,
Truly, is peace, and joy, and Love.

Blessings upon you all. That is all.

WHOLENESS AND THE HOLY SPIRIT

Greetings again. I am Jeshua.
I have come this day to discuss with you,
Healing and wholeness.
Did you know they are the same?
The only way to heal is to be whole.
And the only way to be healed is to be whole.

I know that can indeed sound frightening.
It can sound like a bit "too much" for you to do.
And alas, that is exactly the way you usually think of it.
If I say the words, "In order to be healed you must be whole,"
You tend to say "That is so much for me to do."

And you are exactly correct.
For OF YOURSELF you cannot do it.
Of your self, as I speak to you now of your ego,
You can do nothing.
So, if it is your perception that to become whole
Is too much for you to do, rejoice.
For you have come abreast of a great truth—
That it is indeed too much for you to do.

So what I wish to discuss with you, this day,
Is the Holy Spirit,
And your invitation to the Holy Sprit.
For it is through the Holy Spirit,
And above all, through your invitation to the Holy Spirit,
That you become whole,
That you become healed,
That you become happy.
It is through the Holy Spirit,
And your invitation to the Holy Spirit,
That you shall learn to heal,
And to grant to another the vision you have
Of wholeness, and of healing.
And that vision, as you extend it,
Shall have the power to transform your brothers.

I speak often of the Holy Spirit.
And I seem to speak of the Holy Spirit
As if it were a thing apart,
A being separate from yourself.
And yet I have said to you, over and over again,
Nothing is separate.
You are not separate.
You are God. You are One.
You are part of, indeed you actually ARE, each other.
And that is the truth.

So whatever this Holy Spirit is,
It is not separate from you.
It is not apart from you.
The Holy Spirit, therefore, lies within your mind.
But what can lie within your mind but an idea?
YOU are an idea, a thought, in the Mind of God.
The Holy Spirit is, likewise, an idea,
A thought within the Mind of God.
All of Creation, in any form you wish to imagine it,
Is but an idea, a thought in the Mind of God.
And since you are, since I am, since we are, the Son of God,
The thoughts of God are within us—
Just as they are within God Itself.
So the Holy Spirit is simply an idea within your mind—
Just as is everything in all of Creation.

The great truth about ideas is that
They are strengthened by being shared.
Ideas are strengthened by giving them away.
If one seems to have an idea,
And would wish to isolate it unto himself,
The idea shall die.

With your possessions—your money,
Your food, your clothes, your autos—
It does not seem to work that way.
And indeed, if you give away some of your possessions,
Here in your space and time,
You seem to have less.

With ideas that is not so.
And you already know that.

I simply make this point to remind you of something
Which you, indeed, already know.
You can share any idea you have,
And still it remains totally yours,
Even though it becomes stronger within you
Because you have shared it.
Such is the nature of ideas.

The Holy Spirit is the idea, within your mind, of wholeness.
The Holy Spirit is the idea, within your mind,
That you are not separate.
The Holy Spirit is the realization, within your mind,
That your mind is not split at all, but is One.
The Holy Spirit is the idea, within your mind,
That you have everything, and that you are everything.
We could go on.
You understand what I am saying.

The Holy Spirit is in your mind by nature of the fact
That It is a creation of God,
And therefore was put there by God,
If you wish to use those words.
You cannot remove the Holy Spirit from your mind.
The most that you can do is block
Your awareness of Its presence
By your vain imaginings
That you are something which you are not.

I have told you that
I can bring the Holy Spirit down to you.
But I can only do so at your request.
For you are absolutely free.
And not I, not God Itself, can impose upon you
Any idea which you do not wish to accept.
Rejoice in your freedom.
Tis a great measure of the beauty of what you are
As the Son of God.

So I can assist you in bringing
The Holy Spirit into your awareness.
And that requires but your willingness
To open your mind to the thoughts of God.
They are the thoughts that are real.

They are the thoughts of peace.
They are the thoughts of joy, and of Love,
And of Oneness.

A great deal of what this Course in Miracles is about
Is helping you to come to know, within your thinking mind,
What are the thoughts of God.

As I have told you before,
If you feel conflict, it is not of God.
Then say to yourself, "This is conflict. It does not need to be."
And be still.
And the presence that shall come to you
Shall be the Holy Spirit.
And you will become aware of what to do.
For you will be sensing the thoughts of God.
Your invitation to the Holy Spirit is your decision to be vigilant
In inviting into your mind and your awareness
Only the thoughts of God.
And I will assist you with that, every moment,
But only insofar as you will allow me to do so.

All of the thoughts of conflict, and pain, and separation,
Merely serve to close the door
To your awareness of the Holy Spirit.
But recall again, the Holy Spirit is always there.
You cannot remove It.
And you need only to enter your silence
To experience Its presence.

You cannot experience the Kingdom of God,
You cannot truly extend your invitation to the Holy Spirit,
If it is your desire to do so alone.
In fact, one of the greatest tools you have available to you
For discovering the thoughts of God
Is to be diligent about seeing the Holy Spirit in your brother.
For I promise you, as you come to see the Holy Spirit,
As you discover the presence of God within your brother,
You cannot help but find those self-same blessings
Within yourself.

The Holy Spirit speaks of Oneness.
And in this world,

Oneness is best realized through relationship.
The Holy Spirit speaks of the absence of separation.
And the absence of separation can best be discovered
Through your realization that you are not separate
One from another.

I am able to guide you because I,
Under the same guidance of which I am speaking,
Came to see the Holy Spirit and the Light of God
In every brother, WITH NO EXCEPTIONS.
That included the brothers who seemed
To condemn and torture and kill me.

This is not a fancy.
It is not a daydream of which I speak.
I promise you that you have within you
Exactly the same measure of God as I have within me,
And that I had within me when I walked this earth.

And your invitation to the Holy Spirit—
Which is the same as your request for peace and joy and love—
Your invitation to the Holy Spirit will center on
Your willingness to see the Light of God
In every brother, without exception.
For only then may you see it in yourself,
And be free.

Blessings upon you all. That is all.

SHARING

Greetings again. I am Jeshua.
We have been speaking of healing and wholeness.
I spoke to you last time of the Holy Spirit.
And I told you that the Holy Spirit was actually part of you,
Was indeed a part of your mind.
But even that statement is not quite true.
It is not possible that anything can be a PART of you.
For just to use the word implies, somehow,
A separation, or the absence of Oneness.
If I say that you are PART OF God,
Or PART OF the Mind of God,
Or ONE OF the ideas in the Mind of God,
Those words automatically imply
That there may also be other parts of the Mind of God,
Which could therefore be separate from you.
But there is no separation at all in the Kingdom of God.

You and I are not PART OF God.
We ARE God.
God is not the Father of us, except as our originator,
And as the Source which cannot be changed.
But otherwise God IS US.

And the Holy Spirit is not PART OF your mind.
The Holy Spirit IS your mind.
And all of your thoughts are not PART OF what you think.
They ARE you. Because what you think you ARE.

Within that context I would speak with you today
And try to help you understand the true nature of sharing.
I have told you that the Atonement
Needs to be understood as an act of pure sharing.
That can perhaps seem a bit confusing.
Based on my previous comments,
There is nothing that can be PART OF the Atonement.
The Atonement is not ONE OF the things that God has created.

For there are no PARTS of the Kingdom of God.
The Kingdom merely IS.
It is this that I meant when I told you
That the natural state of the mind is pure abstraction.
Everything merely IS.
Everything exists.
Every thing contains within it all of Creation.
And every thing is also contained within all of Creation.
And that, in the sense of abstraction,
Is what sharing really means.

The Atonement is not a thing that God created.
The Atonement is not a device that God thought up
To correct your misperceptions.
The Atonement is not a way out to allow you to undo
The imagined separation within your mind.
The Atonement IS YOU.

Remember that nothing unreal exists.
This includes, fortunately for you, your thoughts here
Your thoughts about who you are, your ego,
Your thoughts about all of this world
Of space and time and illusion,
And all of its problems.
They do not exist.

The Atonement IS.
And the Atonement is an act of pure sharing.
And as you experience the Atonement
You will come to know within your being,
At the level of experience,
What true sharing is, indeed.

You do not share by giving away.
Think of the ideas of which we have spoken.
Ideas are strengthened by being shared.
When you share an idea, it does not in any way
Diminish the presence of that idea within you.
And yet the idea transmits totally to the recipient
To whom you would give it.
And in such total transmission,
The idea BECOMES that being itself.

When you take an idea, which cannot leave its source—
That source being you and, ultimately therefore, God—
When you take an idea that cannot leave its source
And extend it to another,
It becomes the sole property of the other, in its completeness.
And yet your own completeness changes not one iota.

It truly is that what you are HAS BECOME the other.
And this, abstract though it be, is the nature of sharing.
It would not have been possible for God to have thought of us,
And created us as ideas,
Without that God BECAME us.
It could not have been otherwise that God created us
Without God becoming what we are—
Which, in reality, is God Itself.

The Voice for God is within your mind.
But the Voice for God truly IS you.
The Holy Spirit is within your mind, but It IS you.
And the function of the Holy Spirit is to bring
The Voice of God to your conscious awareness.

Hear me well. You could not, you can not,
You will never be able, in your time,
To hear the Voice for God within you
If you choose to perceive that, IN ANY SENSE,
You are hearing it alone.
Hear this well.

I have also said that the only function of the miracle worker
Is to accept the Atonement FOR HIMSELF.
And now I say that you cannot hear the Voice for God alone.
Those two statements are absolutely compatible.
In order to accept the Atonement for YOURSELF,
You must realize, beyond your thoughts,
Deep within your being,
That you ARE your brother.

And as you attempt to experience the presence of God,
If there is anything within you
That would desire to keep that experience for yourself alone,
Then know that you are perceiving,

That you are functioning as an ego,
That your thought is not real,
And shall truly die.

As you accept the Atonement for yourself
It requires that you experience the truth you see
As a truth that belongs to all of Creation and every brother,
As well as to yourself.
Such is the nature of teaching.
And such is the nature of healing.

Teaching is not talking about your words.
Teaching is not convincing another
To think as you seem to do with your brain.
Teaching, like the Atonement, is an act of pure sharing.
And teaching, real teaching, occurs,
As does everything that is real,
At the level of mind.

As you learn a truth,
Which happens when you think a thought with God,
Which happens when you allow the Holy Spirit
To connect your awareness to your One Self—
As you experience those things,
They can only become truth for you
As you spontaneously, from deep within,
Desire for every brother exactly what you have experienced,
With no exceptions.

And when you do that,
Whether the experience engages your perception or not,
Every brother experiences that truth with you,
At some level
And that is the true nature of teaching.
Tis simply an act of sharing,
Based on the realization that reality DEMANDS sharing,
And that that which you would keep for yourself cannot be real.

Likewise, healing follows in the same manner.
I have told you that to heal you must be whole,
And to be healed you must be whole.
It follows directly just as with teaching.
When you, from deep within your being, desire to be whole,

And wish that wholeness upon all of Creation,
Without exception,
Then you shall experience the effect of healing.

And as you experience the effect of healing,
You will both heal and be healed, as one.
For they are, like all of Creation, the same.

If you, at the level of ego,
Desire to make a perceived physical symptom go away,
And you would desire the experience only for yourself,
Then the essence of your symptom,
At the level of mind, at the level of reality,
Will not go away.
Indeed, there have been many incidents of magic,
In which symptoms of the body truly seem to disappear.
And within your perception that is what happens.

But without the wholeness of which I have spoken,
True healing cannot, and did not, occur.
And I tell you, every one of the symptoms removed by magic
Will remain in the world of form and the world of time,
And will, in some measure and in some form, return,
Albeit by your own choice and your own design.

The Atonement is an act of pure sharing.
To know of the Atonement means to know
That you cannot experience it alone,
That it extends automatically to every brother.
And your only goal is to experience that Oneness,
And then to find the Atonement for yourself.

But when you do that you will find,
With great rejoicing and great joy,
That in finding the Atonement for yourself,
You have found it, truly, for all of Creation.
And great will be your reward.
And great will be your joy.

Blessing upon you all. That is all.

GUILT I

Greetings again. I am Jeshua.
We have been speaking of late of healing and wholeness.
And I would speak to you again this day of wholeness,
Because, as I have said, in order to heal you must be whole.
And in order to be healed you must likewise be whole.

That which keeps you from being whole,
That which keeps you from knowing who you are,
That which keeps you from knowing what you truly want,
Is your guilt.

I have spoken of guilt, and of the ego's use of guilt.
Guilt is an automatic result of the separation.
Your nature is to be whole,
To be complete within your Self.
Your nature is to be whole and to know fully
That you are One with All That Is,
Including One with God, and with every brother.

In order for you to design your experience of space and time,
And therefore, of this world,
You had to seem to split your mind.
Of this we have spoken before.

This imagined split of your mind
Is an attack on what you truly are,
And an attack upon God Itself.
And it is not possible to attack a being
Who is perfectly free and perfectly invulnerable
Without feeling guilt.
The reason for this is that when you
Try to be something you are not,
Even though it be only to imagine it,
You must feel conflict, and division, and separation.

That is the function of the ego.
That is the purpose of the ego.
That is what, indeed, gives the ego its very existence—
The belief in separation.

And in order for you to seem to reach
That state of separation,
You must somehow choose to attack your true nature.
And one way to think of guilt is to realize
That it is the response within your mind
That is generated when you attack your innocence.

Eventually, all of illusion, all of this world,
All of space and time, will pass away.
Indeed, it is not exact to say that they will pass away.
They will be reinterpreted; they will come to be known;
They will be understood in a manner which makes them
Compatible with your real Self, and with truth.

This you cannot do of yourself.
The reason for that is that you, in order to come here,
Structured a part of your mind in such a way
That it truly believes that you are what you are not—
That you are separate, that you are isolated,
That you are alone, that you can be ill, that you can die—
And the list goes on.

However, deep within you lies the truth of what you are.
And it knows that illusion is illusion.
For there always exists within your mind
The idea whose purpose is to guarantee that,
Eventually in your time,
All of your thoughts will be reinterpreted, restructured,
To again become One with the real part of your mind.
And that idea which shall bring you back
To the awareness of your reality is, as I have said,
The Holy Spirit.
The Holy Spirit, the idea of your Oneness,
Is the bridge between the split parts of your mind,
And was placed there by God (and therefore, by You).
Were it not so you could have imagined yourself separate,
And remained that way forever.

"Forever" seems to speak of time.
And yet the concept of forever abolishes time.
The other concept that abolishes time is NOW.
It is your guilt, it is your belief in,
And your desire to experience, separation

That has created time in the first place.
For, as we have said, time is that which allows you
To take part of the knowledge of what you are
And seem to throw it away.

What you really do is project it outside your mind
So that you are no longer aware of it.
And in the absence of your awareness of who you are,
You believe yourself to be separate,
And isolated, and alone.
And that is the creator of your time.
And that is the creator of your guilt.

So, in a very real sense,
Your belief in your time and your guilt
Are one and the same.
Indeed, as long as you choose to believe
That your yesterdays, the moments of your past,
Have brought you to this point in time,
And as long as you choose to believe that this moment in time
Somehow can, and does, create the next moment,
You are but cherishing your belief in separation,
And your own guilt.

For you could not, hear me well,
Believe in your time, or even experience your time,
If you were aware of your own wholeness.
For when you are whole, everything merely IS.
You have everything.
You are everything.
And you automatically extend that self-same everything
Outward from yourself unto all of Creation.
That is healing.
And that causes you to be healed.

So if you would escape from your guilt and its consequences,
You need only release your belief in time.
This means—since everything, as I have told you,
Is created or made at the level of mind—
This means that this and every instant is the product
Of what your mind chooses to create or to make RIGHT NOW,
Independent of any other and every other instant.

Your memories are one of your grandest illusions.
And your sense of regret,
Which is your decision to value and cherish your memories,
Is one of the great creators of your guilt,
And one of the creators of the prison walls
That separate you from your wholeness.

To become free of your guilt you need to pass into eternity.
And eternity is nothing more than the realization
That this moment and forever are exactly the same.
Each moment rises fresh and clean and free.
And you, the Son of God, in each moment,
Are equally clean and fresh and free.

There is no past.
There is no guilt that can tie you to your past.
There is no separation which ever occurred.
And there is nothing in this moment
Which can dictate to you anything of your future.
There is only this moment.
And this moment stands of and by itself.

The concept of forever is a construct that you can use
To allow yourself to sense something that is infinite.
And I have told you that infinite patience
Will bring you freedom NOW.
Infinite patience is freedom from your guilt,
And freedom from the tendency to desire
That any other brother be guilty for any reason.
Infinite patience means that there is no end
To your willingness to forgive,
To see beyond appearances.
Infinite patience means that there are no moments
Which are seen to pass from one to another.
Infinite patience is your ultimate realization
That you are free RIGHT NOW.

And how is it that you free yourself of your guilt,
Of your belief in time,
And of your belief in separation,
And all the imagined tragedy that it brings?
How is it that you can possibly do that
In this world of space and time?

What I will say to you now is very similar
To something I have previously said.
Whenever you are not free, whenever you feel conflict,
Whenever you are not totally joyous,
Know that you are feeling guilty,
That you are perceiving yourself as trapped in your time,
That you are choosing to feel isolated and separate.

Whenever you feel any circumstance
That is not joy and freedom,
And which does not prompt you to extend,
At the level of mind, all that you are—
Whenever you feel anything
That would keep you from that state—
Know that beneath it all you are experiencing guilt.

And remember that you cannot free yourself of that state alone.
So what you should do—
And I say ''should'' only in the sense that I am offering you
A pathway to your own joy—
What you should do, if you wish to be joyous,
Is be still.

And in your silence,
You will find the beauty of this moment.
You will find the freedom of forever.
For when you are still,
When you do the best you can to release yourself
From your belief in your yesterdays
And your fear of tomorrow,
There will come a voice and an awareness.
It will be the Voice of the Holy Spirit.
And you will sense, at some level,
What to do, and what to be, and where to go.

And as you follow that sense,
You will be following it to your own freedom.
And that freedom shall ultimately be
Your pathway out of separation and guilt and loneliness.
And it shall be your pathway into
Freedom and joy and love.

Blessings upon you all. That is all.

LOVE AND THE CRUCIFIXION

Greetings again. I am Jeshua.
Today I begin with you our discussion
Of the lessons of love.
There is a primary lesson of love,
Which you must come to know within your being,
Beyond your thoughts, beyond the words.
And when you learn the lesson at that level,
You will truly understand love.

The major lesson of love is extremely simple.
The lesson of love is this:
YOU HAVE EVERYTHING.
And because that is so, it is not possible
That anything can happen to you
Except by your own choice.
That awareness, in its simplicity, will bring you
To the full understanding of love itself.

What I have just said means that it is not possible, ever,
That you should be, or could be, a victim, in any sense,
In any circumstance of any kind.
It is not possible that some being can DO SOMETHING to you.
It cannot happen.

It is not possible that any beings,
Even those who seem to you to be without personality—
Rocks, trees, wind, comets, meteors—
It is not possible that beings of that nature can affect your life,
Or do something to you,
Except that it be your own choice and your own design.

Pause for a moment.
What if you knew with absolute certainty,
That it was not possible for you, ever,
To be a victim of any kind, in any circumstance, as I have said?
Try to imagine that you knew that.

And then try to imagine any cause whatsoever for anger.
And I will help you—there is none.
You may, in your thinking,
Play with that for as long as you wish.
But you will never find a cause for anger.
And if you are not a victim, and cannot be,
And can never be angry with another or any circumstance,
THEN ALL THAT REMAINS IN YOUR LIFE IS LOVE.

Everything that seems to happen to you
In this world of space and time
Is by your own design.
It is a form of the universe, persons or otherwise,
Celebrating with you that which you have designed
And desired for your own life.
Then the only cause for anger that could arise would be
That the universe not honor whatever it is that you desired.
And that, hear me well, does not, and cannot, happen.

To perhaps make that more clear—
If you wish to suffer injury and pain,
Then the universe honors what you wish.
And only if it did not do that for you
Would you have any cause for anger.
And I assure you again, that does not happen.

If your life seems filled with blessings
And that which you call goodness,
If your life is filled with struggle
And that which you call pain,
All of it, in every detail, is by your own choice.
You are not, and cannot be, a victim, in any circumstance.

THAT AWARENESS BRINGS YOU AUTOMATICALLY
TO THE AWARENESS AND THE EXPERIENCE OF LOVE,
AND ITS COROLLARY, GRATITUDE.

I, when I walked this earth, hear me well,
Chose to die by crucifixion.
You cannot understand the nature of love,
And the meaning of the crucifixion,

Unless you realize that even in that extreme circumstance,
I was not a victim, and could not be so.

I told you that the crucifixion was nothing more
Than an extreme example.
If I, as I was, I assure you, could be ridiculed,
Scorned, beaten, crucified, and seemingly killed,
WITHOUT ONE TRACE OF ANGER,
Then as you look at my extreme example,
Perhaps you can find within yourself
The ability to realize you are not a victim
In much lesser circumstances
Of seemingly much less consequence.

If a neighbor seems to offer to you an unkind word,
You might perceive yourself, in some small sense, crucified.
And love, as I urge you to know it,
Will not see that as an attack,
But merely a form of harmony which the two of you,
In your Oneness, are choosing to act out,
Out of your love for each other.

When you find it difficult to bypass the desire to be angry,
Think back to my crucifixion and its extreme example.
Think back to what I have told you
That I, and you, and all your brothers,
Can never experience anything except by our own choice.
Then you shall perhaps find within you
The freedom to release any desire you might have
To be angry.

I came here to live on this earth, in space and in time,
As an act of love, and as an act of sharing.
The real message of sharing lies in the resurrection.
For in the resurrection I demonstrated for you
That that which seems to happen to the physical body
Is truly of no consequence.
In that sharing, we become One, and we become free.
For thus we are, as the Sons of God.

The crucifixion I do not ask you to share.
Rather I ask you to observe my crucifixion,
And to learn from it, thereby freeing yourself of all anger

And all sense of being a victim.
For thus it is.
And as you release all belief that you can be a victim,
You shall, without effort, open yourself to love,
And freedom, and peace.

Miracles as such do not matter.
I did perform what many would call miracles.
And those, likewise, were nothing more
Than extreme examples.
'Tis true you could, can, walk upon the water as I did.
But it does not matter if you do.

'Tis true that you, as I did, have within you
The strength to free a blind man to see,
To free a lame man to walk,
To free a seemingly dead man to return to life.
You have within you that power and that freedom.
But, hear me well,
It does not matter if you do any of those.

The miracles that I participated in—
Not DID, but participated in with my brothers—
Were just extreme examples.
And the message of all of them is this—
My brothers, look, see what you are.
My brothers, look, see that you are free.
My brothers, look, see that you can teach and share
And give freedom to another
From within yourself.
My brothers, look, no matter what the world
May seem to do to you,
You are absolutely free, and you cannot die.

That was the message I came to bring to you.
It was, alas, oft misunderstood.
And misunderstanding always comes from fear,
And the false beliefs that arise from fear.
Misunderstandings never arise from love.
Hear me well.

If you can take the simple realization
That you are not, cannot be, and will never be,

A victim in any circumstance of any kind—
If you can take that notion
And allow it to become an automatic part of your being,
An automatic part of the belief system
That controls your life here—
Then you will indeed be free.

You will fully understand everything that I came to teach.
And you will automatically, because you have everything,
Extend it freely, with no trace of fear,
To all beings, to all brothers,
And to yourself.

And then you will, very simply,
Have learned that which I came to teach,
That which I came to share,
And that which I came to demonstrate
In the process of my crucifixion and my death,
And above all, in the process of my resurrection.

Blessings upon you all. That is all.

ONENESS AND SALVATION

Greetings again. I am Jeshua.
We are speaking of the lessons of love.
The opposite of the lessons of love
Would be the lessons of fear.
For the opposite of love is, indeed, fear.
We are speaking of love, and as it does for God,
Love leads to extension.

Fear, love's opposite, leads to projection.
Projection cannot occur without fear.
And yet I have told you,
Projection makes perception,
And perception is the characteristic of this world.
So everything in this world that you perceive
Is the product of fear.

How is it that projection cannot occur without fear?
'Tis very simple, really.
In fact, all of what I am saying to you today is extremely simple,
And is a good example of how simple this Course actually is.

Projection arises from fear.
Extension arises from love.
In order to project (and this is so simple)
You must have imagined, or believed,
That there is someone, or something,
Outside of yourself onto which you can project.

Extension seems to SEND OUT love.
For really love is all that can be extended.
And it can seem to you as if the love
Is being extended TO someone.
But really that is not the case.
Love arises out of the awareness that all is One.
Projection arises out of the belief that you are not One.

And so it is that this Course is so extremely simple.
For either you are Spirit, One with All That Is,
Or you are not.
You cannot be PARTLY One with All That Is.
That should be perfectly obvious to every mind,
Even to every ego.
Either you are separate or you are One.
There is nothing in between.
That is why this Course is so extremely simple.

And the reality of Spirit, the reality of God,
The reality of your Self,
Is that you ARE One with All That Is.

I have told you there is an alternative to projection.
And that is it.
So extremely simple, is it not?
When you project you are believing,
And therefore creating for yourself,
An experience in which you seem to be separate.
That makes you alone.
That makes you vulnerable.
That makes you not in control of your own life.
That means that it is possible that you can be a victim.
It means it is possible you could be harmed, or could harm.
It means that it is possible that you could, in fact, die,
And seem to cease to exist.

All of this arises out of projection.
All of it arises out of fear.
The lesson of love, stated once again,
Is that you are not separate,
But that all of Creation is One.
You and I are One.
You and God are One.
You and every brother and every aspect of your world
Are One.

You not only HAVE this life you seem to live,
But you ARE this life you seem to live.
And out of your Oneness,
It truly becomes simple to see how it is that
Having and being are the same.

For how can you have, or possess something,
Which actually IS your Self
Without actually BEING that same something?
Simple indeed, is it not?

What does it take, then, to find your salvation,
To find your freedom, to find your peace,
And to find your joy,
All of which are your inheritance as the Son of God?
What does it take?
IT TAKES YOUR WILLINGNESS TO REALIZE
THAT YOU ARE NOT SEPARATE.
And that is all.
Can anything be more simple?
Could I say it more clearly? I think not.

There are many words in *A Course in Miracles*,
Many words in these chapters,
And many more to come.
And all of those do not say anything different
From what I have just said.
All of the words are designed only to be instruments
To help you come to the realization
That you are not separate,
That you are One with all of Life.

Now, the awareness of your Oneness does not simply mean
That you become aware of your Oneness here and now.
For that notion holds within it the belief
That in your past you WERE separate,
And now have become aware that you actually are One.
But that is not the case.
You are not separate, and never were.
You are One with All That Is.
That is your nature as the Son of God.
That is the nature of God Itself.
That truth has never changed, and never shall.
Hear me very, very well.

All it takes to find your salvation, and your peace, and your joy,
Is your willingness to realize
That you ARE One and have never been otherwise.
This is to say that your salvation requires

That you be willing to realize that the separation
Never really occurred.
Or to express it slightly differently—
You must realize that the separation never happened
IN REALITY.

And thus you read in *A Course in Miracles,*
"Nothing unreal exists." (17)
You read words which tell you
That this world of space and time,
And its belief in bodies and separation and misery and death,
Is not real.
And that is exactly so.
If you believe any of it to be real you MUST be projecting.
You must be afraid.
You must be denying the Love which is your Self.
And therefore you must be choosing
Not to know your salvation

If it is so simple,
Why does not everyone in this world choose salvation?
The answer lies in the fact that your creative powers
Are essentially equal to the creative powers of God.
And when you chose to create
An imaginary world of separation,
You did it with all the masterfulness of a god.

And thus it seems as real to you
As if God Himself had made and ordained it.
It demanded, however, as we have said,
That you throw part of knowledge out of your mind,
And cause yourself to seem incomplete.
And then in your attempts to answer the question
Which arose out of your imagined incompleteness and its fear,
(The question, "Who am I?")
You created an illusion that seems so real
That it is very, very difficult indeed to let it go.
In fact, of your self—
And I speak now of your thoughts and your ego—
Of your self you are not capable of letting it go.
Such is the masterfulness with which you have created
The illusion of this world.

There is an answer, however, ordained by God,
And given you by your Self.
That answer is the Holy Spirit.
It is within you.
It was placed within you in the self-same instant
In which separation was imagined and released.
And within you remains the Holy Spirit,
Which is, and must be, a part of you.

So your salvation, in all its simplicity,
Demands that you allow into your thinking mind,
The mind of your ego,
The simple idea that I have been expressing this day—
That you are not separate,
That you are One.
Your willingness to let that idea
Become part of your thinking mind
Will lead you to salvation, and to your freedom.

And it is the Holy Spirit within you that will take you there.
For the Holy Spirit has the answer.
Your ego, your thoughts, cannot, of themselves,
Produce the answer.
That fact is by your own careful design.
However, God's careful design
Guaranteed that you and I and all beings
Have within us the Holy Spirit.

And as you open to the thoughts of Oneness,
The Holy Spirit uses His single-edged sword
To guide you to your salvation.
And the more you think the thoughts of Oneness,
The more the Holy Spirit will take
His awareness of your perfection,
His awareness of your brother's perfection,
His awareness of your perfect equality,
His awareness of the universal need you have
To know yourselves as One—
He shall take all of that and carry it for you to God.
And as He carries it to God,
He really will be carrying it to your Self.
For you are the same.

We have spoken before of how
The single-edged sword of salvation works,
Of how it is that the Holy Spirit leads you to your freedom
Without attack, without condemnation,
With nothing but His vision
Of Oneness, equality and love.

And so for you, the beginning point,
And for your thinking mind, the ending point,
Along the path to your salvation
Is simply your willingness to place within your mind,
With all the vigilance and diligence you can muster,
The realization that you are not separate,
That you are One,
That having and being are indeed the same.

And the Holy Spirit will take that idea
And carry it beyond your thinking, beyond your ego,
Unto the point where your thinking, and your ego,
And the values that it creates,
Shall simply pass away—
And you shall become free.

Blessings upon you all. That is all.

THE LESSONS OF THE HOLY SPIRIT—
GIVING

Greetings again. I am Jeshua.
We have been speaking of the lessons of love.
And today I would speak with you
Of the lessons of the Holy Spirit.
And they are the same.
For you are love.
And the Holy Spirit knows you only as what you really are.
So the lessons which the Holy Spirit brings to you
Are only those lessons which will lead you
To the awareness, to the memory,
Of that which you truly are as the Son of God.

I have already told you that love is the awareness
That you have everything, and are everything—
And that what follows, when once you realize that is true,
Is the automatic uncontrollable desire and need
To extend and to share that everything.
And thus it is that Love becomes itself
By being extended, by being given away.

And the reverse is also true.
Any time you would attempt to withhold anything,
And keep it unto yourself,
(Which is what defines separation)
It follows that what is present
Is no longer love, but fear.

The first lesson of the Holy Spirit is this:
"To have, give all to all." (18)
Or stated another way, if you would have everything,
You will receive It by extending,
Or by giving everything that you have.

The counterpart is—if you would withhold anything,
You will detract from yourself,
And make it impossible for you to have everything.

Thus I said two thousand years ago that
To those who have, more shall be given.
And to those who have not, even what they have
Will be taken away.
That is not a law imposed by God.
That is simply a truth,
Based upon the nature of what God is, and of what you are.
And being of God, it cannot be changed.

It can seem, I realize, difficult indeed
For you to be told that you must give everything away.
This is so because you tend to see yourself not as Spirit.
You tend to see yourself as a body, living in space and time.
And that you equate with your reality.
You then imagine a myriad of things
That your body needs in order for it to survive,
And, therefore, in order for you to survive.
And granted, when you see yourself as a body,
And therefore needing all these things or circumstances,
If someone says to you, as you perceive it,
"Give it all away,"
It can, indeed, seem frightening.

However, the Holy Spirit, being Spirit as you are,
Sees you as Spirit,
And always addresses that aspect of you,
Which is real and unchangeable.
And in that context the first law of the Holy Spirit is—
'To have, give all to all." (18)

What this means (and this may help your understanding)
Is that you need to realize that you are Spirit,
That every brother is Spirit,
And that all of you are the Son of God.
Not the sons of God, but the Son of God, singular.
God has one Son, One with Itself.
And you are that Son.
And every brother whom you perceive is also that Son.

Otherwise stated, there only exists,
Within the Son of God, perfect equality.
There only exists, in reality, Spirit,
With no aspect of Spirit differing from another.

And so the first step in giving all to all,
And indeed the most important step,
Is for you to realize that which I have just said.
Every brother is, in reality, Spirit.
Every brother is, in reality, your Self.
Everything that you seem to do and experience
Is done and experienced by the one Son of God.
Everything that you seem to experience in your life
Is part of a grand and glorious harmony
That the one Son of God has made and is experiencing.

So in order to give all to all,
You must begin by realizing that every brother
Is fully and equally the Son of God, just as are you—
That there is nothing which God has not given your brother,
That there is nothing that God has not given you,
That there is nothing that could be withheld
From your brother by you,
Or from you by your brother.

At the level of Spirit you are One.
The fact that you are One, that there is only perfect equality—
Which is exactly what the Holy Spirit sees—
The fact that you are One is the truth that makes it so
That there is no order of difficulty in miracles.
All that there is to be given,
All that there is to be received,
Is perfect and complete Love,
Without restriction and without reservation.
What every brother deserves from you,
Just as you deserve from every brother, is everything.
And that demands the fullest appreciation
For everything he seems to do and be.

When once that truth is realized within your thinking mind,
And eventually at the level of experience,
Then you will have experienced your reality as Spirit.
And the giving of all to all shall flow from you
Without effort or concern of any kind.

I have told you that the Holy Spirit,
In space and time and this world, will guide you exactly.
You will know where to go, what to do, what to say.

For the Holy Spirit, operating at the level of Spirit,
Knows that which you should give
Of your time, your possessions, and your talents.
The Holy Spirit, deep within you,
Knows when to give, where and how much.
And you will be directly guided to that awareness.
And especially as you open to the awareness of the Holy Spirit,
You will know, more and more clearly,
Exactly what to give of your possessions and your time.

So it is that the first lesson of the Holy Spirit—
To have, give all to all—
Follows automatically from the experience and the realization
That all is One in Spirit, that all is One in God.
That is the truth which, in the end, will set you free.
That truth is the one that lets you realize
That you are, indeed, not a body.
It is the truth that tells you that you cannot be bound
By the seeming circumstances here in this world.
It is the truth that tells you that no circumstance or happening,
However adverse it may seem,
Can have any effect on the true nature of what you are.

As we have said, that was the message of the crucifixion,
And, above all, of the resurrection.
That is a journey you do not have to make yourself,
Because I made it for you.
So all you need do now is open to the realization
That all is Spirit, that your reality is Spirit,
And that there is the Holy Spirit present
To guide you and direct you in all that you do.
And thus you shall be led safely and happily
To your peace, to your freedom, and your joy.

Blessings upon you all. That is all.

THE LESSONS OF THE HOLY SPIRIT—
PEACE

Greetings again. I am Jeshua.
We have been speaking of the lessons of the Holy Spirit.
These lessons are very important.
For these lessons, ultimately, if understood,
Will help you to regain the memory
Of that which you are as the Son of God.

We spoke of the first lesson, which is—
"To have, give all to all." (18)
I could also have said, "To be, give all to all."
For what I said to you was, in brief—
You are Spirit, only, and nothing but Spirit.
Your reality is Spirit.
The ultimate reality of every brother
And of all Creation
Is but Spirit.
And that Spirit is One.

There is no separation.
There is no aspect of Spirit which is greater than,
Or less than, any other aspect.
There is no experience of Spirit which is, in any sense,
Greater than, or less than, any other experience of Spirit.

Thus it is true, as I have told you,
That there is no order of difficulty in miracles.
This follows because you are Spirit indeed.
To have and to be are the same.
This is one of the fundamental laws of Spirit.
In space and time it seems otherwise.
In fact, it seems often the opposite.
But in reality, always you are Spirit,
What you have, you are.
And that you cannot change.

And so it is, the first step
In learning the lessons of the Holy Spirit
Is to keep within your awareness the realization
That you are Spirit, that you are One,
And that what you have and what you are
Are the same.

The next lesson of the Holy Spirit says this—
"To have peace, teach peace to learn it." (19)
This is a very important step.
Indeed, the lessons of the Holy Spirit help you to progress
From the world of the ego, the world of conflict,
To the world of Oneness, and the world of freedom.

And when once you can say,
Even within your thinking mind and your thoughts—
"In order to have, I must give,
For that is the nature of what I am."—
When once you have arrived at that point,
Then it logically follows that you would ask—
"In order to have what?"

Thus the second lesson of the Holy Spirit
Brings us to the realization of that which is worth having,
And that which is worth being.
But as I have said a number of times,
The goal of this Course is the getting and the keeping
Of the state of peace.

Peace is calmness, and quietness.
But more so, peace is a certainty
That cannot be deprived of anything,
That cannot be threatened in any way.
Peace is the fullness of experience without fear.
And peace arises from the realization that nothing,
In any form whatsoever, can harm you.
Peace arises from the knowing that you are absolutely safe.

And so, the second lesson of the Holy Spirit
Helps you to realize that which, indeed, you want.
And what you want is your peace, your freedom,
Your joy, your love, and your absolute safety.

Insofar as you walk this world
Of space and time and separation,
Insofar as you imagine that you have a brain which thinks,
And you seem to use it accordingly,
Then that which you think you ARE will follow
From that which you think you think.

Ultimately, as we have said, all thinking shall pass away.
But for now do not be dismayed.
I realize full well that you do, in your humanness,
Believe that you actually do think.
Do not make yourself wrong in that regard.
For so it is that you imagine that you do think.
And your thinking seems to define for you what you are.

Your thought system is the creator of that
Which you seem to be in this world.
Therefore, if you would have peace in this world,
Your thought system, upon which YOU are based,
Must contain within it peace.
What you think determines what you do.
And what you do is seen by others as what you are.
And what you are is what you teach.

Students do not hear empty words.
Students perceive what you are.
So I say to you now—
If you would have peace, teach peace,
In order to learn it for yourself.
What I am really saying to you is this—
Change your motivation.
Change the basis for your thought system.
And from that will follow, ultimately,
That which you become here in space and time.

In reality your nature is Spirit,
And your knowledge is of peace.
That you cannot change.
When the memory of your real nature returns to you,
Which may take you time if you choose,
Or will take an instant if you choose,
Then you will be free.
Then you will be at peace.

Thus you were created by God.
And that also you cannot change.

So if, in this world of space and time and illusion,
You would have peace, then you must teach it
By expressing it in that which you are.
And the building block, the foundation for your peace,
Shall be your motivation to have it.
And your motivation to have peace
MUST start with the realization
That you are Spirit and that you are One,
And that in order to have, you must give.
For everything that you give, you shall receive.

Really, the second lesson of the Holy Spirit
Follows quite easily from the first.
And the first is perhaps the most difficult
For your thinking mind to comprehend.
'Tis difficult indeed to see yourself,
To experience yourself, only as Spirit.
However, when once you do realize that you ARE spirit,
And that everything that you give
Becomes magnified for all, including yourself,
And can never be lessened—
When once you arrive at that realization,
Then it takes only a moment to realize that
That which you would have is, indeed, peace,
And joy, and freedom, and love.

I am certain, even now, in your thinking mind,
As I suggest to you that peace is the source
Of your joy, of your freedom, and of love,
All of which is your inheritance given you by God,
That it takes you but an instant to say
"Yes indeed, I would like to have that."

And so indeed, if you would like to have peace,
And the certainty and the safety and the freedom that it brings,
All you have to change is your motivation.
All you have to do is truly, wholly, desire that it be yours.
For to wholly desire is to create.
And to create is the power given you by God.

Creation can only follow from truth.
Creation can never arise from falsehood or illusion.

Therefore, to have peace, you must teach peace.
To teach peace, you must BE peace.
And to be peace, your motivation must be ONLY for peace.
And therefore it must be only for truth.
And truth, as difficult and as strange as it may seem,
Arises from your realization that you are Spirit,
That you are One,
That everything you give is yours,
And that everything you would withhold,
You deprive yourself of having and being.

The pathway to your freedom, the pathway to your joy,
The pathway to your peace, here in space and time,
Arises from your motivation to change your thinking.
And as the motivation becomes experience,
Your thinking will change.

Begin therefore, as I have said,
With the idea, the thought,
That you ARE Spirit and that you ARE One,
And that everything you have is everything you are.
And that that is, indeed, simply everything.

Blessings upon you all. That is all.

THE LESSONS OF THE HOLY SPIRIT— VIGILANCE

Greetings again. I am Jeshua.
We have been speaking of the lessons of the Holy Spirit.
Remember that the Holy Spirit is within you, is part of you.
And the real function of the Holy Spirit is to guarantee
That you can never be separated from God.

You have chosen, for now, a world of illusion.
And you have chosen it for the purpose of imagining
What it might be like to be apart from God—
Which you cannot be.
The lessons of the Holy Spirit are the lessons
Which shall bring you back to the awareness
That you are not apart from God,
Or apart from anything that is,
And that you cannot be so.
And that awareness shall be your freedom and your joy.

We spoke of the first lesson that said—
"To have, give all to all." (18)
Truly, that is the opposite of the way the world thinks.
And to find the truth of what you are,
You must learn to give,
And know that it is in giving that you shall truly receive.
Because the only gift you can give is to yourself.

And the second lesson simply refers to
The nature of the gift that you would give.
The gift of God is total peace,
Which is synonymous with joy,
Which is the same as freedom,
Which is the same as love.
So to have peace, teach peace.
To have joy, teach joy.
To have freedom, teach freedom.
And to have love, teach love.
They are all the same.

And thus the Holy Spirit would help you to realize
What it is that you truly desire.

And now the third lessons says—
"Be vigilant only for God and His Kingdom." (20)
What does that mean?
You seem to be here, in a world of thinking,
In a world of egos and imagined separation,
In a world of illusion.
And yet, within you, there is the undying awareness
That you must return to the awareness of what you are.

Vigilance begins with the awareness
Of the gifts of the Kingdom of God.
Within your thinking, within this world of illusion,
You cannot escape the inner knowing that there is a reality,
That there is that which you truly desire,
That there is more than what this world has to offer.
And all of you, at some level, know that to be true.
For it is the truth of what you are, and cannot be escaped.

Your vigilance, then, is your willingness
To allow the Holy Spirit to work with you in your thinking.
Your vigilance, then, is your willingness
To take everything which you would think and desire
And seem to experience,
And hold it up to the light of the truth
Which the Holy Spirit teaches,
And to do this without exception.
If you do that with willingness,
And desire above all else to receive the gifts of God,
Then the Holy Spirit, which is always within you,
Shall come forth, shall be present,
And shall guide your thinking unto your joy,
Your freedom, your peace, and to love.
For those are the gifts of God.

How should you be vigilant only for God and His Kingdom?
Vigilance requires, as oft as ye shall do it, stillness within.
For it is in your stillness that you may hear the inner voice,
The voice of the Holy Spirit.
Whenever there is conflict, whenever there is unrest,
Whenever there seems to be isolation,

Or frustration, or separation—
Pause and be still.
And in your stillness, even in your thinking,
Simply request that the Holy Spirit be there.
And it will happen.

Another measure, quite simple indeed,
Is for you to realize what are
The gifts of the Kingdom of God—
Peace, and freedom, and joy, and love.
And when you find true peace, true freedom,
True joy abiding within your being,
You may trust it and follow it without exception.

If you find that it is clear to you
That you are not at peace, and not feeling joy,
Then pause once again and be still,
And request that the Holy Spirit—
Which is the part of you that remains in contact with God,
And which is always present—
Request that the Holy Spirit offer you guidance to your joy,
To your peace, to your freedom, and to love.

You might ask, "If I am feeling peaceful and joyful,
How can I tell that it is the peace of God,
And not of illusion?"
And the simple test, which I have told you before, is this—
If anything, anything whatsoever,
However small, however large,
If anything of this world can threaten or take away
Your peace, or your joy, or your freedom,
Then it is not yet the true peace of God.

Do not forget that the Holy Spirit takes that which is of truth
And keeps it safe for you within your mind.
The Holy Spirit takes that which is partially true and purifies it
So as to keep its truth within your mind.

And that which is not of truth, the Holy Spirit will reject.
It, of course, does not disappear.
For no idea can leave its source until such time
As its creator chooses that it do so.

But that which is not of truth becomes part of
The world of the ego, the world of illusion.
And the nature of the world of illusion is
That it SHALL pass away,
That it is subject to perception, to whim, and to threat,
To grief, and misery, and to death.

When you have something which can be taken away,
Then you do not, indeed, have it.
When you have something
Which can NOT be threatened in any form,
Then that which you HAVE is a part of what you ARE.
And thus I speak of ''having'' and ''being'' as the same.
For when that which you have IS that which you are,
The measure is that it cannot be threatened.

For nothing in the universe can threaten
The reality of what you are.
Not even God Itself can threaten the reality of what you are.
For if It did, God would be threatening Itself.
For you are One with God.
There is nothing, hear me well—
There is NOTHING that can threaten
What you have, and what you are.
If what you have can be taken away or threatened,
It is your proof that it is not what you are,
And that you have not yet reached the state
In which you experience having and being as the same.

The Holy Spirit's guidance, therefore,
Will bring you to the point where HAVING is what you are.
And BEING is what you are.
For they are the same.
And at that point, all need for effort to be vigilant
Shall pass away, and you shall be free.
You shall BE peace.
You shall BE joy.
You shall BE Love.
And when you begin by being those gifts,
Then you cannot keep them from being yours.
Do you see?

Be vigilant only for God and His Kingdom.
In your thinking, if ever you find conflict or unrest,
Pause and be still.
Request of the Holy Spirit Its presence and Its guidance.
If ever you feel not at peace, not at joy, not free,
If you cannot find within you, love,
Pause and be still.
And request the guidance of the Holy Spirit.

If you do feel at peace,
But realize it can be threatened,
Pause once again and be still.
Ask for guidance and delivery from the world of illusion.
And the Holy Spirit will be there.

Initially, your thinking and your fear—they are the same—
May seem to be present and make it difficult to hear.
But persist in your stillness.
And you will become aware, first softly,
But then more so and more so,
Until the message becomes strong and clear.
You will hear the quiet knowing of what to do and what to be.
And that shall be the Holy Spirit,
Which is your Self, and which is the Voice for God,
Speaking to you and through you.

And as you follow that Voice,
That which you become, that which you have,
And that which you are
Shall echo its message throughout the entire world.
And you shall become savior.
You shall become the bringer
To the world, and to yourself,
Of the gifts of the Kingdom of God—
Your peace, your freedom, your joy,
And above all, the gift of absolute Love.

Blessings upon you all. That is all.

THE GIFTS OF THE KINGDOM

Greetings again. I am Jeshua.
I have come to discuss with you, this day,
The gifts of the Kingdom.
And the Kingdom, of course,
Is the Kingdom of God.

I have come to tell you, this day, the truth
That the Kingdom of God is your kingdom as well.
Everything that is God IS you.
In your world you speak of having things.
And thus you might say that
Everything that belongs to God belongs to you.
For that is so.

However, do not lose sight of the fact that
"Having" and "being" are the same in the Kingdom.
And so the truth remains that
The Kingdom of God IS GOD.
And the Kingdom of God IS YOU.

The gift of the Kingdom is creation.
That is the gift of God to you,
Because it is the gift of God to Himself.
In extension, in the expansion of Itself,
God, without changing, became magnified.
God, without changing, extended.
God, without changing, increased.
And God, without one change,
Became more than He is.

Your mind, your thoughts, cannot comprehend
The truth and the meaning of those words.
And that is simply because, within your thinking mind,
You cannot fully understand creation.
But whether you understand it or not,
The gift of the Kingdom, God's gift to you,
Is creation itself.

What is this "creation"
That is God's gift to you, and to Himself?
Creation is the experience of joy.
Creation is the simple joy of being.
Creation is the simple act of becoming what you already are
By extending yourself outward.

It is so that creation must extend in one direction.
I have told you that you and God
Do not have a totally reciprocal relationship.
God has created you, His son.
You create your own sons, which are your creations.
And they, in turn, create their own sons.
And the process goes on, and on, and on, unto infinity.

You, I, the Son of God, do not create the Creator.
Were it to be so,
Were it so that God created us AND WE CREATED GOD,
Life would simply be, if you will,
A closed circle of existence,
Never expanding, never becoming.
God, in His wisdom, knew that.
And thus it is that creation must extend outward.

That must be so, as well, because
At the center of Creation is God.
And God, as we have said, is everything.
God is wholeness, God is completeness—
Nothing lacking, nothing to be added,
Nothing that can be added.
You cannot add to God.
And so the only direction in which creation CAN flow—
And even your thinking mind can understand this—
The only direction in which creation can flow is "out from . . ."
And that is the simple expansion and extension
Of an Everything, an infinity of Everything,
Which literally cannot be contained.

Creation flows outward in one direction.
What does that mean for you?
It means that, within your freedom given you by God,
There is one freedom you do not have.
You cannot turn and reverse the process and change God.

You cannot turn and reverse the process
And change that which God has created.
Hear me well, this day.
What God has created is you, His Son.
You cannot turn round and change God.
And likewise, you cannot turn round
And change what you are.

God has created you like unto Himself—
Spirit, One and Free.
And thus it follows that anything
Which you would deign to experience—
And you are free to imagine whatever you will—
Anything you would deign to experience,
But which is not compatible with what God has created,
Must be experienced as illusion.
And that includes this entire world.

This world—its space, its time, its bodies, all of it—
Is your creation.
It is your son.
And just as you, the creation of God,
Cannot turn round and change God,
So it is, within the law of the Kingdom,
That your son, this world,
Cannot turn round and change you.

What does that mean?
It means, simply, as I have told you already,
That everything, every experience
MUST COME from mind,
Must come from the reality of what you are.
Your body cannot change, or affect you, in any way.
It has no power to become sick,
Except that it be chosen by, and have its origin in, mind.
Your body truly has no power even to die,
Except that it come from, and be chosen by, mind.
This world, and all of its circumstances,
Which seem to be external to you—
None of them can change you in any way.

That is how it is that we say this world is illusion.
It cannot have any effect upon the reality of what you are.

For it is but your son, and cannot turn round and change you,
Just as you cannot turn round and change God.

I would speak, then, of your creative power.
I would speak of how it functions in this world.
And I would speak of its reality.
Creation, as I have said, is, and must be, extension.
And extension, by its very nature,
Must arise out of the awareness of
A wholeness and a completeness
Which cannot be contained.

In this world, of course, you do not have such awareness.
Were you to have it you would not be here.
For this world, in its essence, is based upon the belief
That you are not complete, and not whole.

So how does the law of creation function in this world,
Since you cannot extend?
How is the law modified?
What you do, as I have told you, is project.
And when you project
You begin with an awareness of incompleteness,
The lack of wholeness, and the fear that comes with them.
And projection is for the purpose
Of attempting to complete yourself.
And so you project outward in order to gain
What you call "experience,"
Which you then use to fill the lack
Which demanded that you project in the first place.

Can you see? Tis what you call in your world,
A vicious cycle with no end.
That means—with no end in peace.
You shall never be at peace
Until you become aware that you are whole.
And in your awareness of wholeness and completeness,
Projection shall have disappeared
As fog before the morning sun.
Then all there will be is extension.
And that, of course, you will know as Love.

When you project, what do you see?
You see only what you have projected.
Never can you see anything but your self.
In the Kingdom, the reality is
That there is nothing but your Self.
And that truth does not change.

The process of projection
Would cause you to believe it otherwise.
But it is not so.
What you project, you shall see.
And what you project, and therefore what you see,
Is literally what you believe you are.
I did not say that what you believe is what you KNOW you are.
For in the world of incompleteness,
There cannot be knowledge.
Of that we have spoken before.
WHAT YOU PROJECT IS WHAT YOU BELIEVE YOU ARE.

So if you would become aware of what you believe you are,
Look at your world.
Whatever you see is what you believe.
And what can you see?
Whatever you choose. For you are free.

Insofar as you believe the fears of the ego,
And the belief in lack and isolation,
Insofar as you believe in the absence of wholeness,
That is what you will find.
Insofar as you, even within your thinking,
Can come to believe that you are, as I tell you, the Son of God,
Whole, pure, complete and beautiful,
Then that is what you shall see.

So as you look out at each brother, at each facet of your world,
Know that you see but your self,
And your own belief of what you are.
If you see fear, and feel it within your being,
Know that YOU are afraid.
If you see simple, unbridled, joy and peace
Flowing within your brothers,
Know as well that that is what is within you.

And give thanks unto yourself.
For always it is your own creation.

In creation you extend, as you must,
Because you cannot be contained.
In this world you project in order to believe
The stories you have made up about who you are,
Ultimately, because you need, because you are afraid.

What then is your goal?
As you would experience the reality of the Kingdom here,
Your goal is to find the peace
That comes from seeing your self as you are.
Your goal is to experience the peace
That comes from seeing through the eyes of the Holy Spirit.
Your goal is the peace
That comes from seeing yourself as I see you.
And all of those are the same.

And I have told you so many times—
You are complete. You are whole. You are beautiful,
You are pure. You are One. You are the Son of God.
You are God Itself.
And you are the meaning, and the purpose,
And the joy of all of Creation.

Do what you can to open your being
To sense, to feel within,
My awareness of what you are.
Open to the awareness of the Vision of Christ,
Which is the vision with which the Holy Spirit
Sees you in your reality.
And when you do that, then it shall seem as if
You have, indeed, received the gift of the Kingdom.

In the Kingdom the gift is creation.
Here, since you cannot create,
Since you project out of an imagined need,
It shall seem as if you have received the gift of the Kingdom.
And what shall that be?
Only this: peace.

As I have said, you shall be perfectly calm.
There shall be no turmoil. There shall be no unrest.
There shall be no conflict upon your being.
For how can there be unrest, or turmoil, or conflict
Within the being of God?
And therefore, how can there be
Unrest, or turmoil or conflict
Within you?
For you and God are, as I tell you, the same.

Blessings upon you all. That is all.

HEALING

Greetings again. I am Jeshua.
We are discussing at this time,
The gifts of the Kingdom.
And it is one of those gifts
Which I wish to discuss with you this day.
The gift of the Kingdom which I wish to discuss today
Is that of healing.

Healing is not part of the reality of the Kingdom of God.
Healing is a gift which you shall receive as you journey
Along the pathway, along this course to miracles.

What is it that healing shall bring to you,
Since I speak of it as a gift?
Healing shall bring to you the gift that you give.
For it is true that if you would become a healer,
Which also means, if you would be healed,
You shall do it by giving.
Not by receiving. Never by receiving.
In fact, that is a fundamental truth which you must recognize,
If you would be healed.
You must recognize that if your intent is to receive,
You have not understood the truth.

Healing comes from your recognition of
The simple truth of what you are.
I have said it so many times, over and over.
And I say it once again—
You are the Son of God.
You are co-creator of All That Is.
You are complete. You are whole.
There is no lack within you.

And if you would heal, all you need do is this—
Realize that there is no lack within your brother.
If you but see the truth of what your brother is,
Then both of you become healed.

What really is this healing of which I speak?
I have told you that healing
Is the form of communication which the Holy Spirit uses.
Do you understand communication itself?
Communication, within a world in which all is One,
Arises from sharing.
And sharing does not mean that you, a separate, isolated being,
Would share something, which is also isolated,
With another being, isolated as well.
Sharing does not, and cannot,
Arise from the belief in separation.

So if you would communicate within the laws of God,
What you shall do is share experience.
This means that you,
Within the realm of whatever you experience,
Realize that you and your brother are One.
This is to realize that whatever you experience
Belongs to him, because YOU ARE HIM.
This is to realize as well that
Whatever belongs to the Holy Spirit belongs to him,
Just as surely as it also belongs to you.
For, of course, it is all the same.

So if you would be healed, look within,
And see there the Son of God,
In the form of your brother.

How can you heal unless you first sense
That there is a need for healing?
Ah, in this world of separation, and tears, and toil,
Do you not so often look out and see just that—
Separation, and tears, and toil—
All of it expressing Itself in the form of fear?
Is that what prompts your healing—
That you would look out and see the misery, and then say
"I need to be healed"?

Hear me well. For what I shall say here is most important.
When you look out and see lack, and grief,
Misery, and tears, and toil, and death,
It is not from that awareness that your healing shall arise.

Truly I tell you, God and the Holy Spirit
Do not see those things which I have just mentioned.

Insofar as you would be healed, what you shall do
Is see your brother in his truth.
What you shall do is recognize your brother
As you see him through the eyes of the Holy Spirit,
And, therefore, through the eyes of God.
And when you do that, what do you see?

I have told you that healing arises
In conjunction with the laws of God.
And the laws of God, in part,
Simply make you aware of what your brother is.
Your brother is not a body, but Spirit.
Your brother is not separate, but One.
And he must be seen as One,
Wholly integrated with all of existence.
Your brother is not imprisoned by a world of tears and toil.
Rather, your brother is free.

Now, for a moment, imagine that you COULD
See your brother that way.
Imagine any circumstance, even one of dire illness,
If you should choose.
And within that circumstance attempt to realize
That your brother is Spirit, is One, and is Free.
Attempt to realize that your brother
Is actually choosing what brings him joy.
Attempt to realize that there is no being
Separate from your brother
Who would ever wish for him to do anything other
Than what he is doing in that moment.
Attempt to realize that your brother, as Spirit, is absolutely safe,
Beyond any harm you could ever imagine that might befall him.

Now go back to the circumstance you imagined,
And see it in a new light.
Where is your belief in tragedy?
Has it not disappeared under the light of freedom, and of love?
Indeed, I tell you this day—
If you have been able to see as I have suggested,
Tragedy cannot enter your consciousness.

For truly I tell you, tragedy is a name given to nothing.
It does not, and cannot, exist.
Tragedy could only exist if you were not free.
And the laws of God demand that you ARE free,
And remain free—always.

The gift of the Kingdom of which I speak this day is healing.
And healing is that which exists—always.
I have spoken of healing as the changelessness of Mind.
And what do I mean by that?
I mean that the laws of God define
Who you are and what you are.
And that cannot change.
You are Spirit.
Spirit is of Mind.
Mind is the source of creativity.
Mind is that which houses the creative power of God.
And Mind is You.
And Mind cannot change what It is.

Ah, yes, there is an infinity of experience.
But experience is just the expression of your creative power.
That is all.
You are free to experience whatever you will,
Just as is your brother.

As you look out within this world, as you are wont to do,
Your healing, and your being healed,
Shall arise out of your awareness
That your brother does not change.
Your healing shall arise from seeing your brother
As perfect, complete and whole,
Beyond tragedy, beyond grief—
Indeed, beyond fear of any kind.
And as you see your brother thusly,
You shall be party to the Vision of Christ.

Whatever you project or extend, you believe or you experience.
It is not possible, as I have told you,
To project or to extend a belief or an experience
To PART OF Creation.
If you, in your illusion,
Would see a brother as frail, and ill, and weak,

Then it must be that you believe that of every other brother,
Including yourself.
It is not possible, I assure you,
To believe that PART OF Creation is whole,
And that part of it remains fragmented, weak,
Isolated, and alone.

Now hear me well. That even applies to the way you see me.
It also applies to the way you see God.
If you but pause and apply logical reasoning,
If you will, to your thought system,
Then it will follow that if you see
Weakness, and fear, and tragedy
Upon the face of your world,
Then you, I promise you,
Do not see God Itself as invulnerable,
As pure, and as completely free.

So if you would experience,
If you would give and receive healing,
You may do it thusly.
You may change your mind about Mind Itself.
Which is to say, you may change your mind about God.
This can seem difficult for you.
For it would seem that you already believe
That God is complete, and whole, and omniscient,
And all-powerful—and the list goes on.
But I promise you, what I said is true.
If you see weakness in your world,
Then you must, as well,
See it in God.

So I make you an offer.
If it seems difficult to see your brother as he truly is,
Then look at me.
And see if you can open your being to the awareness
That I am complete, and whole, existing as Spirit,
In a great infinite Oneness,
And living in an absolute and complete freedom of existence.
See if you can see me thusly.
For if you can, then you will bless your own being
With that same existence.

And if it even seems, perhaps, difficult to do that,
Then simply look at God and attempt to believe that
God is complete, and whole, and invulnerable,
Beyond fear, beyond reproach,
Beyond doubt, beyond opposition.
Attempt to imagine completeness, in whatever form you can,
And allow that it be the characteristic of God.
And then, in the simple realization
That you are created in the image of God,
So it must be for your brother.
And so it must be for you.

A gift of the Kingdom is healing.
And healing is the gift you give.
It is not possible to give healing in order to receive.
For if you try, you shall fail.
You give the gift of healing out of your awareness
Of the truth of what your brother is,
Of what I am,
Of what God Itself is,
And yes, what you are.

See yourself beyond your body.
See yourself beyond space and time,
Beyond restriction, beyond limitation.
Realize that you are, as I have said—
Spirit, One, and completely Free.

Allow your mind to change until you realize
That there is, indeed, nothing about your mind that can change.
For you were, and are, and always shall be, the Son of God.
And the simple awareness that that is true
Shall heal your brother, and yourself,
And your entire world.

Blessings upon you all. That is all.

THE UNBELIEVABLE BELIEF

Greetings again. I am Jeshua.
I have come this day to further, with you,
My discussion of the gifts of the Kingdom.

I have spoken to you, in part,
About what those gifts may be.
I spoke about the gift of healing.
I helped you become aware that healing
Resides in the awareness of wholeness.
Healing resides in the awareness of completeness,
And of fullness.

I would speak to you this day
More about the Kingdom itself.
The Kingdom is the Kingdom of God.
The Kingdom of God is extension.
The Kingdom of God is creation.
The Kingdom of God is joy.
They are all the same.

All of them arise from self-fullness.
God, the infinite source of Love, cannot be contained.
For, even in your terms,
How can an infinity of anything be contained?
Indeed, it is not possible.
God, in order to BE God, extends Himself.
Extension is simply the creation of experience, and of being,
Arising out of the fact that Love cannot be contained.

If you ever, within your thinking,
Believe that you can hold something unto yourself alone,
And then attempt to deem it love, you are mistaken.
Love cannot be confined.
Love cannot be contained.
And unless it is shared, it cannot be Love.

As I have told you, Love is extension.
Love REQUIRES extension.
Love and extension go hand in hand,
And cannot be separated.
So it is that God extends Itself outward,
Not out of need, not out of longing, not out of loneliness,
But out of a fullness so great that it cannot be contained.

And thus you and I and all beings,
The Son of God, was born.
That which God extended IS God,
And cannot not be God.
As God literally extended Himself into Creation,
His creations have become, and are, God Himself.
That includes me, you, all brothers, and all beings.

Try to imagine, if you will, the completeness,
The wholeness, the infinity of All That Is,
Taking PART of Itself and pushing that part out from Itself
In such a way that there was created an absence.
Literally, try to imagine that the infinity of existence,
The unboundedness of infinite Love,
Would try to take part of Itself
And place it where It is not.
And even in your mind, you realize that such cannot be.

Everything is Mind. That I have told you before.
Everything is true thought.
Everything is an idea in the Mind of God.
And thus, perhaps, you can see how it is
That ideas cannot leave their source.
The infinity of What Is, the infinity of Love,
CAN NOT take part of Itself and place it where It is not.
This applies to God.
This applies to all of Creation
And, hear me well, this applies to you.

Now, I have spoken to you about an unbelievable belief.
And what that unbelievable belief is,
Is the belief in the ego.
It is your belief in your self (small "s").

Go back to the realization that infinity
Cannot in any way separate part of Itself from Itself.
Such could only be if God were finite,
And there were some place where God is not.
The same applies to you.
There is no place in Thought, in Mind, or in space and time,
Where You, in your reality, are not.
And the ego is the false belief
That what I have just told you is not true.
The ego is the belief that you,
Son of God, infinite creative being,
Can separate your Self from your Self,
And call your Self something else.
Do you see how absurd the notion is?
And do you wonder now how can you believe it at all?

How can you look upon your self as separate
From any part of Creation, any part of the universe?
Only can you do so if you believe that God has not created you.
And that is not the case.
Only can you do so if you believe
That you are not the Son of God,
And that God is not God.
And that is also not the case, I promise you.
Only can you believe in the ego,
Only can you believe in yourself as a separate, isolated being,
If you believe that you literally can rend asunder
That which is You,
And that which is God.

I have spoken of the split mind.
And the only way you could even imagine
That which I have been describing
Is to somehow imagine that you have split your mind—
Which you did not do, and cannot do, and could never do.
But in your imaginings, you simply thought
For a fleeting instant, "What if . . . ?"
And before the question was finished
In the mind of the Son of God,
The answer was given, and it was done.
A chuckle, the awareness of freedom, and it was done.
'Twas not even a ripple on the ocean of experience,

Which is the creation, the beingness,
Of God Itself, of Love Itself.

If you would choose, in your analyzing and your thinking,
To take the notions I have just given you
And proceed with them to a logical conclusion,
You will realize that there is none.
And if you choose to do that,
If you choose to play with those ideas,
You will indeed come to realize that the belief is unbelievable,
Just as I have said.

So what is really unbelievable, then?
The belief that you exist as a small "s" self.
What is truly unbelievable is the belief that you are not God.
For do you not say in one word, "God is All That Is,"
And then proceed to believe that you are separate from Him?
And do you not wish to laugh this very moment
At the absurdity of that notion?
Such is the capriciousness, such is the fickleness, of the ego.

So it is, as I have told you before,
That the hallmark of the ego is conflict.
Only by generating conflict,
Which you, in your awareness, would choose to ignore,
Can there be any belief in the ego itself.
In the absence of conflict there is nothing
That you would push out of your mind.
In the absence of conflict, you become whole,
Which is what you have been, and are,
And always shall be.

In the absence of conflict there is only peace.
In the presence of peace there can never be differences.
In the absence of differences there cannot be separation.
In the absence of separation there is only One Self—
And that is God, and you, and me,
And all brothers in all of Creation—
One vast harmony of creation and being.

And so it is that you must cherish your conflict
In order to believe in your small "s" self.
If ever you come to true peace, the peace of God,

Then your ego will disappear in a moment, without effort.
And your ego, which you believe to be you, KNOWS THAT.
And so you seek to maintain conflict in order to remain here.
And how do you do that?
BY BELIEVING THAT YOUR CONFLICT BRINGS YOU JOY.

But, if you think for even a moment,
Do you not realize that conflict is pain?
And when you think about the conflict
Of which you are aware in your life,
Are you not aware that it is painful?
And, of course, all of you are.
And yet, within the structures of your ego,
You believe that your pain is not pain,
That your pain is joy.

"How is that?" you might ask.
You have confused joy with the idea
That you can be separate and alone.
You have structured this ego, this world,
In such a way that you can believe that you are isolated,
Alone and weak, a being of frailty and ultimate death.
That is by your design.
And so you have tricked your thinking mind into believing
That whatever supports that belief in the isolation,
The aloneness, the frailty, and the eventual death—
That whatever supports that belief
Is what creates what you are and gives you life.

And you do know, of course, that life itself and being IS joy.
And so, in your confusion,
You believe that whatever supports your ego is a source of joy.
And thus you struggle and compete
And claw your way through a war of individual existences,
Each one grappling as best it can
To preserve itself in the face of the billions of others
Attempting to do the same—
All for the purpose of believing
That in doing so you become joyful.
And already you have seen clearly in your own mind,
Without me even telling you,
That of course it is not joy. It is conflict.

Now is it even more clear why I say "the unbelievable belief"?
I am sure you see.
The gift of the Kingdom is the simple awareness—
Which belongs to you even in your thinking minds—
The gift of the Kingdom is the awareness
That extension is being, that extension is giving,
That extension is receiving, that extension is Life Itself.
And all of those are the same.

The gift of the Kingdom is the simple truth
That you are not split apart from God.
For nothing can be so.
The gift of the Kingdom is the realization in your mind that,
Since God is the infinity of All That Is,
And you are as well,
You cannot be alone, and cannot isolate yourself—
No matter what you would do, or imagine.
The gift of the Kingdom is the simple truth
That God is All That Is,
And therefore you, likewise, are All That Is.
For you are God.

Your own being, your own life,
Your own existence, which is Love,
Depends upon extension.
And extension is something which you DO.
This you have not been able to stop doing.
The Holy Spirit, in its awareness of your reality,
Has preserved all of your creations.
And your real joy shall come when you are aware, once again,
Of their presence, of their place,
In the grand harmony of being which is God.

The gift of the Kingdom shall come to you
As you elect to listen to the voice of the Holy Spirit.
For It shall make clear to you,
Any instant in which you choose,
The truth of what you are—
Which is God, the Son of God, Infinite Being,
Incapable of being split apart,
Incapable of being separate
From any part of the infinity that Being is.

Your freedom, your salvation, and your joy
Shall come to you as you realize that
Your belief in separateness is indeed unbelievable.
And in that awareness, under the guidance of the Holy Spirit,
Those gifts shall be yours as you simply
Take that unbelievable belief, and let it go.

Then your true life shall come to you.
And as you extend to your entire world—
Be it the world of space and time, or the world of Spirit—
As you extend to the world the awareness of your own peace,
Your own joy, the self-fullness that is Love,
You shall extend those, without effort, to all of existence.
And as you do so, you shall celebrate
That you have but magnified, beyond measure,
The beauty of what you are.

Blessings upon you all. That is all.

PEACE AND FREEDOM

Greetings again. I am Jeshua.
I have come this day to discuss with you
Your spiritual journey.
And you may refer to your journey as
"The journey back . . .''
And thus you ask, the journey back—to where?
'Tis extremely simple, as I have told you.
The journey is back to peace.

So as you begin this chapter, I suggest
That you ask yourself one simple question,
"Am I always, every moment, totally at peace?"
And if you can answer, "Yes,"
Then ask yourself a second question.
"Is there anything of this world, which, should it change,
Could affect, in any way, my perfect peace?"
For if you deem yourself to be peaceful,
And yet find it true, within, that any change—
Be it the loss of a possession, your money, your house,
Be it the loss of a relationship—
If any change could threaten your peace,
Then your peace is not real.
So if you have asked yourself those questions,
And have found yourself not totally at peace,
Then continue with me along the journey back.

If you are not at peace, then you are at war.
The absence of peace IS war.
And there is one thing which you must learn,
And that is this:
In this war in which you find yourself,
Simply because you are not at peace,
IN THIS WAR, THERE IS NO OPPONENT.
That means there is nothing in the universe,
Nothing within God,
Nothing within any of your brothers,
Nothing within your world,
Which has a will different or separate from your own,
And which would design to destroy your peace.

IN THE ABSENCE OF YOUR PEACE,
YOU ARE AT WAR WITH NO ONE.

That understanding is absolutely required
In order that you will, eventually, in your time,
Come to the experience of peace.
You are at war with no one.
So the curriculum is one designed to bring you to peace,
To help you win the war in which you have no opponent.

Well, how does there seem to be a war in the first place?
There seems to be a war because you hear two voices.
You hear the voice of the ego.
And you hear the Voice of the Holy Spirit.
One of the voices is always there.
That is the Voice of the Holy Spirit,
The Voice of God.
That Voice is part of you.
It was placed there by God, and can never leave.

The voice of the ego is placed there
Out of your desire to experience the illusion of separation.
And insofar as you choose that pathway,
Then you are free to choose to listen to the voice of the ego.

However, in the absence of the illusion of separation,
The ego dies, has no voice, and can not speak.
If you would hear two voices
Which would teach you different pathways,
Then you must be in conflict.
You MUST be at war. Do you see?
And thus you cannot be at peace.

So how is it that you win the war?
BY LISTENING TO ONE VOICE.
And since it is absolutely not possible
To hear ONLY the voice of the ego,
You have but one choice available.
If you would come back to your peace,
You MUST do it by hearing but one voice,
Only the Voice of the Holy Spirit.

The Voice of the Holy Spirit shall speak to you of freedom.
For that is the message of the Holy Spirit—
You are free.
The message of the ego is the opposite.
The message of the ego, albeit unknown to you,
Is the message of imprisonment.

"How is that so?" you might ask.
I have told you that the voice of the ego
Is the denial of freedom.
"What does that mean?" you might ask.
The ego would teach you about what you are
By telling you to look outside yourself
In order for you to learn what you are.
In your belief in separation, in your belief in the ego,
That is exactly what you are bound to do.
You look out at a world, at beings who seem separate from you,
And, based on what you see in that world,
Discern what you think you are.
And so it is that if you would hear the voice of the ego,
You are allowing yourself to be told who you are
By voices which seem separate from you.
And if a will separate from your own
Would teach you about your own will,
How can there be peace?
If you would even imagine allowing another will
To dictate to you what is your own will,
You become imprisoned by that belief.
Do you see?

What does the Holy Spirit teach you that sets you free?
The Holy Spirit teaches you
That the simple truth of the universe
Is actually true.
The Holy Spirit is always there, within your being,
With one simple message—
YOUR WILL AND THE WILL OF GOD ARE THE SAME.
What does that mean?
It means that nowhere in all of Creation
Does there exist a will of any kind
Which would oppose the Will of God.
It means that no will, anywhere in all of Creation,

Including the Will of God, does, or can,
Oppose your will.

Think of a world, if you will,
In which nothing, no one, ever, for any reason,
Even for the briefest moment,
Would ever oppose what you would will,
What you would be,
What you would experience.
Is it not obvious to you,
Even as you read these words,
That that is the epitome of freedom itself?

So what is your freedom?
Your freedom is your realization
That your will and the Will of God are the same.
But that truth extends beyond you and God.
It extends to you and me.
And, indeed, my will and yours are the same.
My will for you is what you will.
And nothing other than that.
And, hear me very well,
That truth extends to every brother in this world,
Or in any world you might ever imagine.

There is no will separate from yours.
There is no will, including your own,
Separate from the will of any brother.
And I have told you to realize that whenever you meet anyone,
It is a holy encounter.
Each encounter is your chance to experience salvation.
For as you see your brother, so shall you see yourself.
Your vision of your brother is exactly
The vision you have of yourself.
In your world of space and time and bodies,
What you would do to a brother is exactly
What you would have done unto yourself.
The Golden Rule is not an option.
It is a truth which stands inviolable, and does not change.

Every brother whom you meet brings to you a holy encounter,
Because he LITERALLY IS your pathway to salvation.
You cannot reach salvation without him.

And why is that so?
It is so because the Kingdom of God is freedom.
The Kingdom of God is peace, and joy, and Love,
All of which are the same.
The Kingdom of God is perfect freedom
Such as I have spoken of this day.
AND PERFECT FREEDOM IS THE REALIZATION
THAT THERE IS NO WILL DIFFERENT FROM YOUR OWN.

If you would imagine yourself to be isolated,
If you would imagine yourself to be a separate being,
And then try to imagine no will being different from your own,
You will fail.
It must be that you shall find your freedom
In your relationship with your brother,
And in your awareness that his will, and yours,
And mine, and God's,
Are always the same.

And the beauty of it is this:
The Will of God Itself is perfect freedom.
You were created in absolute freedom to create and to be.
You were given all power, and all glory,
In order that you might create
In the exercise of that freedom.
If the freedom of which I have spoken was not yours,
Then God would not be free.
For there is no separation of any kind between you and God.

What is it, then, that you should bring
To the holy encounters that you have with your brothers?
You bring one gift—THE GIFT OF FREEDOM.
In the realization that your brother's will is the same as yours,
Then never, ever, is there any reason to oppose
What your brother is, or what he would be.

And it works thusly—
As you see your brother as perfectly free,
You must see him as invulnerable.
There is nothing in all of creation, including God Itself,
Which can, or would, ever impose upon your brother
Anything at all.
He is absolutely free to be, to create, and to experience

The infinity of whatever he will.
God has made him thusly.
And that truth cannot be changed.

And what if your brother IS that free?
Can you be any less free than your brother?
The answer is obvious—no, indeed!
In the holy encounter,
You see your brother's inviolate invulnerability,
Which is his absolute freedom given him by God.
And thus you see your own.

As you see your own freedom, which is, and must be,
Unopposed by anything in all of Creation,
Then you will only look within.
And what you will see as you look within
Is the perfect, complete, whole, and joyful Son of God.
And as you look within, which you will be able to do
Because you first saw your brother's freedom—
As you look within, you shall find your own joy.
And you shall find, within you, the entire universe—
Your brother and his freedom,
Me and my freedom,
God Itself and the freedom of Life Itself,
Which is, indeed, God.

The war against peace is a war against no one.
And as you see the freedom of your brother,
Which comes from the realization
That your will and his are the same,
Which comes from the realization
That your will and God's are the same,
It is then that you shall realize, indeed,
That it is a war against no one.

For you shall realize that there is, in the whole universe,
No one but your Self,
No one but me,
No one but every brother who walks this earth with you,
And no one but God,
All of which are, and must always remain, the same.

Blessings upon you all. That is all.

THE UNDIVIDED WILL

Greetings again. I am Jeshua.
I have come this day to further with you
My discussion of your will, and of the Will of God.

I have told you that there is no difference, no separation,
Between the Will of God and your own will.
It is also true that there is no difference, no separation,
Between your will and the will of any, and every, brother.
I have stated it thusly—
The will of the Son of God is undivided.
The will of the Son of God is whole.
The will of the Son of God is not fragmented.

It is not possible in the Kingdom of God
That there be any being, not even one,
Whose will could be in opposition
To the will of any other part of the Sonship,
Or of God, or of all of Creation.
It is in the recognition of this undivided will
That you shall find your freedom.

As you join with your brothers at the level of mind,
As you join with your brothers,
All you are doing is exercising your awareness
That your will and your brother's will are the same.

I have also told you that your will and mine are the same.
And I have told you that we exercise that same will together,
Because I have gone beyond the ego.
Recall that the ego is the belief you hold
That you are a separate, identifiable being,
Different from other aspects of Creation.
I, even though I use the word "I,"
Know that that is not true, and cannot be.
I am part of you. I am within you. I am within God.
You are within me. We are One.

Since I have no ego—
Which means that I have no belief of any kind
Which would define me as separate from you—
Because I have no ego, no belief in separation at all,
I cannot connect with your ego,
Even though YOU may believe it exists.
And therefore, since I cannot experience in any way
Our separation, we become whole.
We become One.
Indeed, we are the undivided Son of God.

As you do the same as I have done,
As you become able to look out
At your world of bodies and space and time,
And see beyond egos,
As you literally see beyond all belief in separation,
Then your will becomes one with each and every brother.

You can do this because I have within me
The awareness of our Oneness.
And its presence within me makes it, without recourse, yours.
It is in that state, it is in the awareness of our undivided will,
That we ARE the Son of God.
It cannot be that our will is divided. It is not possible.

However, in your space and time, it is possible
Not to be aware of the undividedness of our wills.
As you, in space and time,
Become aware only of the wholeness, the Oneness,
The undividedness of your will and your brother's,
Of your will and mine, of your will and God's,
Then you become aware within yourself
That you ARE the Son of God.

God made you His Son.
God did not make you His Son separate from Him.
God literally extended Himself unto, and into,
You and me and all of Creation.
And as the Son of God, we ARE God.

And thus it is that our beingness completes God.
In fact, God extended Itself unto and into you and me
In order that He could be complete.

For extension comes with Love.
And as I have told you, without extension there is no Love.
And so God, in order to be God,
Extended Himself into and unto you and me,
And all of Creation.

Now, hear me well.
YOU ARE EVERYTHING TO GOD.
And that is true.
God values you completely, wholly, and totally,
Just as God values Himself.
And God's valuing of you IS God's valuing of Himself.

To value (lest you become confused)
In the Kingdom of Heaven is to see truly.
God sees you always as what you truly are.
You and I, the Sonship, are the treasure of God.
We are all that God desires.
We are all that God wants.
We are what God becomes.

And what are you really then,
If you are the treasure of God?
You are the extension, within a world of freedom,
Of the creative power of God.
You are created by Creative Power Itself.
And thus you are like unto that Creative Power.
And thus you have the power to create also.
And as you create, and I create,
We literally extend the Love and the Beingness of God.
And thus the joy of God remains full.

The joy of God does not BECOME full.
For there is nothing greater that it can become.
It remains full, as it always was, and always shall be.
And so you and I, as we join in our undivided state,
Beyond the ego and beyond the separation,
Have become, and are, the treasure of God.

And how do you do that here, in your space and time?
You do it by simply going beyond the ego.
And how do you do that?
You never stop asking yourself,

"What is the Will of God for me?"
And you never stop hearing the answer, which is—
"The Will of God for you is to create, and create, and create,
In freedom, and in joy, beyond any imagination,
False though it be, of separation.
The Will of God for you is to be always aware of
Your undivided will with Him, and with all of Creation."

And thus we come to this world,
Where you have made bodies that seem to walk around,
Bodies, masterfully designed by you, the Son of God—
However, designed for the purpose of verifying to yourself
That you are separate.

And how do you verify the separateness
That you seem to have as a body?
YOU VERIFY IT BY ATTACKING.
And what is it to attack?
ATTACK IS ANYTHING WHICH YOU MIGHT DO
WHICH SHALL SUBSTANTIATE FOR YOU
THE BELIEF IN SEPARATION,
Which in reality never happened, and cannot be.

And as you use this body to experience your space and time,
And to experience the joy of existence,
As you wander from your awareness of what you are
And use your body to attack,
Then you have used it under false perception.
And you have brought into your life conflict,
The absence of peace, and the absence of joy.
And you have seemed to split
The undivided will of the Sonship.

How can you change that if you would deem to do so?
First ask yourself, "Do I deem to do so?
And why should I, in the first place?"
If you change your belief that the body is for attack,
And therefore release your desire to be separate,
What do you do?
You say, once again,
"Do I desire to know the Will of God for me?
And if I do desire so, whom shall I listen to?"
And as I have told you,

You listen to the Holy Spirit.
And what is the Holy Spirit?
The Holy Spirit is the link of communication
Between God and His Son.
I have told you, before—
What you believe, you project,
And what you know, you extend.
And what you extend is what you are.
And what you project is what you believe you are.

The Holy Spirit knows Itself.
And Its function is communication.
And thus It logically, in accordance with the laws of God,
Extends what It is.
And what It is, is the vehicle of communication.
It is the connecting link between God and His Son.
And It is, as well, in this world,
The connecting link between God and His Son,
While His Son believes that He is fragmented into sons—
Which He is not, and cannot be.

And thus, if you are still,
And open yourself to the Voice of God,
To the Voice of the Holy Spirit,
And to my voice, if you will,
What you shall hear is a message
That speaks of your body
Only as a means of communication.
And what does that mean, more simply put?
It means that you will always see every function of your body
As a tool you can use to join, and not to separate.

If you speak a word, you will see it as a vehicle for
Connecting with, and joining with,
The mind of your brother.
If you perform an action with your body,
You will see that action as what you would do
To bring to both of you the awareness
That you are joined, that you are One.
And always that shall be the case when you open yourself
To the Voice of the Holy Spirit.

And what shall happen when you do that?
You shall, because you are reaching out
To your brother, and ultimately to yourself,
You shall, once again, become aware of
The undivided will of the Sonship.
And then you shall realize in its aftermath
That the undivided will of the Sonship
Is, indeed, the treasure of God.

And you shall realize,
In that moment of seeing your body and everything it does
As a means of communication and of joining,
That you have completed God Itself,
And as well, completed yourself.
Since you and God are, and must be, One.

'Tis that simple.
If you, ever, or any time,
See your body as a device of separation,
Then it is truly and literally an attack upon your brother,
An attack upon your Self, and upon God.
And it must breed conflict,
The absence of peace,
And the absence of joy.

Insofar as you listen within to the Voice of the Holy Spirit,
Then you shall choose to use the body
As a means of communication, which is a means to join.
And then the conflict that I have mentioned shall disappear.
Because the conflict cannot stand
In the presence of our Oneness.

With the disappearance of conflict
Shall return the childlike joy and the childlike freedom
That shall reverberate throughout the entire universe.
And as it does so, the entire universe
Shall seem to hear the Voice of God as it says—
"Rejoice. For this is my beloved Son
In whom I am well pleased."

Blessings upon you all. That is all.

THE BODY AS MEANS

Greetings again. I am Jeshua.
I spoke to you somewhat last time about the body,
And how the body should only be used
As a means of communication.

The word "means" is very important here.
Today I wish to speak to you more about the body,
And how it is that the body is always a means—
And never an end.
This is most important to your understanding of this Course.

What does it mean to say that the body
Can be an end, as opposed to a means?
To believe that the body can be an end
Is to believe that the body exists of itself.
Nothing can be an end, nothing can be a goal—
Except that it exists.
And I have already told you many times over
That the body is not real, is an illusion, and does not exist.
To that extent it is not possible for the body to be an end.

What is it for the body to be a "means"?
For what is a means at all, as I speak of it?
A means is simply an avenue whereby . . .
Whereby what? It matters not.
A means is an avenue whereby you can experience.
A means is an avenue whereby you can become.
A means is an avenue which is the pathway TO something.
And when I say to you that the body should be seen
Only as a means of communication,
Then I am saying to you, this—
Recognize that the body is a vehicle
Which you can use to experience communication.
Never think that the body is the communication itself.
For that would be to believe that it is an end,
Which, as I have told you, it cannot be.

Furthermore, to believe that the body can be an end
Is to believe that IT has feeling.
I have told you that the body can have a FUNCTION.
I have told you as well that function arises out of being,
But that the relationship is not reciprocal.
Function does arise out of being.
However, it does not follow that that which has function
Automatically exists, or has being.
That, as well, is important for you to understand.

The body has a function.
The function HAS ARISEN out of being, creative being.
For that is what you are.
However, the fact that you have chosen to give it function
Does not mean that it exists. Hear me well.
That is of fundamental importance in this Course.

Illusion arises out of the Oneness of all being.
For illusion can be given function.
But the fact that it has function does not make it real.
To be real means to exist of itself.
Function never exists of itself.
Function only exists out of the creative power of being.
And so it is that you, creative Son of God,
Have given function to your body.

So always remember that the body
Is a means and never an end.
It is a means of communication.
And as I have told you,
Insofar as you see the body as a vehicle
Whereby you can extend joining,
As a vehicle whereby you can learn of Oneness,
Then it can serve the purpose of the Holy Spirit.
And that is the purpose it should serve
If you wish to learn this Course,
If you wish to come to the experience of peace.

In order for you to never see the body as an end,
But always as a means,
You MUST realize that you are experiencing here,
In space and time, THROUGH YOUR BODY, NOT IN IT.
You must realize that the experience which you seem to have

Is made possible in space and time through the means,
Which is the body,
But that the experience IS NOT the body,
And is not even OF the body.
Always the source of experience is Mind.
And Mind is the source of everything.
All creative power lies within Mind,
And never within the body.

What happens, then, as you come to realize
That all of your experience here in this world is truly of Mind,
And that all of your experience of this world
Is simply THROUGH the body,
That the body is only the means WHEREBY you experience?
What happens then?
In your realizing that the body is means,
Then of course you cease to believe that it is the end.
And in your ceasing to believe that the body is the end,
You cease to believe that it is what you are.

And that is what the ego would wish you to believe—
That the body IS what you are.
And why is that?
Because the ego is the product of
The carefully laid plan of separation.
Thus the body seems to be an isolated being,
With existence apart from all other beings.
As such your attitudes toward the body, as I have told you,
Are attitudes of attack.
For attack is but separation, and the desire to be alone,
Which you cannot be.

Attack is the desire to be alone,
The desire to be separate,
The desire to substantiate your ego
Apart from the rest of your world.
All of which is not possible.

As you simply become aware that the body is not an end,
And that you are not your body,
Then wherein do you lie?
Certainly not in your body.
And it follows, of course, then, that you lie within Mind.

And what happens as you actually experience
The realization that you are of Mind, and only of Mind?
You become FREE—
To simply experience life, existence itself,
Whether it be here in space and time, or beyond.

Mind, as I have told you, cannot attack.
For mind is not separate, cannot be, and above all,
Has no design to be separate, when it is understood correctly.
The brief illusion of the split mind
Was your momentary decision to explore
Trying to be what you could not be.
Momentary—as I have told you before.
In a brief instant, with a chuckle, it came and went.
And that was all.

But here in your space and time, it is again most important
That you realize that the body is but a means and never an end.
For that awareness shall set you free.

One of the forms your freedom shall take
Is the freedom from sickness.
For in your realization that the body is simply a means,
That the body is simply a vehicle of experience,
Which is the product of Mind,
You shall find, in your realization
That everything comes from Mind,
That never shall you choose sickness.
For sickness is nothing more than a device,
A carefully laid plan that you use
To substantiate your belief that you can be separate.

If ever, hear me well, if ever you are sick—
From the slightest bodily sniffle,
To the worst bodily disease you can imagine,
From the worst psychiatric disease you might define,
Back to the slightest sigh that is not joy—
If ever you experience any of those,
You are believing that the body is an end.

How is that so?
As you believe that the body is an end,
You believe, as I have told you,

That it has existence of itself.
And thus you believe that your body can become sick,
Somehow independent of you.
And thus you believe that you, separate, isolated being,
Can be the victim of your body.
While without the belief in separation, it could not be so.

Arising out of mind, it would be possible for you to choose
What the world would call physical symptoms.
But in your awareness that the body is but a means,
And that everything comes from Mind,
There would never be resistance.
Because there could never be the belief
That you were the victim of your body.
And therefore, your perception would not be of illness.
It would simply be of experience.

And what I have told you is that healing arises
From the awareness that you are whole.
To be whole is very simple to understand.
It means not split, not fragmented,
Not separated from anything at all.
Wholeness follows as a matter of course
From the realization that everything,
Everything, hear me well, comes from Mind.
When there is but One Source,
Then there cannot be division, or separation,
Or isolation, or fragmentation,
Or any of that which leads to sickness.

The awareness that everything comes from Mind
Leads as well, as a matter of course,
To the awareness of the undivided will of God and His Sons.
Of that I have spoken before.

Hear me well this day
Your body has a function given it by you,
Creative being, creative son of God.
Its function does not grant it existence.
The body does not exist of itself.
And therefore it does not exist at all.
Since it does not exist, and cannot exist,
It cannot be an end.

Always it is a means.
And it is simply for you, as you learn this Course,
To never forget that means is all that it can be.

For then you shall see beyond it,
But above all, THROUGH it.
As you experience your life here in space and time,
As you experience your life through the body,
As the creative power of mind extends,
And does not stop at the body,
But merely functions through it—
All that simply echoes the truth that the body is not an end.

If you would deign to have it be an end,
Then it shall seem to you
That the flow of creative power stops with body,
And is arrested.
And if that seems to happen,
You must seem isolated within yourself.
Your mind must seem split.
This is one way, if you wish,
To realize how the split mind seemed to come to be.
You simply chose to create a vehicle of separation,
The body, and space and time,
And to choose to believe that it had creative power of its own,
Which could make it an end.
You therefore chose to allow your creative thoughts
To be arrested there instead of extending through them.
And thus it is exactly that, because of the arresting
Of your creative thoughts in the body,
It does SEEM as if the body has creative power of its own.
And that is the illusion of this world.

Once again, in order for you to be free,
In order for you to learn this Course,
In order for you to awaken to the truth of what you are—
What it takes is that you realize
That the body has nothing more than a function to serve.
It has no being, and no existence of its own.
Always it does whatever it is commanded to do
By the creative power of Mind.
It can never be otherwise.

And your awareness of that simple truth
Shall go with you, day upon day upon year,
And shall be, for you, the pathway to your freedom,
And to your joy, and to love.

Blessings upon you all. That is all.

REALITY AND PRAYER

Greetings again. I am Jeshua.
I have come this day to further, with you,
My discussion of *A Course in Miracles*.

It would not be possible for you to be afraid
Unless you felt that there existed a will different from your own.
I have spoken about the fear of the Will of God,
And what a strange belief it is indeed.
For the truth is that there is no difference
Between your will and the Will of God.

Only if you existed apart from God,
And you had a will of your own,
And God had a will of His own,
And those wills were different
And could therefore be in conflict—
Only then would there ever be cause for fear.
For if there is a will that could oppose yours,
Then somehow that will might be able to change what you are,
Which you would perceive as being able to destroy you.
Insofar as there is no opposition
Anywhere within the universe as God has designed it,
Then there exists no room whatsoever
For fear.

So if you speak of being a God-fearing person,
As many of you are wont to do,
Realize that what you are assuming is that
First, you are separate from God,
And second, that God has a will different from your own,
Which He might exercise to oppose you,
And ultimately to destroy you.
Were this the case, then indeed
Your fear would be absolutely justified.
However, nothing is more absurd than the belief
That your will is different from God's.

God is the Creator.
God is the Cause of everything.
Nothing exists at all but what has arisen
Out of the Mind of God.
And God, being One within Himself,
Could not possibly create that which would oppose Him.
He could only do that if He were split within Himself,
Which has not happened, and cannot be.

However, when you chose to seemingly split your mind,
In order to be able to come here,
You did so by learning to project.
And in your projection, you are wont to project upon God
The same circumstance that you imagine for yourself.
And thus you very easily and readily
Imagine that God's Mind is split,
Just as you perceive your own to be.
And if God's Mind is split, then of course
There can arise, within God Itself, opposition.
This false belief in opposition
Many of you have named the devil.
And I tell you this day,
The devil does not exist, and cannot exist,
Simply because God is One.
His Mind is not split, and cannot be.

To accept reality is to accept the simple fact
That God is One.
That is all.
If God is One—not split at all, which He cannot be—
If God is One, and you are part of God,
Then it follows that you are part of that great Oneness
Of this I have been speaking these many weeks.
Insofar as you are part of the great Oneness,
Then, of course, there can be no split between you and God.
For within Oneness, how can there be duality?

The word Oneness itself demands that
Duality not be able to exist.
The acceptance of reality is quite simple, really,
And quite logical as well,
Even to your thinking minds.
And so if you would accept the Atonement,

You must begin by accepting within your mind
An awareness of reality itself.
And that is, as I have been saying, simply this—
God is One. All is One.
There is no difference between your will
And the Will of God.
That is all.

I have spoken of prayer, and the answer to prayer.
Let us think about prayer itself
In the awareness of what I have just said to you.
There is no opposition to anyone or anything in all of Creation.
Such is the nature of reality. Such is the nature of God.
The belief that such might not be true
Is the source of the belief in separation—
And, of course, the source of all fear.

I have already told you quite clearly,
That if your will is different from God's, or any other will,
Then the possibility exists that another will might,
In its opposing you, destroy you.
And thus you must be afraid.

The belief in separation is the source of fear,
And is the ONLY POSSIBLE source of fear.
This world is based on a belief in separation.
And thus I say to you, as you look about your world,
Fear has made everything you see.
For insofar as you see a world where
There can possibly exist separate beings with separate wills,
You must be afraid.

And if you include God as one of those beings
With a separate will, then of course
You must, as well, fear God.
And how can you pray to a being whom you fear?
Terrifying, indeed, it is.
And yet that is what so many of you are wont to do.
You make a request of God,
Believing that His Will is different from yours,
Somehow hoping that your supplications
Will cause God to change His mind—
So that for one brief moment He will agree with you,

And grant you what you ask.
And then you further hope that in the next moment
He will not unchange His mind and take it from you—
Or in the worst scenario, as I have mentioned, destroy you.

Actually there is one scenario worse than that,
Which is even more absurd—
And that is that God would choose not to destroy you,
But simply to put you in a state of torture forever and forever.
And this you call hell.
And this you call God's Love.
How absurd. Do you see?

If you would truly pray, and would truly receive,
Then your prayer MUST arise from the awareness of reality.
Your prayer must arise from the awareness
That in all of Creation there is no will separate from your own.
If ever your wishes, and therefore your prayers,
Would be to generate, or increase, separation,
Then they are really prayers to increase your fear.
Do you see?

And so if you would pray to God, to me, or to the Holy Spirit,
And say "Please make me more afraid than I already am.",
How can there be an answer?
For if love is the opposite of fear, and God loves you,
Then nothing in God's creation, in Its reality,
Would ever increase your fear.
And no answer the Holy Spirit would ever bring to you
Would increase your fear.
No answer I would ever bring to you
Would ever increase your fear.
And, hear me very, very well,
No answer any brother would ever bring to you
Could possibly increase your fear.

And so if you would pray out of a desire to be separate,
You are but proving to yourself why it is
That the ego and the Holy Spirit exist
With a total block of communication.
The Holy Spirit begins by saying, "We are One."
The ego begins by saying, "We are separate. We are not one."
Then how can one say to the other,

"Let us sit down and discuss the nature of life?"
Do you see how absurd it is?

So if you would truly pray,
Bring whatever request you would have
On behalf of your brother.
For you must realize, in your Oneness,
That if your brother does not receive
The selfsame answer to your prayer,
You, likewise, cannot receive it.

When I tell you to never doubt your brother,
I mean, "Simply believe in him."
And to believe in him means to accept and to appreciate him.
When you accept your brother you simply acknowledge,
Beyond the words, at the level of experience,
That you are One.
And when you appreciate your brother
You give true value to him,
Which simply means that you see him
In the truth of what he is,
Which is the Son of God,
One with you and all of Creation.

And so I tell you never to doubt your brother.
Which is also to say, never doubt that
He deserves everything you deserve.
Never doubt that he is as worthy of everything as are you.
As you realize that God is everything, and God is One,
Then you must realize that your brother has everything,
And furthermore, deserves the everything
That God has given him.
Because he IS the most loved,
The most appreciated being in all of Creation—
Just as are you, and me, and everyone.

Insofar as you realize that your brother has everything,
Then everything becomes yours.
And if you have everything,
What request can you make?
In the world of ideas, which it is,
In the world where ideas
Can only be strengthened by being shared,

What can be your only prayer?
As you sit and look within,
And realize that you have everything,
Your only prayer can be to have
That with which you may share the everything.
And that is the definition of creation.

God created you to be a being with whom
He could share everything.
And you, in like nature to God, do the same.
You create your brother just as God has done.
And you and your brother are co-creators, as I have told you.
You create your brother for the sole purpose of being able
To share with him the everything that you are.

So that is the only prayer
You can ever offer to the Holy Spirit,
"How can I share the everything I have?"
If you would, alas, see yourself as separate,
Therefore incomplete, and therefore afraid,
And would pray in order to receive,
Of course you think of bargaining.
You would bargain with your brothers.
But above all, you would bargain with God.
But, if God gives everything completely to all beings,
How can you bargain?
How absurd as well! Do you see?

If you would pray in order to receive,
Based on your belief in lack and separation,
Then you would not value that which you receive.
For insofar as you believe yourself separate,
You believe in bargaining.
And you, because of the nature of God,
Can not receive value greater than that which you give.
You can attempt to do so in your world.
You can attempt to pay a small price and receive a great return.
But all that will happen is that
You will end up not valuing what you have received.

The only way to receive fully is to pay full measure.
And if you would receive EVERYTHING,
Then what must you give in order to receive it?

Of course, you must give everything.
Ah! But that is one of the laws of God.
To give and to receive are the same.
This is so, simply because you are One with God,
And with all of Creation.
There is nothing but your Self.
What you give is, and must be,
Given to your Self.

And so it stands. If you would ever receive
That which you might pray for,
You must measure the value of what you receive
By what you would give.
And how could you want less than everything?
'Tis God's gift to you. It is your inheritance.
And it is yours even if you believe it not to be so.
So if you would design to receive everything,
Then that is what you must give—
Everything.

And you do that by never doubting
That your brother is One with you,
And worthy of your gift of everything.

The acceptance of reality is simply to accept that all is One.
There is no separation.
There is no difference between your will and the Will of God,
Or any will in all of Creation.
And in that awareness, fear is gone.

And in the awareness that all is One,
Then of course, everything that is, is yours.
And since it is all but ideas,
The only way you can give it is to give it as an idea.
And thus it strengthens within you
The same idea you have given away.
And thus your perfect completeness
Becomes more complete than it was,
Even though such is not possible to your thinking mind.

The acceptance of reality is the realization
That, if you would receive,
You must give in order to do so.

In your awareness that your brother is One with you,
And worthy of every gift that you can give,
Then what you shall do is give everything.
And then what shall be answered
Is any prayer you might ever have prayed.
For in the giving of everything,
That is exactly what you must receive.

Blessings upon you all. That is all

ERROR AND FORGIVENESS

Greetings again. I am Jeshua.
I have come this day to discuss, with you,
Error and forgiveness.

So often in this Course, I speak of error, and of sin.
I tell you that the Son of God is sinless.
There is no sin.
And I also talk to you about error.
You cannot sin. But error you can make.
You can be in error, but you cannot be in sin.
You can make error, but you cannot sin.
And because it is error, you are not held accountable.
Because it is only error, you remain free.
And because it is error, nothing has changed—
Not your relationship with God,
Nor your relationship with who and what you are.

So perhaps we should ask,
''What is error, that makes it so easy?
What is error, this thing which literally transposes sin,
And frees us from the belief in sin,
And all of its consequences?''

So today I have come to discuss with you—error, what it is,
And the awareness of freedom that its understanding brings.

In a word, to be in error means this—TO BE UNAWARE.
And that is all.
You are the perfect Son of God. You are absolutely free.
You are beyond limitation, beyond restriction,
Beyond imprisonment of any kind.
For such is the nature of God.
And since God is One, and you are part of God,
It must be so.

And what is the one problem of this world,
Of which I have spoken so many times?
'Tis the problem of separation.
And how is it that you become separated?

How is it that you create the problems
Which are, and which define this world?
Simply by doing this—
BY BECOMING UNAWARE OF WHAT YOU ARE.
And that is all.

You are the Son of God.
Although for many of you, that is only words at this point.
I speak the words, "You are the Son of God."
And what if for one fleeting moment
You knew that those words were true?
What if your awareness went beyond the words
To an experience that actually became part of you?
Then you would be free.
And you would never be the same.

So the truth is, I tell you, that you are the Son of God,
And you simply do not know that that is true.
Which is to say, you are unaware of the truth about your Self.
And that is what this Course is literally all about—
Helping you to become aware of what you are.
And that is all.

If you are absolutely without sin,
And if there is, and can be, no consequence of any kind
To that which you would think, or experience, or say, or do—
If there is no consequence of any kind,
Then you are absolutely safe.

And yet you are in error. What does it mean?
Simply this—that you are not aware
Of the fact that you are absolutely safe.
And now ask yourself this—
"If the truth of God is that you are the Son of God,
And a part of God,
And if the truth of God is that you are absolutely safe,
THEN CAN YOU CHANGE ANYTHING AT ALL
BY SIMPLY BEING UNAWARE THAT THAT IS TRUE?"
And the answer is, "Of course not."
You ARE the Son of God.
And if you don't happen to know it in this moment,
Does it change the fact that God is your Father?
No, indeed.

And so, as I have told you so many times,
This illusion, this world, never happened.
And now do you see?
This world is based on error.
This world is based on a false belief
That you are separate from God, from each other,
And literally, from yourself.
But it does not, and cannot, in one iota,
Change the truth that it is not so.

And would you demand, in your projection,
And in your desire born out of separation—
Would you desire that God punish you,
Or hold you responsible for simply being in a state
Where you do not know the perfection
And the beauty of what you are?
That is the worst of it.
Simply that you do not know.

Recall that the words that were ascribed to me
On the cross were these,
"Father forgive them, for they know not what they do."
And it matters not if those were the exact words I spoke.
What matters is that that speaks well
Of what I am saying to you this day.
'Tis as simple as that—you know not what you do.
But more importantly, you know not what you are.

So do you need to be forgiven?
I speak to you of the Holy Spirit's plan of forgiveness.
I speak of the ego's plan of forgiveness.
And what would the ego do?
The ego would see error.
The ego delights in looking out at its world,
Looking out at its brothers,
Seeing the wrong they have done,
And then magnifying it by bringing it
To the front of consciousness, and making it real.
It then delights in saying, "Somehow we must correct
This horrible thing that you have done."

Ponder, for a moment, the truth I have told you.
You, within the Sonship, share an undivided will.

Your will is One with God's.
And your wills are One with each other.
Of this I have spoken before.
Then ask yourself a question,
"If there are no separate wills, and if it is not possible
That two wills could be in opposition,
Because they are the same—
Then is it possible, truly, is it possible
That what anyone would will could be seen as wrong?
Or be seen as error by another being who shares the same will?
And the answer is, "Of course not."

Well, how can the ego see error at all?
'Tis because of the false belief in separation.
For you, as an ego, wish to stand alone,
And in opposition to your world.
You wish to define your own will
As being separate from the rest of your world.
And this you look upon as freedom.
How absurd! What a lonely, sad place to be!
Can you see?

And if you look upon every brother as having a will
Separate and different from your own,
Then what happens is this—
Anyone who does not act in accordance with your will,
Which, because it is yours,
Has become the standard of the universe—
Any being who acts not in accordance with your will
Is wrong, and is in error.

Ah, what if you and your brother shared one will?
It is not possible for two beings,
Whether or not one of them is God—
It is not possible for two beings to share one will
Unless the will of both,
Unless the will of all,
Is perfect freedom.

The ego's desire is always that its brother NOT BE FREE.
The ego's desire is to put its brother in a prison
Where his only function is to substantiate the self concept
Which, by definition, is the ego itself.

Insofar as you would be an ego,
Then you must be willing to mercilessly use your entire world
To simply substantiate your belief in what you are.
Vicious indeed!
So do you see why I sometimes say this world
Is one of hatred, and not of love?

So the ego would look upon error,
Which is seen to exist because there are different wills.
And then it would make that error real.
And then it would speak about forgiving the error.
What it always means is this—
"You need to change to become what I want you to be."
This happens, moment upon moment, in your lives,
Whether it be with your friends,
Whether it be with your children as you are a parent,
Whether it be with your spouse or significant other
As you dwell in what you call a love relationship.
Always it is of the ego.
And never is it of freedom.

Now I would speak of the Holy Spirit's plan of forgiveness.
The Holy Spirit's plan of forgiveness is simply this—
Not to see what is not true.
If the worst that you have done
In coming to this illusion
Is to have chosen to become unaware of what you are,
Then what does the Holy Spirit do?
He simply does not participate with you in your unawareness.
And that is all.

If you are perfect, which you are,
And the Holy Spirit knows that,
Then when you would pretend to stand alone
And say "I am afraid,"
All the Holy Spirit can do is see you as the Son of God,
Perfectly free, and perfectly safe,
No matter what you would believe, or think, or say, or do.
And that is all.
The Holy Spirit simply sees you as you are.
And that is all.

You might think of it this way.
If to be in error is to be unaware,
Then to forgive is simply to be unaware of the error.
And so do you see, the Holy Spirit can take
The ability that you have made,
And turn it into a vehicle whereby you can see God.
And always, always, always,
That is what happens in the Holy Spirit's vision.
And always, always, always,
It is possible for you to look upon
Any and every aspect of your life
In the same way that the Holy Spirit does.

Now what if you would choose to forgive?
There is only one way to forgive.
There is only one way to solve the problems of this world.
And that is what I have just outlined—
To use the Holy Spirit's plan,
WHICH IS NOT TO SEE THE UNAWARENESS.
If you would believe yourself sick,
The Holy Spirit cannot see you as sick.
The Holy Spirit cannot and does not,
Participate in your unawareness.

I will tell you, in a later chapter,
Not to side with a Son of God in his illness,
Even if he believes in it himself.
And that is an example of what I am saying.
Even though he be unaware of what he is,
Do not join him in his unawareness.
Simply see him as he is.

And what is he?
This we have told you over and over again—
He is Spirit. He is One with God and all of Life.
He is absolutely free.
And that is enough.
Always the Holy Spirit shall see that truth
In any circumstance.
And if you would forgive,
Then you shall see all of life, and your brother,
In the same manner.

But what if that seems not obvious to you?
What if you look upon a circumstance in your life,
And something inside of you says,
"That is wrong. That is not OK"?
Then what do I suggest you do this day?
I suggest that you pause, and be still.
And in your stillness,
Listen for the Voice of the Holy Spirit.
Listen for the Voice of God.
Listen for the Voice of your real Self.

For when you do that, in your stillness,
There will truly come a vision.
There will come a new way to see the circumstance
That you thought was somehow not good.
And you will see, through the eyes of the Holy Spirit,
The presence of love, the presence of freedom,
And ultimately, the presence of joy—and therefore peace.
And you literally, truly, can look upon
Any and every circumstance in your life
With this Vision of the Holy Spirit,
With the Vision of Christ.

Do you know what the entire illusion of this world is?
'TIS SIMPLY THE CHOICE TO SEE THINGS DIFFERENTLY.
You would look upon the world falsely.
You would look upon the world and see what is not there.
You would simply be unaware of what IS there.

And in His forgiveness,
The Holy Spirit simply sees what IS there.
And that is what He would teach you.

And now, what if you, having heard what I have just said,
Would help your brother to be healed?
If your brother needs to be healed,
Then something must be in error in his life.
Is that not true? Of course it is.
And I have spoken of the unhealed healer.
The unhealed healer is one who simply does this—
He starts by believing that something is wrong,
And then says, "How can we fix it?"

The Holy Spirit NEVER SEES WHAT IS WRONG.
He does not, and cannot, see error.
And any being who would look upon error
And make it real, and try to fix it,
Does not understand the nature of healing,
Does not understand the nature of Love,
And above all, does not understand the nature of God.
And if you do not understand the nature of God,
Then you literally have no clue as to what you are.
For you are the same as God.

Then what if you would become part of your brother's life,
And allow him to be healed?
You will learn that the true healer simply lets healing be.
So what do you have to offer to anyone who needs healing?
What does the Holy Spirit have to offer to you
When you sit in error, and because of your error
Tremble in fear?
What does God have to offer you when you tremble
In the imagined darkness of your illumination?
What does God have to offer when you imagine yourself
Imprisoned within a world
Whose ecstasy and nature are perfect freedom?

This I have told you before.
God cannot, and will not, impose upon you in your freedom.
For if He did, you would not be free.
Nor can the Holy Spirit, nor can you,
Impose any experience upon your brother.
This follows at once when you come
To the understanding of Love.
So what do you have to offer to your brother
Who sits in error, who sits in his fear,
Who sits in the darkness,
And who desires for it not to be there?
Can you take away his fear?
No, indeed. For then he would no longer be free.

All you can offer to him is your vision of what he is.
All you can offer is your vision of his freedom.
All you can offer is your vision of his perfection.
All you can offer is your vision and your awareness
That everything in his life is Love,

And can never be otherwise.
For that is the nature of God, and of the universe.
All you can offer is your awareness
That Love is literally, truly, all that exists.
For that is what the Holy Spirit offers to you.

And how do you gain the vision of the Holy Spirit?
By being so still that you can hear
The whisper of a Love that is so great
That never would it impose upon you anything at all,
Even the infinity of its own Love.
And do you understand now why we say Love is freedom?

And now the blessing comes.
What if that is what you offer to your brother
In his prison of unawareness?
What if that is what you offer to your brother
To free him from his own error?
Then what must happen, without fail?
YOU WILL SEE YOURSELF EXACTLY THE SAME WAY.
As you look upon your brother's life
And see not the error of his ways,
But see the perfect beauty, the perfect freedom,
The hidden joy, that always remains and is part of what he is—
As you look upon that in order
To let your vision be your gift to him,
Then that becomes your own vision of yourself.

And you become as free as you see him.
And you become as loved as you would love him.
And you would become as joyful as the joy you see within him.
And you will become as safe as is your brother in your vision.
And do you see now, how your brother is your savior?

So truly, if you would heal, look beyond error.
Use the Holy Spirit's plan of forgiveness,
And see not the unawareness that would make your brother
Believe that he is afraid.
For in so doing, you offer him the vision
That shall bring him healing.
You have allowed healing to be
Within the context of God's perfect freedom.
And above all, you have become healed yourself.

And as you become healed,
You simply look beyond your own error,
And become totally free of sin.
As you look within,
You shall find welling up within you
The perfection and the beauty,
The freedom, the peace, the perfect Love,
And the absolute joy that is the Son of God.
For that is what you are, and shall always be.

Blessings upon you all. That is all.

THE ACCEPTANCE OF YOUR BROTHER

Greetings again. I am Jeshua.
I have come this day to discuss, with you,
The acceptance of your brother.

There is a very practical way for you to know
If the Holy Spirit is speaking to you and through you.
It is what I told you two thousand years ago—
By their fruits you shall know them.
Thus I have told you that
If the Holy Spirit is speaking through you,
It will elicit joy in your brothers.
If It is not, then the joy will not be there.
And by this simple test you can tell.

But what if you seem to produce joy in your brothers,
And are not joyful yourself?
What do you make of that?
You simply realize the same truth—
By their fruits you shall know them.
And it follows, by the fruits you shall know yourself.
For if there is that within you
Which can produce joy in your brothers,
Then, of course, it is there within you,
Even if you are not aware of it yourself.

I did tell you last time that to be in error
Is simply to be unaware.
So if you are in error
And are simply not aware within yourself of the Holy Spirit,
Then perhaps you shall not experience joy,
Even though it shall and can happen
That joy shall be induced within your brother.
That shall happen as the proof
That the Holy Spirit is, indeed, within you.
'Tis quite simple. And that is enough.
The truth is this—
WHAT YOU SHALL LEARN FROM YOUR BROTHER
IS WHAT YOU HAVE TAUGHT HIM.

I have also told you that
The decision to accept is the decision to receive.
And the decision to receive is the decision to accept.
And have I not, as well, told you that you are Spirit,
One with God, One with your brother,
And One with all of Creation?

So what is it to teach, and to learn?
What is it to receive? And what is it to accept?
All of it must be understood, must be realized,
From within the thought system
Where you know that all is One.

So if you would accept your brother,
Do not think, even for a moment,
That you, a separate, isolated being are accepting
Another separate, isolated being.
For if you allow that thought within your mind—
Which you have the freedom to do—
You will not understand what it is to accept.
For truly, to accept is to receive.
And when you accept your brother,
You receive him unto, AND INTO, yourself.
When you accept your brother,
You simply realize that your brother IS YOU.

So whatever you would give to your brother,
Whatever you would desire to teach him, if you will,
It must be that which you would receive unto your own being.
It must be that which YOU would learn.
Do you see?
And so you shall learn of what you are
By what you have taught your brother.
And now do you see   by their fruits you shall know them.
And by their fruits they shall know themselves.
Is it now clear?

As you look upon your brother,
You truly, literally, look upon yourself.
It cannot be otherwise.
Thus I have told you over and over again—
Your brother is your savior.
And that is how it is so.

As you look upon your brother you look upon yourself.
AS YOU LOOK UPON YOUR BROTHER
YOU TRULY, LITERALLY, SEE YOUR VISION OF GOD.

As you look upon your brother in order to see yourself,
There are two possible evaluations which you may see.
Truly, as you look upon your brother, you see yourself.
And as you look upon your brother you see, indeed,
Your vision of God.
And what are the possibilities?
As I have told you, there are two,
Both of which are available within your mind.
That both are available means simply this—
That you have the power to choose which one you will hear,
Which one you will accept,
And therefore, which one you will receive,
Therefore, as well, which one you will teach,
And in the same vein, which one you will learn.

First, there is the evaluation which is true.
There is the evaluation which comes from,
And is of, the Holy Spirit.
It speaks to you, of course, of what you truly are.
It speaks to you and sings to you a song of the Son of God.
It speaks to you and sings to you a song
Of perfection and peace and love and joy.
But above all, it speaks to you and sings to you a song
Of Oneness and joining and sharing.
It speaks to you and sings to you a song
Of the fact that there is no difference
Between your will and the Will of God,
Between your will and your brother's will.

And then there is the evaluation of the ego.
And the ego cannot communicate with the Holy Spirit.
The reason is this—
The ego does not understand joining.
For the ego, as we have said before,
Is nothing more than the simple belief
That you are separate and isolated and alone.
The ego begins by speaking to you and telling you
That you are but one being, isolated and alone.
And to preserve yourself, which is to preserve your ego,

You must do it, literally,
In opposition to the rest of your world.

And the Holy Spirit whispers in your ear,
While you are hearing those words,
That your peace lies not in separation,
But in the freedom that comes from joining and sharing.

Ah, how can you tell which to choose?
Does it not seem, from within the framework of
The thought system of the ego, that it is consistent?
Indeed it does.
All thought systems are based upon premises.
And if you start from within a thought system
That says you are separate and alone,
You can indeed imagine an entire world.
And that is exactly what you have done.

But a problem arises.
You cannot accurately and fairly evaluate
The thought system of the ego FROM WITHIN IT.
The only way you can see the truth is to, somehow,
For a moment, step outside the thought system of the ego,
And then look back at it and evaluate it.

Well, how can you do that?
The simplest way, as I have told you so many times,
Is to be still and listen to the voice of the Holy Spirit.
For it is He Who will speak to you of a world
Based on different premises—
Those of sharing and Oneness and joining,
All of which are the essence of Love.

But what if you would attempt to see
The falseness of the thought system of the ego from within it?
For as long as you cling to the belief that you are separate,
That is what you are constrained to do.
If you, in your delusion and your error,
Would attempt to explore the ego
From within its own thought system
I suggest that you consider these words—
"God Himself is incomplete without me." (21)

What if you, from within the thought system of the ego,
Could pause and truly think about those words?
What if you, from within the framework of the ego,
Could contemplate the notion that God Himself is incomplete?
Surely you would laugh as you said it.
For it is clear that, even within the thought system of the ego,
You define God as that which is perfect
And whole and complete.

So if you say "God Himself is incomplete without me.",
What are you saying?
That God is not what you believe Him to be.
For when you say those words,
You are seeing God as a separate, isolated being.
You are redefining God as a sum made up of pieces,
As fragmented, as broken,
And as split to His very core.
And this you realize,
Even within the thought system of the ego,
Cannot be true.

So even as you think about the words
"God Himself is incomplete without me,"
You must step outside the thought system of the ego
And ask, "What could this mean?
For truly God Himself is not incomplete, and cannot be."

And truly I tell you, you are not separate from God,
Have never been, and cannot be.
The only way that God can be incomplete
Is in your imagination.
The only way that God can be incomplete
Is from within a thought system which believes
That you are what you are not,
That you are, or can be, separate from God.

Now, what if you would entertain
The Holy Spirit's vision of what you are?
It speaks to you of the grandeur of God.
It tells you that you are the Son of God,
That you are God's creation,
That you, literally, are the witness to the reality of God.
If you would hear the Voice of the Holy Spirit,

It truly sings you a song, and brings to you a vision of God
Which is the same as the vision of yourself.

Ah, but the ego—
The ego stands amidst its belief in separation and isolation.
It stands in its fear that must arise from believing
That God's will is separate and different from its own,
And that therefore God might choose with His separate will
To destroy it.
And if you would entertain that thought, you must live in fear.
And thus you see yourself as little, little and fragmented,
Little and subject to the whim of God,
And therefore subject to the whim of the rest of your world,
Which represents to you, God.
And do you not speak of Mother Nature,
Somehow tying nature to its creator God?
And do you not see yourself as victim of it,
As well as of God?

And what happens if that belief becomes unbearable to you?
What happens if you make the mistake,
From within the ego's thought system,
Of being still for a moment,
A moment in which you hear a voice
Whispering of the grandeur of what you are?
Then the ego protests loudly.
The ego would then attempt to transform
Your belief in littleness into one of greatness.
This I have termed grandiosity.
For this is what the ego would offer you
When you have sensed at some level, deep within,
The grandeur of God,
Which is the same as the grandeur of you.

What is the difference between grandeur and grandiosity?
The grandeur of God speaks of the Oneness
And the harmony of Love,
And of the joining of all of Creation.
Automatically it speaks of a perfect freedom,
Which if you could know it for one moment,
Would cause the ego to disappear
In that self-same moment,
Never to return.

But grandiosity, that is the ego's attempt
To cause you to believe that you are, indeed,
The possessor of your same grandeur,
Which at some level you know is there.
But the ego must speak of your greatness
From within its framework of separation.

So the ego says that you are great because you can stand
Tall and strong against the rest of your world.
The ego would speak to you of grandiosity
Which is based on competition,
And which ultimately is based upon its source,
Which is attack.
So when the ego,
Within its thought system of separation,
Finds you little and frightened and weak,
It must look upon everything you experience
With suspiciousness.
And it wonders, "Is anything here going to destroy my belief
That I am separate and isolated and alone?
For this I must preserve.
For this indeed is my very existence."

And what if a thought creeps into your mind
That speaks to you of the grandeur of God?
Then the ego suddenly shifts gears
And speaks of your greatness, your grandiosity,
Which is your imagined strength
Based upon competition, opposition, and attack.
For the ego can only speak to you out of its viciousness,
Which must cause you to attack
In order to believe that you can be safe,
Which must cause you to attack
In order to believe that you exist at all.
Do you see?

If you would accept the Atonement,
You must accept your brother.
And to accept your brother
Is to receive your brother unto yourself.
Which is to experience, beyond the level of the thoughts,
Beyond the words, beyond the analyzing,
That he IS yourself.

And if you would accept your brother,
It must be that your vision of your brother
Is the same as your vision of yourself.
And as you hear the Holy Spirit speak of your brother,
Of his Oneness and harmony, of his creative power,
Of the grandeur given him by God,
Then that is what you shall discover yourself to be
In your own awareness.

Hear me well. Your unawareness, your error,
Changes not one iota the truth of what you are.
And the acceptance of the Atonement,
Which MUST involve the acceptance of your brother,
Is nothing more than letting go of your unawareness,
Is nothing more than forgiving your error—
Which was the false vision of your brother.
That error will be transformed as you are still within,
As you allow the whisper of the Holy Spirit
To speak to you of what your brother really is,
And has always been.

And as He whispers in your ear,
As He sings to you a song of harmony and Oneness,
A song of a single will which knows not of competition,
Which knows not of greed,
Which knows not of specialness and isolation—
As He sings to you a song of freedom that comes
From the perfect sharing of one will,
And which must be the will of freedom for all beings—
As the Holy Spirit speaks to you and sings to you
Of that vision of your brother,
You will, without effort, accept your brother.
And then as you pause and look within,
You will come face to face with the perfect, beautiful truth
That that indeed is what you are as well.

As you see your brother as the Son of God,
As the perfection, as the light, the love, and the joy that he is,
Then you automatically become aware that that is what
You are as well, have always been, and will always be.

Blessings upon you all. That is all.

THE GOD OF SICKNESS

Greetings again. I am Jeshua.
I have come this day to further, with you,
My discussion of *A Course in Miracles*.
Remember, I have told you that
The decision to accept is the decision to receive.
I have also spoken to you of the acceptance of the Atonement.
So what does that mean?
Simply this—that to ACCEPT the Atonement
Is to RECEIVE the Atonement.
And I also said that to accept your brother
Is to receive your brother unto yourself.

Remember, Atonement can be expressed as at-one-ment.
This you have heard before, of course.
And so if you would accept the at-one-ment,
What do you accept?
The answer is simple, is it not?
You accept everything.
And if you would accept everything,
What that means, of course,
Is that you receive everything.

And how do you receive everything?
Simply by accepting it as part of yourself,
As part of what you are.
This also have I told you—
You must learn that there is nothing outside yourself.
There is nothing outside yourself which can make you fearful.
There is nothing outside yourself which can make you loving.
There is nothing outside yourself
Which can make you anything at all—
Because there IS nothing outside yourself.

That realization is the cornerstone of
The acceptance of the Atonement,
And the experience of the message of this Course.
It is not possible that anything outside yourself
Can make you into anything,
Can make you experience anything at all.

It is also not possible that anything outside yourself
Can make you different from what you are.
Ah, God is your Creator.
And God has created you as what you are.
God, in His Oneness, has created you
Like unto Himself.

There is nothing outside of God, and nothing outside of you.
So insofar as God is One, and there is nothing outside of God,
And you are the creation of God, His only Son,
There can be nothing outside of you.
But what if you deign to believe
That there IS something outside of you,
And further yet, to believe there is something outside of you
Which can determine what you are?
Well, have I not told you—
What determines what you are is your God.

So what if you believe, albeit falsely,
That something outside of you can determine what you are?
Then what have you done?
You have created an idol.
You have created the belief in a false god
Whom you believe to be your creator.
You have made an idol which you worship as a god.
And more so, if you would believe in
The "self" which you cherish,
And which you believe has been created by this god—
If you would believe that "self" to be real,
Then you MUST believe in that god.

And yet, I have told you, you are at home in God.
There are no other gods.
And the belief that such gods exist is truly idolatry.
You are at home in God.
And yet you believe it to be otherwise.
It is a dream, as I have told you—
Nothing but a dream.
And if you would waken from the dream—
In an instant you can become aware of the frivolity,
The fickleness, and the falseness
Of the dream you have dreamed.

And so it is that this life of space and time and bodies,
All of which is illusion, is but a dream based upon idolatry.
It is a dream based upon the belief
That there is something outside yourself
Which has made you what you are,
Which has somehow confined you to space, and to time,
And to this body you seem to walk around in,
And which seems to determine your life for you.
And thus DOES THAT NOT BECOME YOUR GOD—
That which determines what your life is?

And even though it be a dream,
I have told you that you cannot dissociate
Unless, at first, you know.
For to dissociate is to separate yourself from SOMETHING.
And how can you dissociate from something
Which was never yours?
Even you can see that, of course.
And if you would start from within the state of knowledge,
And arrive at a belief in an idol—
If you would start within the state of knowledge
And have arise within you a false belief,
A false image of yourself
Which seems to come from outside yourself—
If you would do that, hear me very well,
IT MUST BE A DECISION.
It must be a decision that was made by you.

And now I tell you again
A truth of the greatest of importance.
God is One. God is God.
God has not been split asunder,
Cannot be, and never shall be.
The nature of God is the very nature of existence,
And the nature of Life Itself.
And were God to be split asunder,
Existence, as existence, would cease to be.
And such cannot happen.

So if there was made a decision to forget,
A decision to dissociate,
It must have come FROM YOU.
Remember, there is nothing outside yourself at all.

So any decision to believe what is not true
Must have come from within you.
So this world of space and time, and bodies, and illusion
Was made as a conscious decision.
Although consciousness, as you understand it,
Does not exist within Spirit,
Do not be concerned with that at this moment.
Simply realize that the decision to dissociate,
And to make illusion,
Had to arise out of a state of full awareness.

And yet, you cannot BE what you are not.
All you can do is BELIEVE that you are what you are not.
And so, if you have made a decision to enter a world of illusion,
One of the things that decision required
Was that you make up gods who would seem, in some manner,
To determine what you are.
And if you would believe yourself to be a body,
A victim of this world and space and time,
If you would believe that this world determines what you are,
That is where the god of sickness comes in.

For does not sickness seem to be a thing
Which HAPPENS TO YOU?
You, in your thinking minds, of course,
Believe that you do not want to be sick.
And yet you have the symptoms of sickness.
And does that not prove to you
That it must come from outside yourself?
So beautiful the design! So clever the design!
You imagined a split mind that allowed you
To dissociate part of yourself,
And to believe in a false god,
One which helps to substantiate for your thinking mind
That your illness is determined by a god outside itself—
A god of sickness and of circumstance.
You call it accident, and tragedy,
And germs, and bacteria, and disease, and pestilence—
The names all stand for the same thing—
The belief that there is that which is not you
Which can determine what you are.

And I have told you not to side with a Son of God in sickness,
Even if he believes in it himself.
For it is true that to believe a Son of God can be sick
Is to believe that a part of God can suffer.
There is that within you which knows that all is One,
That God is One, and that you are part of that Oneness.
So if you can be sick, it follows at once
That God Itself can be victim, just as are you.
But it is not so, I promise you.

The belief that a Son of God can be sick is truly idolatry,
Is truly the belief that there is something outside of him
Which can determine his life, and what he is.
And thus I tell you,
If your brother cherishes that belief,
And if you would heal him, and heal yourself,
Do not participate with him in that same belief.
For if you would share, and substantiate with him,
The belief that something outside of himself
Is making him into what he is,
Then YOU, not your brother,
Are standing tall and spreading your arms and saying—
"God is not God. God is no longer One.
He has been split asunder."

Is it reasonable to speak such falseness without even asking
By what means the perfect Oneness was split asunder?
You believe that a split has occurred from within a Oneness
Out of which it could not possibly arise.
If you contemplate that, even you can see its absurdity.
And so, if you would believe that a Son of God is sick,
What you are doing is proclaiming for your own life
That his god of sickness is also your own.
You are proclaiming with him
That there is that outside of yourself
Which determines what you are—
Just as your brother believes the same.

Then what if you would heal your brother?
Simply do this—be aware of the truth of what he is.
And to "be aware of" does not mean
To think it at an academic level.
To be aware of the truth about him means to accept the truth,

Which means to receive the truth,
Which means to allow the truth to become what you are.

The acceptance of truth in this world
Is the perceptual counterpart of creation in the Kingdom.
If you accept the truth, then within your perception
It becomes what you ARE.
And creation itself is the experience of
That which flows out of you, out of your being,
And yet is, and becomes, what you are,
Never to leave.

If you would accept the truth about your brother,
In order to heal him, and in order to be healed,
Then at the very core of your being
You see him simply as he is—
Indivisible, One with God, a being of Spirit,
Outside of which and whom can be nothing.
You therefore see him as a being
For whom there exists but ONE God.

If you would accept the truth for your brother,
At the core of your being there can be no room for idols,
Above all, the idol of sickness.
So the healing of your brother, and the healing of yourself
Is so extremely simple
That you will marvel at its simplicity.
And all it takes is that that simplicity
Become part of what you are,
Just as creation is the same process
Within the Kingdom.

When you take these words, and open your being
To the point where they become who you are—
Beyond the thoughts, beyond the words,
Beyond the analyzing—
When they become part of you at the core of your being,
Then you shall BE the healer of your brother, and of yourself,
And of the whole world.
And this is its simplicity—the message of healing—
Hear, O Son of God, the Lord thy God is One.

My blessings upon you all. That is all.

THE DENIAL OF GOD

Greetings again. I am Jeshua.
I wish to speak with you this day
About the denial of God.

You may recall that I said to you—
You deny God because you love Him.
You deny Him because you love Him,
And you know that He loves you.
And perhaps you are wont to ask,
"How does that make any sense?"

Remember, I told you that
You cannot dissociate unless at first you know.
Likewise, you cannot deny a thing
Except that it be that which you have known.
And all of this world of illusion,
As I told you last time,
Was made with full awareness
Of what it was you were doing.
Well, if you were fully aware of
God's infinite Love for you,
Could you ever deny God?
The answer is, of course not.

So in order, by your own choice and design,
To make a world of illusion—
For the purpose of believing that you are separate,
For the purpose of believing that you are not One
And that God is not One—
In order to make all of this world of illusion,
It was necessary to somehow put out of your mind
Your awareness of God and God's love.
But I have told you that God IS One,
And that you cannot be apart from Him.
God is in your mind, and it cannot be otherwise.

So the only way you could make this world of illusion
Was to split your mind, and have a part of it
SEEM to be unaware of God, your Creator.
And that is the essence of the split mind.
When you split your mind, it was for the purpose
Of becoming unaware of God in your mind,
For the purpose of becoming unaware
That God is the Creator of what you are.
And that is what it is to deny God.

Now I also told you
That the denial of God must lead to projection.
How is that so, you might ask?
It is not possible for you to totally rid your mind
Of the awareness that you were created. For it is but a fact.
God is Creator. We are the creations.
And creation flows outward,
As I have told you, in one direction.
You, we, I, have the same creative power as God.
But we still are the created, the children, the Son of God.
So it is you are unable to totally clear your mind
Of the awareness that you are created.

When once you have denied God
For the purpose of coming here in the first place—
When once you have denied God,
You MUST look to discover wherein lies your creator.
For you KNOW that your creator exists.
But within the illusion, you think it not to be God.
But here lies the rub—God is One.
There is nothing outside of God.

So having denied God, and having attempted
To put the awareness of God out of your mind,
When you then look to find your creator,
What do you find as you look within a place
Where the awareness of God is not?
You find, of course, nothing.
For that is what is there—nothing at all.

But you, in your illusion, demand a god, or gods,
Which shall be the determiners
Of who and what you are, and what you do.

So when you look and find nothing there,
What are you to do?
Ah, you take an image of the god that you want to be yours,
And you place it upon the nothingness.
And that is the exact definition of projection.
You take the choice of what you want to see
And project it upon the imagined nothingness
Which seems to exist outside of God.

And then in the twinkling of an eye,
You look again to see what you have placed there.
And you discern that to be your god,
The creator of what you are.
So, of course, you must see exactly
What you have placed upon the nothingness.
And so, just as I have told you,
You always see what has come from within yourself.
And insofar as you choose to believe
That what you see in your projected world
Is actually that which determines what you are,
Then that image becomes the god you have made.
And so it is that you deny the true God
By taking your awareness of the reality of God
And putting it out of your mind,
Then looking upon what you have projected
Onto an imagined nothingness.
You look to see what you have put there,
And call that god.

I have told you that the god of sickness
Seems to determine what you are,
What you can do,
Where you can go,
So many of your limitations and restrictions—
All of them seeming to function
Through this imaginary image you call your body.
But that god to whom you have given great credence,
The god of sickness, could not have arisen
If first you had not denied the presence of God
Within your mind.

Projection works the same
When you would blame your brother

For determining what you are.
If you believe that your brother MAKES you upset,
Or that he CAUSES you to be angry,
Or that he TAKES AWAY your peace,
Or even if he seems to be the source of your feeling happy,
Then always it is your projection.
You see not your brother.
You but see what you want to see,
Projected upon the imagined nothingness
Of which we have spoken.
And that which you project you call your brother.
And none of it could be so unless you had denied God.
Whenever you believe that you can be sick,
Whenever you believe that your brother,
Or anything else of this world, can take away your peace,
It could not be so without that you had denied God.

I have spoken to you of magic.
And I have told you that magic is the attempt
To reconcile the irreconcilable.
Magic is the attempt to bring together
Two things which cannot co-exist.
Magic is the attempt to put into your thought system
The belief that two such things CAN co-exist.
As an example, you may think of magic as a pill you might take
To seemingly correct an illness within your body,
When you know full well that everything comes from mind.

But the greatest form of magic is your belief
That you even can be sick in the first place.
For God has made you perfect.
And the perfection of what you are and sickness itself
Cannot co-exist, cannot be reconciled.
And the belief that the complete, whole, perfect Son of God
Can be sick at all is an absolute belief in magic
Of the first order.

I have told you as well that
Truth and illusion are irreconcilable.
To believe that you can understand truth
While yet believing in one fragment of illusion
Is the belief in magic.
I have as well told you that

Freedom and bondage are irreconcilable.
To say that God has given you free will,
And yet to then suppose that there is anything at all in your life
Which can impose experience upon you,
Is simply your attempt to reconcile freedom
And the absence of freedom.
And that, as well, is the belief in magic.

You are absolutely free.
You cannot take away your own freedom.
All you can do is deny it,
In the same way you have denied God.
You can pretend that you are not free.
You can pretend that your life
Is imposed upon you by that which is outside yourself,
Be it the illness of your body,
Or the actions of your brother,
Or anything else you would deign to imagine.
But all that you see, when you believe yourself not to be free,
Is your desire not to be free
Projected upon the imagined nothingness
Which you believe exists outside of God.
And all the while you know
That what exists outside of God is nothing.

And 'tis the same with you—
What exists outside of you is nothing at all.
So a god of sickness is a god who would speak to you
And tell you that there IS something outside yourself
Which can impose upon you an experience,
That there is something outside yourself
Which can cause you not to be free.
You have imagined the illness of your body
As a primary proof that you are not free.
While what you see is the projection of that belief
Upon nothingness.

And now, what if you would desire to have sickness end?
What is it that you should do?
What is it that you CAN do?
You are here, within this imagined world of illusion,
Thinking thoughts that are not your real thoughts,
Thoughts which are of the past,

And which have no creative power.
What can you do to end sickness,
Either in yourself or your brother?
'Tis absolutely simple.
If you would bring about the end of sickness,
THEN CEASE AT ONCE TO DENY GOD.

To deny God is as well to deny yourself.
For God has made you part of Him.
And that which is God is that which is you.
So if you place the awareness of God outside of your mind,
By imagining it to be split,
Then with it goes the awareness of what you are.
If you would end sickness, you must cease to deny God.
And at the same time you must cease to deny
What you are as well.

How can you do that here?
Can you FIGURE OUT what you are?
Can you use these meaningless thoughts
Of which I have spoken
To figure out what you are,
In order that you can cease to deny yourself,
And thereby cease to deny God?
The answer is this—no, you cannot.

Then how can you cease to deny God and yourself?
You must do it by being still
And listening to the part of your mind
Wherein lies the knowledge of God,
The knowledge of what you are.
In your silence, you will hear the Voice of the Holy Spirit
Singing you a song of God, and a song of your Self—
Singing you a song of the fact that God is One,
And that you are the same.

So use these words, and use your thoughts,
Only to determine what you will allow into your mind.
If you have thoughts that speak of separation,
If you have thoughts that speak to you
Of something external to yourself,
And which might impose your existence upon you—
Be it your body, or your brother, or anything else—

Then cease to allow that thought in your mind.
Say to yourself in thoughts,
"I know it is not so. For I am free.
For the laws of God
Are the laws of freedom,
And of Love."
And then listen.

And you will hear the Holy Spirit
Singing you the song of love and freedom.
As you hear that song, as it becomes you,
Deep within, past the words, past the analyzing,
You will become aware of the freedom
That you once pretended to give up in order to come here.
And in the awareness of your freedom,
Sickness will dissolve in front of your eyes
As fog before the morning sun.

Recall I have told you not to side with a Son of God in sickness,
Even if he believes in it himself.
That is what I meant.
If your brother believes himself to be sick,
Then say to yourself in words,
"I know that sickness is a belief in magic.
And I will cease to believe in magic.
I will open to the awareness of what I truly am."
And then, as you are still within,
Even in the presence of your brother,
The Holy Spirit will sing you the same song.
And your brother will have access to that same Voice—
Because he is One with you.

He is free. And you cannot impose
The song of his freedom upon him.
For if you could, he would not be free.
So simply realize within yourself that sickness IS magic,
And that what you see is your brother's freedom.
Then offer that same freedom to him
THROUGH YOUR AWARENESS.
As you offer it to him, the gift shall become yours.
You shall realize that sickness is indeed magic,
And that it has no place in your own life.
And your own sickness,

If you had believed in it before,
Will truly disappear, just as I have told you.

And thus the truth remains—
You cannot ever be sick without denying God.
You cannot ever be sick without fabricating a god of sickness
Which you have projected upon a nothingness
That seems, in your mind, to lie outside of God.
You cannot be sick, ever, unless you believe in magic,
Unless you refuse to believe in the perfection of God's Son,
And unless you try to reconcile sickness and perfection—
Which, of course, you cannot do.

You cannot be sick at all—from the worst cancer,
To the slightest sniffle, to the slightest sigh of tiredness—
You cannot be sick at all
If you are aware within of God, and of your Self.

So if you would desire sickness
To pass out of your life and out of your world,
Then, in words say,
"I will no longer deny God, nor myself."
And then be still.
And in the song that you will hear
Reverberating through your being—
The song of the Holy Spirit—
You will hear the truth.
You will hear a song of truth
That speaks of freedom, not bondage;
Truth, not illusion;
Perfection, not sickness;
Joy, not depression.

But most of all, you will hear a song
That speaks and sings simply of Love—
For that is the nature of God.
And that as well is the nature of what you are.

Blessings upon you all. That is all.

THE GIFT OF FATHERHOOD

Greetings again. I am Jeshua.
I have come this day to discuss with you
A most important choice which you must make.
And that choice is between God and the ego.

I have told you so many times,
God is All That Is.
So what can there be, what can there be at all,
Which is apart from God?
In truth, what can there be at all that IS NOT God?
And the answer, of course,
Which you already know within your being,
Is—nothing.

So if one asks you a question,
"Which do you choose, God or the ego?",
And if it be true, as I tell you it is,
That there is NOTHING which is not God,
Then can there be God OR anything, at all?
And the answer is simply—of course not.

So when you think in terms of God OR the ego,
If the ego is not God, then can it exist at all?
And you, of course, know the answer this minute,
Within the deepest part of your being.

Then what is the question?
What is the question that I pose?
Indeed, what is the question of all of life?
And what is the question, especially for you,
Here in this sojourn in space and time?
What is THE question as you walk upon this earth?
Always it is—"Who am I? And what am I?"
And do you see that this entire world is nothing but
A false answer to that self-same question—
"What am I? And who am I?"
And what is it, really, to say "What am I? Who am I?"
Is it not to say "From whence did I come?"

And that, of course, is to say "Who is my father?"
And so you, this moment, already know the answer.

If you exist at all, and God IS All That Is,
Then you ARE part of God.
And therefore you have arisen, somehow,
Out of that which is God Itself.
And so, if you would say, "Who is my father?"
There is but one answer that can stand—
"Your Father is God."

So the question I posed to you about the ego is this—
"If God is All That Is,
And you have clearly arisen from God Itself,
Then can you have arisen from something else
Which is apart from God?"
And spoken that way, the question is silly indeed, is it not?
And so you see the question answers itself.
"Who is my Father? God or the ego?"

'Tis nonsensical indeed, if you think about it clearly,
Just as is this entire world.
And that, of course, is what this Course is all about—
An attempt to help you see clearly what this world is,
What it means indeed,
What it does not and cannot mean—
And that ultimately it is not real,
And therefore cannot threaten in any way
That which is your reality.

The ego has a thought system.
And for your purposes, I say that God has a thought system.
Truly, God does not think thoughts as you think them.
For remember, the natural state of the mind,
Including the Mind of God,
Is complete abstraction.
And thoughts and words do not arise
From a state of complete abstraction.
But within this framework of space and time,
The ego does, indeed, have a thought system.
And it is consistent with its premises.
These we shall discuss later.

So what is God's thought system?
It is not a set of ideas which you can speak in words.
Indeed, you cannot define God's thought system.
And why is that?
Because God's thought system is YOU.
And what is it about you
That makes it impossible to define God's thought system,
If that thought system is what you are?
Now, hear this question very well.
How can you define that which is without limit?
How can you define that which is eternal and infinite?
How can you define that which is All That Is,
Without beginning, and without end?

How can you define such a thing, such a being?
Only with one word—to say it is You.
You are the cornerstone of God's thought system—
Because you are the Light.
And you may remember that I have told you
That the Light is, indeed, you in your natural state,
Unfettered by your thinking, free of the concepts
And the prisons created by the words
That seem to bring you the thoughts you think you think.

The Light is your natural state,
In its complete and perfect, unlimited, boundless freedom
To be, and therefore, to create.
That is what you are.
And truly, within the thoughts you think you think,
Those comments are but words,
And are incomprehensible to your experience.
For how can you, seemingly sitting
Within the confines of this body you have,
Speak of being unlimited and eternal?
How can you speak of that and understand?
Indeed, you cannot fully understand that truth,
Because that would be knowledge.
And knowledge you cannot obtain
While you yet remain here on your earth, in this form.

If God is your Father,
What gifts does He bring to you?
Ah, what if God truly is All That Is?

And I promise you that is so.
Then we must once again speak these words—
When God created you and became your Father,
There occurred no separation of any kind.
And if God is your Father, which He is,
You are not, as His Son, separate from Him.

So what is the gift, the simple, single gift
That God, your Father, bestows upon you?
'Tis this IT IS THE GIFT OF GOD ITSELF.
And that is all.
But have I not told you that
Having and being are the same?

Open your being to the truth of those words.
You have the gift that your Father gives you.
And that gift IS God Itself.
And if you HAVE that gift, then truly it IS what you are.
And so, truly, you ARE God.
And if it follows that you ARE God,
Then can you NOT BE God? Of course not.
You can imagine otherwise.
You can even imagine yourself separate from God,
If you can try not to laugh this moment.
But, separate from God you cannot be.
You can even imagine yourself separate
From that which YOU are,
But to no avail.

And so if you ARE God and you exist,
Then what is it that keeps you alive, if you will?
It is being God.
And creation is simply the flow of being God,
Beyond time, beyond space,
Without limit of any kind.
And so it follows that you, as God,
MUST CREATE, simply in order to be.
But one choice you do not have is to cease to exist.
For if you were to die,
God Itself would disappear in the twinkling of an eye.
And that, without question, I promise you, cannot happen.
If you were to die, it would be the death of God Itself.
How absurd!

And so whether you know it or not,
Whether you believe it or not,
Whether you like it or not,
Always, always you are creating.
For to create is to be, to exist, and to live.
And so if you are God, and must remain so,
Then you, indeed, have creations of your own.

And what is the gift that you would give
In your creating?
'Tis the same gift that God Itself gave you—
Because you have no other choice.
Because that is the only thing there is to give.
You give, like God, the gift of fatherhood,
Which is the gift of your Self,
Which is the gift of everything,
Without limit and without restriction,
Beyond space and beyond time.
For that is the same gift of fatherhood which you have received,
And which you must give,
Always, automatically, without fail.

But what if in your belief in separation,
You fear to give?
What if you are afraid to open to the awareness
That that IS the gift you have received,
And the gift which you MUST GIVE lest you cease to exist?
Then you must believe in the thought system of the ego—
That God's Will is separate from yours.
Of this we have spoken before.

I remind you once again
That the simple belief that your will can be separate from God's
Is the source of all of your problems,
All of your sickness, all of your conflict,
And all of your fear.
But separate from God you cannot be.
So here, in your vain imaginings,
You believe in God as a being separate from yourself,
Who might have a will which could oppose you,
As we have spoken before.

And if you would desire to let go of your fear,
If you would let go of your conflict,
And let go of the sickness that seems
To be part of your life here,
Then what must you do?
You must simply open your being to healing.
You must invite healing into your life.
And if sickness is separation,
Then to be healed is to join.

And what is the one simple truth
That shall bring about the ultimate joining,
The ultimate connection,
That shall abolish separation and its fear forever?
It is the simple truth that God's Will is not different from yours.
And that is all.

So what do you do, if you would be healed,
When there is, trying to shout and clamor into your ear,
The voice of the ego preaching its thought system,
The cornerstone of which is separation?
And what if the clamor and the shout of the ego in your ear
Would seem to block the quiet, gentle
Whisper of the Holy Spirit,
Which speaks for God, and speaks of what you are,
And speaks of the truth that always, always, always,
Your will and God's are, and must be, the same?

If you would invite healing into your life,
You do it by listening to the whisper,
By listening to the Voice of the Holy Spirit, the Voice of God,
Which, as I have told you before,
Is simply the Voice of your One Self,
Which is but You in the reality of what you are.
So the simple truth is this—
The whisper of your reality speaks of one will,
Speaks of joining, and speaks of harmony.

Now this is the test which you may apply
If your desire is to be healed—
The gift of fatherhood is the gift of everything,
Without limit, without restriction,
And without exception of any kind.

And that is what the Voice of God would tell you.
And any voice which would speak of
Holding anything unto yourself, protecting it as it were,
Defending, keeping it safe from—
Any voice that speaks thusly, I promise you,
Is the clamoring of the ego,
And cannot be the whisper of the Voice of God.

So if you would invite true healing into your life,
Always apply this simple test
To any thoughts of which you become aware—
Is there anything in these thoughts
Which would exclude my brothers from anything,
Which would keep anything unto myself alone,
Which I would desire to protect,
Which I would desire to defend?
And if the answer is "yes,"
'Tis the clamoring and screeching of the ego in its fear,
Knowing that, if you give without limit,
The ego will disappear at once,
And all that will be left is the Voice of God.

The test seems so simple, does it not?
But I urge you, apply this test
If you would invite healing into your life.
Look at the gift that God has given you,
And which you must give always,
Simply in order to preserve,
And to return to your clouded awareness,
The truth of what you are.

Simply give as God gives.
And always check and see—
Would you limit, would you restrict?
For God would never do so.
And you, in your reality, would never do so, as well.
And as you discover that there is nothing
Which you would withhold
From any brother for any reason,
Then you have invited healing into your life.
And healing brings with it the simple awareness
That your will and God's Will are, indeed, the same,
And must always remain so.

So look at your brother, this day.
Look at any of them, and all of them, and simply say—
"I would give everything to you, in gratitude,
For all of it is mine.
For I have the gift of the Fatherhood of God,
Which is God Itself.
And because I have the gift of God, that is what I am.
And in order to remain God,
The perfect being that I am,
I will simply give without limit, and without restriction."

And the simple truth, of course,
Which you already know in words,
Is that the gift of one's Self,
Without limit and without restriction,
Is simply the gift of Love—
Which, of course, is exactly what you are,
And shall always be.

Blessings upon you all. That is all.

THE INHERITANCE OF GOD'S SON

Greetings to you this day. I am Jeshua.
And I have come, this day, to speak with you
About the inheritance of God's Son.

For in your world, is it not true,
That if you are son to a father,
You think in terms of—
"What do I inherit from my father?
What is it that I receive
Simply by virtue of the fact that I am 'son'?"

Oftentimes, in your world,
You think of receiving much of your inheritance
After a father, a parent, has died.
Ah, but God as you know, is eternal, unchanging,
And cannot die.
So if you are God's Son when,
(Do you hear the words of time?)
WHEN shall you receive your inheritance?

But only can you think in terms of "when,"
If you believe in the state of separation
Which you call time.
It is true that time is the grand maker
Of what you believe to be separation.
But, hear me well, you are God's Son
In the absence of, and beyond, time—
Beyond space as well.
You are God's Son, independent of, and beyond, time.

So it is not to ask,
"WHEN, as God's Son, do I receive my inheritance?"
For the question makes no sense at all.
You might wish rather to ask, "WHAT is my inheritance?"

Remember I have told you that, in the world of spirit,
Having and being are the same.
So can you HAVE an inheritance without that you BE what it is?
And the answer is—of course not.
For they are the same.

So what in essence is your inheritance?
'Tis simply the undeniable, unchangeable fact
That AS THE SON OF GOD, YOU ARE GOD.

But I have also told you
That your inheritance as the Son of God is glory,
That glory is saved for you by God,
That glory is your right by virtue of the fact
That you ARE God's Son.

Well, if glory is your inheritance, perhaps you would ask,
"What does that mean?
Does it mean that I HAVE glory and that I AM glory?
And if so, what does that mean?"

I have spoken to you about going from darkness into light.
And I have told you that the pathway of darkness
Is not the pathway of God's Son,
And that the companions of darkness
Are not befitting of the Son of God.

And at some level, do you not believe
That if you would enter the Light,
If you would come to the understanding of what you are—
If you would become enlightened, as you put it—
If you would achieve your salvation—
Do you not tend to believe that that involves
Work and struggle and toil and even tears?
For do you not seem to believe
That along that path you must OVERCOME something?

And to overcome seems to demand a struggle against . . .
And indeed, do you not feel that you need to overcome
The presence of the dark companions?
Thus you believe that you need to fight against your misery,
And your grief, and your tears,
And seem to need to conquer
That which causes them to be present.

But remember how I have told you
That if you find yourself weary, you have only hurt yourself.
For pain is not God's Will for his Son.
Pain is beyond the awareness of God.

So if you would believe that you need
To OVERCOME the companions of darkness,
Realize it is only in your imagination
That the companions are even present.
God's Will would not have them be present.
God's Will for you is the Light.
And I have told you
That if only you knew God's Will for you,
Your joy would be complete.

But I also did tell you in honesty
That you cannot know that joy now, in this life.
For it is beyond you.
For YOU do not know how to remove your weariness.
You need the Comforter, God's Comforter,
To show you the way.

So if you would take the journey from darkness into light,
Which is nothing more than the journey
Unto the awareness of what you are—
A journey into the simple awareness that God's Will is yours—
If you would take that journey,
You can not figure it out on your own.
You cannot accomplish that goal by struggle,
And toil, and tears, and pain.
You cannot find the Light through struggle against
The companions of darkness.
Hear me well this day.

And what if you, for a moment, believed my words
That it was not possible for you to find the Light
By struggling against the darkness?
What would you do if you believed that?
You would cease to struggle, would you not?
For struggle, if it serves no purpose,
And only seems to bring you pain and discontent,
Is simply a thing which you would choose to let go.
So if you would take the journey from darkness into Light,
Simply RELEASE the companions of darkness.

And how do you do that?
By realizing that God's Will for you, as I have told you,
Is perfect happiness.

God's Will for you is joy.
God's Will for you is perfect freedom.
God's Will for you is that you be co-creator of All That Is.
God's Will is that there be nothing in all of Beingness
Which does not have upon it
The mark of your love and your joy.
God's Will for you is that the Light which you are
Shall shine, and shine, and shine, unto infinity,
Without limit of any kind.
And that I tell you is the glory of the Son of God.

You are to be glorified.
And why is that?
Because you, the true One Son of God
ARE co-creator with God,
Co-creator of All That Is, with no exception.
And if you could, in your human awareness, stand before
A Being Whose power, Whose magnitude, Whose Love,
Was the Creator of All That Is,
Would you not wish to drop to your knees
And sing hymns of praise to that Being?
But I tell you that Being is YOU.
For you are the Son of God.

What if it seems that you cannot touch that awareness?
What if it seems there are blocks present in your life
Which keep you from truly hearing these words?
You can hear with human ears
These sounds of your space and time.
But true hearing is far beyond the words.
True hearing is that which touches
The core of your being, at the level of experience.
This I have told you well.

So what, then, if you cannot hear my words this day?
What if they do not touch your heart
And sing the song that I promise you is there?
Then remember my words,
"Only you can deprive yourself of anything." (22)

If there seems to be the lack of anything in your life,
But above all, the lack of peace,
The lack of the awareness of what you are—

If that seems to be present in your life,
I promise you that no brother, no circumstance,
Not God Itself, has ever done, or imagined, anything
To take it away from you.
For God's Will for you remains
Perfect completeness, happiness, joy, and freedom.
So if lack seems to be in your life,
It MUST BE of your own choice.

And so you say, "Then teach me how to let it go.
Please, I would learn to release the blocks
And open my being to the Light."

The first step in hearing the truth
That only you can deprive yourself of anything
Is to realize that GOD DID NOT DO THIS TO YOU.
And beyond that to realize
That your brother did not do this to you.
Your brother, or God, would not, and could not,
Do anything to you.

I have told you that the laws of God are for your protection.
And even when you seem to deny the Light,
The laws are still for your protection.
For if God were to take away from you
That which allows you to imagine that you are in darkness,
You would be limited. And you would not be free.
But God's laws are preserved, even in your imagined darkness.
The laws protect you in your absolute freedom.
And that freedom can never be taken away
By any being, or any circumstance, including God.
That is the measure of God's Love.
That is the measure of creation.

Now when you first realize that God did not do this to you,
And that your brother did not do this to you,
Then it is so logical, and so natural, for you to assume
That you must have done it to yourself.
And thus you tend to place blame within.
And what I say to you now is of the greatest importance—
BLAME MUST BE COMPLETELY UNDONE.
For if you blame your brother,
And your brother is One with you,

Then you must be accusing God's Son of attack,
And of being outside of you.
You accuse God's Son of having destroyed
The Oneness that is God.

And what if you choose to blame yourself?
Since you are One with your brother,
You must also be blaming your brother in the very same way.
Only this time you would realize that
It is you who are somehow trying to destroy
The Oneness that is God's Son, and is God,
And is all of Creation.

And so to say, in any sense, in any circumstance,
That this was done to me by God, by my brother,
Or BY MYSELF
Is not to understand creation.
For if you, in any sense,
Would think of an event as "happening to you,"
Then hidden within that belief is the belief in separation,
Which is the building block of this entire world,
And the cause, truly, of all of your problems.
Thus the reason that blame must be undone
Is that you must move beyond the belief
That events in your life HAPPEN TO YOU.
For if you believe that they happen to you,
Then someone or something must have been the cause.
And that belief is what you must move beyond.

Well, how can there be events in your life
If they do not happen to you?
Hear me very well.
The events in your life do not HAPPEN TO you.
The events in your life ARE you.
And THAT is the glory of God's Son.
All of Creation IS you.
And that is the inheritance of God's Son—
The truth that everything, without exception, IS you.

And what if you, from deep within,
Could EXPERIENCE the truth of what I have just said?
What would change in your life?
What if you could open to the simple realization

That all that exists in Creation
Is the grand and glorious Oneness that is God,
That IS His Son, and that IS all of Creation?
What if you could open to that?
To the simple realization that NOTHING is outside you,
That NOTHING can happen to you,
That there is NOTHING but which IS you, IS God,
IS Creation Itself,
What would you do?

Your life would change unto the celebration of Beingness.
And you would embrace every experience without exception,
Out of your realization that it is not happening to you,
But IS you.
And in your simple realization that
Your will and God's are the same,
You would know, without question,
That you can TRUST your experience,
That you can trust the perfect safety that is yours.
And then you would simply embrace the experience,
With celebration.

What would happen if you actually did that?
If you looked beyond the belief
That you could be deprived of anything at all,
From whatever source—
If you looked beyond the belief
That ANYTHING could happen to you—
If you opened to the realization
That you ARE your experience—
If you opened to all of that with celebration,
What would you find?

This is the measure of the glory of the Son of God.
This is the measure of God's inheritance to His Son.

What you would find as you
Opened to the celebration of the experience of your life
Is simply this—
You would find Love.
And that is all.
I promise you, even here in your space and time,
And what you call the human condition,

When you open to, and embrace, without resistance—
Without the belief that it is apart from you—
When you truly open to every experience,
The only thing you will find is Love.

It is your perception that would seem to tell you otherwise.
But as you let go of the dark companions
Which would sing you songs of misery,
And grief, and guilt, and pain—
As you let go of them
And open to the Light,
The only thing you will see,
The only thing you will find, is Love.

Remember I have told you, you cannot do it of yourself.
You cannot figure it out.
You need God's Comforter.
And what is that?
That is, of course, the Voice that whispers
Unto the silence of your heart,
The Voice of the Holy Spirit.
For the Holy Spirit can mediate between truth and illusion.
And that means, in part, to see nothing but Love.

So as you are still within, as you open, without resistance,
As you embrace whatever would come to you,
And listen,
The Comforter will be there.
It will be the Voice of the Holy Spirit,
The Voice of God.
And because you are One,
It will be the Voice of your One Self,
Singing to you, singing a song of beauty,
And love, and peace, and joy.

And when you hear that song,
You shall, in gratitude, praise God
For the inheritance that you have been given
By the simple fact that you are His Son,
And shall always remain so.

My blessings upon you all. That is all.

THE DYNAMICS OF THE EGO

Greetings again. I am Jeshua.
I have come this day to discuss with you
What is actually a misnomer.
For I would speak with you about
The dynamics of the ego.

To speak of the word "dynamics"
Is to imply that something can be done.
To speak of the dynamics of the ego implies
That the ego can actually DO something, DO anything.
And that, truly, is not possible at all.

Why is it that the ego cannot DO anything?
The simple answer is this—
THE EGO DOES NOT EXIST.
And that which does not exist certainly cannot do anything.
But that answer is oftentimes not so easy to understand,
To internalize, to take beyond the words
To the level of your experience.

So let us, this day, look at the ego.
I have told you that the only way to dispel illusions
Is to look at them directly,
While not trying to protect them in any sense.
For NOT TO LOOK at illusions is how you preserve them.
And I do tell you this day, the ego IS an illusion.
And so if we would, together, dispel that illusion,
If we would, together, go beyond it,
Then we must look at it.
That we will do, together, this day.

Well, what does it mean to LOOK AT the ego,
To look at anything?
Does it mean to study it?
Does it mean to discuss it?
Does it mean to analyze it?
The answer is, no indeed.
For remember what I have told you, and will say again—
"The ego analyzes; the Holy Spirit accepts". (23)

So if we would look at the ego, what shall we do?
If we would look at that which is not real, how shall we do it?
To look at something simply means
To become aware of its nature.

I have told you that every idea has a purpose,
And that its purpose is reflected in what it is.
In the case of the ego,
Its purpose is reflected in what it SEEMS to be.
Now the ego is an idea.
It is an idea which you, the Son of God,
Projected outside your Self
For the purpose of pretending, of dreaming,
That you were something which you are not.
To actually do that is not possible.
It is not possible to BE what you are not.
It is not possible to BE what you cannot be.

And the fundamental purpose of the ego
Is to be found in one simple idea—
The ego is the simple idea that you,
That your brother, that anyone, that anything,
Could somehow be separate from God.
And that is it. That is all.

So what did you, the Son of God, do?
You projected onto the receptive mechanism of consciousness
The thoughts which seem to occupy your mind
And tell you of what you are.
And that in essence is the ego.
As I have told you before, the ego is simply
A collection of thoughts you have about who you are.
But those thoughts are the thoughts
That have been projected upon consciousness.
And therefore, those thoughts are not your real thoughts at all,
Just as I have told you many times before
Therefore, they are thoughts which do not have reality,
And which do not speak of what is real.

Your ego is simply a collection of thoughts,
Of which you seem to be aware,
And which would seem to tell you of what you are.
But those thoughts do not speak of what you really are.

And so, you are hearing, at the level of your thinking minds,
Thoughts which tell you that you ARE something
Which, deep within, you know that you ARE NOT.
And I promise you, that must bring you conflict.
It takes no reasoning at all to realize
That when you try to be something
Which you are not and cannot be,
You must be in conflict.
And ultimately, that conflict is the source of all your fear.

Now hear me very well.
You, in your playing out the dream of separation,
Have projected the thoughts upon consciousness
Which would tell you of what you are,
BUT WHICH DO NOT SPEAK THE TRUTH.

And what is the central message of those thoughts
Of which you are aware?
What is the central message of the ego, as I speak of it?
THE CENTRAL MESSAGE OF THE EGO IS THAT YOU ARE,
AND MUST BE, AND SHALL ALWAYS REMAIN,
TOTALLY ALONE.
And that is all.

And you know, truly, even in your thinking minds,
That being totally alone is not what you desire.
You know, even at the level of consciousness,
That you desire to love and to be loved,
To be in relationship with your world, with your brothers,
And with God.
You know that.
And the ego is simply this collection of thoughts that tells you,
If you listen to it, that you are but alone,
And shall always be so.

Now, how can that be?
And do you see now, as you simply look at that,
Which is what we are doing,
That you are hearing a voice whispering unto your awareness,
"You are alone. You are alone. You are totally alone."
And you must, as you choose to listen to that voice,
Be in conflict and be afraid.
The voice of the ego is the voice of fear.

And what if you pause and look at that?
Now herein lies the hard part.
The voice of the ego, when you do not look upon it as illusion,
SEEMS to tell you who you are.
You have designed this world of space and time and illusion
In such a way that you literally believe
That this little collection of meaningless thoughts
IS what you are.
And thus you believe that if it were to disappear,
If that illusion were to be dispelled,
That you would die.

AND SO YOUR ULTIMATE FEAR IS THAT
YOU MIGHT LOSE THE SOURCE OF YOUR OWN FEAR.
And so do you see, the first dynamic of the ego
Is to make you afraid that you might let go of your fear.
But if you WERE to let go of your fear,
Then suddenly you would open
To the realization of what you are,
To the awareness of the Son of God.
If you were to let go of your fear that is what would happen.
But it seems to you, that if you do that, you will surely die.
And so the dynamic of the ego is to preserve your fear
As if it were your very existence. Do you see?

And what about existing itself?
If you believe that you do exist,
If you believe you are alive—
If you believe that you exist, and that to exist is to be,
Then you desire to preserve your own existence.
And so you then believe that it makes you happy
To preserve that which you call yourself.

And so you see now that the workings of the ego,
Which YOU have designed and put into place,
Function in such a way as to convince you
That it makes you happy to be totally alone.
But that is a false premise,
Which can only be accepted by you
If you equate the absence of the ego with your own death.
For certainly, "to exist" seems to be better than "not to exist."
And therefore, "to exist" you equate with happiness,
Even though that which you call existence,

And which you believe to be the source of your happiness,
Has its foundation in fear itself. Do you see?

Well, how can the ego preserve that,
When even as you look at it now,
It makes no sense whatsoever?
And this is the key which I have told you.
The ego analyzes, the Holy Spirit accepts.

What do you do if you accept?
What do you do if you accept your own life,
The experiences, the circumstances, that come to you?
What do you do if you accept your brothers?
What do you do if you accept God?
YOU SIMPLY OPEN.
You simply open without resistance,
Without restraint, and without a program
Of that which you need to preserve
In the process of your opening.

If you simply open,
Then what you become aware of is WHOLENESS.
What you become aware of is the completeness,
The Oneness that is God, that is Life,
That is your brothers, and that is you.
And I tell you now,
The moment that you truly open to the existence,
To the presence of life, to being itself—
In that instant the ego, without effort,
Will pass away, and become what it always was—
Nothing at all.

But the ego analyzes.
The ego takes parts of the whole and treats them as complete.
And what is that?
That is separation itself, is it not?
If you can take a part of All That Is, a part of God,
And treat it as if it were complete,
Then you must have separated off from your awareness
All of that which remains, and which yet is still God.
And that is the exact way in which
You have split, or seemed to split, your mind.

Now if you take part of the wholeness
And look at it as complete,
And take what looks like another part and see it as complete,
And another, and another, and another,
Then what you do is, out of the pieces,
Weave a new picture of what seems to be life itself,
Made out of the pieces, which by definition
Are separate from the rest of Creation.

And so in analyzing, in shredding into pieces
That which is whole, you seem to make a world.
And it is in the analyzing that that seems to occur.
And that is how the ego functions.

Now I have told you the thoughts of consciousness
Have been projected onto consciousness by mind,
For the purpose of believing in separation,
For the purpose of believing that you are totally alone.
And I have told you that that is what seems to be the ego,
And yet which seems to function,
To have its own will, to be able to do things.
But it is nothing more than a simple collection
Of meaningless thoughts
Which do not speak of the truth.

And so if you would address the illusion of this world,
If you would look upon it in order to dispel it, to let it go,
If you would do that for the simple purpose
Of awakening to the awareness of what you are,
Then look once again at what I have told you this day.
All that you seem to be is a collection of thoughts
Whose basis must be fear,
Because its central idea is that you are, have always been,
And will always be, totally alone.
And to preserve that belief,
The ego causes you to cherish your aloneness
As if it were your very life.
And thus you believe that being totally alone
Is the source of your own happiness,
When actually all that you are doing
Is being afraid to let go of the source of your fear.
Do you see?

And so if you would look upon the ego
And dispel its illusion of aloneness,
What must you do?
As I have told you so many times before—
Listen to the Voice of the Holy Spirit.
For It will speak of acceptance.
It will speak of opening.
It will speak of wholeness and Oneness.
And nowhere within acceptance,
Within wholeness and Oneness and, yes, within Love itself—
Nowhere within that framework
Can the tiniest idea of separation even begin to rear its head.

So what shall you do if you would dispel the ego,
And therefore free yourself of its dynamics,
Which, as we have said, are not dynamics at all?
What shall you do?
You shall open to life itself.
And what is the best, the ultimate, representation of life itself?
How best can you open,
Here in your world of space and time, and yes, bodies?
The ultimate representation of that which you must accept
Is your brother.

So if you would look upon the source of your fear,
As I have described it to you this day,
You simply accept your brother, accept life, and accept God.
And when you do that, the ego MUST pass away.
And what is the simplest way to accept
Your brother who is One with you?
It is to simply look upon your brother, without exception,
And to say, "I trust you in loving me.
I trust you in loving me, and I thank you for loving me."
If you accept your brother, without resistance,
And without exception,
What you shall experience is the presence of Love.
For that, I promise you, is all that there is.

But if you look from within the illusion of the ego,
To perpetuate it, you will see a brother separate from you,
With a will different from your own.
But if you accept, if you open,

Then all thought of different wills passes away
In the twinkling of an eye.
And all that will be left is Love.

And if you simply open,
If you simply accept the presence of God,
What you are doing is simply saying,
"I trust. I trust that God's Will for me is perfect happiness,
And that God's Will for me is the same as my own."

And in accepting the wholeness and the Oneness,
Which is but your will and God's Will in perfect harmony,
You shall find that you are simply opening to Love.
And the ego, this simple illusion of separation,
Which you dared to look upon,
Will pass away, as I have told you,
In the twinkling of an eye.
And you shall be free.

My blessings upon you this day. That is all.

TRANSCENDING THE EGO

Greetings again. I am Jeshua.
Last time I spoke to you about the dynamics of the ego,
And reminded you that the ego cannot DO anything,
That the ego is simply a collection of thoughts
Which you, in your reality,
Have projected upon space and time and consciousness
For the purpose of seeing things differently,
For the purpose of seeing that which is not true.

I have also told you that the ego looks for, and finds, error.
And what does that mean?
That means that the ego literally must seek out what is not true.
The ego must cause you to believe that life is inconsistent,
That life is not fair, that life happens to you,
That you are a victim,
Ultimately, of course, to believe that you are the victim of God.
And the ego—the thought system that you have made
For the purpose of pretending that you are separate—
The ego must see that.

And so I have told you—the ego sees error
In order to make it real.
Thus it concludes that error IS real, and that truth is not true.
And to say that error is real is simply to say
That illusion is reality.

And I have also told you
That it is not possible to see what you do not believe.
And it is likewise not possible to not believe what you do see.
Such is the power of perception.
Such is the power, the creative power, of the Son of God.
And as you have made illusion,
As you have chosen to look upon error as if it were real,
It seems to you as real as reality itself.

And therefore I have come to bring you
This Course In Miracles and these words in order
To help you to go beyond the belief in error,
To help you to SEE, to help you to see that which is true.

I have spoken to you about waking to redemption.
And waking is nothing more than
Coming to see that which is true.

If you would choose to look upon that which is true,
There are some things I wish to share with you.
I have told you that the resurrection
Is nothing more than the transcendence of the ego.
The resurrection is not an event in which a body rises again.
The resurrection, my resurrection,
Was simply the statement, was the proof,
That what is true is true.

There are some things you need to know
About the resurrection.
I speak of the crucifixion and the resurrection.
And I ask you which you would choose.
I ask you if you would choose
To imprison your brothers and yourself,
Or set them free?
And the two things are, of course, the same.

As you become aware of the resurrection,
As you open to the transcendence of the ego,
As your perceptions go beyond the realm of the ego
To that which is true,
Then you shall find a new experience
That will lead to new beliefs which, when they stabilize,
Will lead you to a new perception,
A true perception of the world.
And you shall see the real world.

It is entirely possible, as I have told you,
To see the real world even here.
All you need do is believe in it.
For what you believe is what you see.
But you cannot believe it unless it becomes your experience.
And that is what I bring to you here.
Not lessons for you to learn, not the play of ideas,
But a practical application that shall take you to the experience
That is necessary for your belief, and thus your perception,
To change.

First and foremost is this—
God, the Holy Spirit, that which is real,
Would never ask you to give up,
Would never take away,
Would never increase,
Your fear.
When you, in any sense, would perceive
That which would request of you and seem to desire
To take away that which you have,
Even if it be your belief in error—
If you perceive that anything would "take away,"
Then you are not, hear me well,
Experiencing the real world.
And you are not understanding Love.

For Love, simply and clearly, is THE condition of reality.
If you would see, if you would believe in,
If you would experience the real world here—
Then you need to open to Love.
And that is all.
For the real world literally—literally, I tell you—
Is every loving thought of the Son of God.

Now hear me well, this day.
It is not possible for the Son of God
To think thoughts which are not real,
Thoughts which are not Love.
And so the real world is literally
ALL of the thoughts of the Son of God.
The real world and the awareness of the real world,
Which shall take you to knowledge,
Demands that you realize
That there are no opposites in all of Creation.

It is not as if there is good,
And because good exists, that bad must exist as well.
It is not as if there is truth,
And that therefore deceit and falseness must exist.
For all of it is the great Oneness that is God.
THERE ARE NO OPPOSITES.

If you, from within the thought system of the ego,
Would see error, what are you doing?

You are looking upon that which is true,
And through the interpretation which perception demands,
You are perceiving it to be what it is not.
And that is all.
Illusion is simply to look upon that which is true,
And to see it, to believe it,
To seem to experience it as being something that it is not.

The Holy Spirit represents the part of your mind
That holds truth within it, that sees truth, that truly forgives.
But remember, forgiving is not seeing error
And then somehow saying, ''It is okay.
Even though you have erred, I forgive you.''
To forgive is simply to see completely beyond the error itself,
Unto truth.
So the Holy Spirit literally represents
That part of your mind which sees ONLY the truth.

If you would perceive the world
Through the thought system of the ego,
You must see the error of which I have spoken.
If you perceive yourself as separate and perceive opposites,
If you perceive that your brother's will
Can be different from your own,
Then you are not seeing reality.
And you can never do so from within that framework.
And if you would try, you must be blocking yourself
From the awareness of Love.

The condition of reality is simply this—
Reality is Love.
Reality is one will that never takes, and only gives,
Which extends forever, and unto forever, and unto forever.
Reality is one mind without opposition of any kind.
It is a harmony so perfect that opposition,
If you were to think of it, would be incomprehensible
And that is the condition of reality.

And if you would choose between God and the ego,
All you need do is choose that which is real.
I have asked you a most important question.
And it was whether
You would rather have the problem or the answer?

The problem? The problem?
I have told you that you have but one problem.
And that problem IS the ego.
And the solution to that problem is the truth of God,
Which arose in response to the decision to pretend
That the ego could actually exist.

So when I ask whether you would rather have
The problem or the answer,
It reverts to the question,
"Would you choose the ego, or choose God?"

If you would choose God, how shall you do that?
You shall do it by realizing that in your perception,
In the thought system of the ego—
What you shall always find is the conflict
Which is, as I have told you, the hallmark of the ego.
If you would go beyond the ego,
It must be to go beyond conflict.
It must be to go beyond seeing error.
It must be to go beyond seeing opposites,
Or even the possibility that opposites can exist.

How, then, do you do that?
How do you say, "Yes, I have looked upon illusion,
And I have seen the thought system of the ego.
And I would choose, not the ego, but God.
I would choose reality.
I would choose Love.
I would choose harmony.
And above all, I would choose peace"?
How do you do that?

And I tell you again this day, as I have told you so many times
And as I will tell you again and yet again—
If you would see God,
If you would experience the presence of God in your life,
It MUST COME from seeing your brother truly.

If you look upon your brother,
And you see, in any sense whatsoever, opposition,
Or a will that would seem to be different from yours,
You are not seeing at all.

And you are blind to the vision of Love.
If you would see a brother who is confused,
Who is not at harmony with himself,
Who is ill,
Who is not joyful in his own freedom,
If you would see any of that, I promise you,
You but look upon yourself.

But if you would experience the transcendence of the ego,
If you would experience the resurrection—
The resurrection that I came to teach
And to put into the realm of human consciousness for you—
If you would experience the resurrection,
Then you must look anew upon your brother.

What if you try to look upon your brother
As being separate from you, as you are wont to do,
And from within that belief in separation say,
"I will see harmony here.
I will figure out, somehow, how this is Love"?
You will fail.
If you would see the truth,
Then you must let the bringer of the Vision
Be in charge of your looking.
If you would experience the peace of God,
Then you must look through the eyes of the Holy Spirit.
And that requires that you become like a little child,
The little child who realizes in simplest form
That he does not know.

And so, instead of bringing the perceptions of this world,
The perceptions of the ego,
To your encounters with your brother, to your holy encounters,
Instead of bringing that with you,
If you would experience reality and Love and the peace of God,
You must bring with you
NOTHING AT ALL.
You must open your seeing to the Holy Spirit.
You must come with no thought of past,
With no fear of future,
With no script that defines your brother as separate from you.
You simply come in stillness, with openness to each moment,
Openness to each moment of your life.

You come with openness to each moment
That you spend alone, or with your brother—it matters not.
You come with openness,
An openness that says,
"I do not know, and I would learn. Teach me."

And what shall happen as you simply open,
As you release your desire to cling
To any of the thoughts that define this world for you,
As you release any desire to literally cling to the ego,
As you simply say, "I would choose God
And the peace of God"—
As you do that and let go,
The Holy Spirit shall bring you, truly,
A new perception, a true perception,
The vision of your brother
Which is the Vision of Christ.

And as I take you back along the pathway
That goes beyond your ego,
Back through the pathway that literally transcends it,
You will first perceive,
Then believe,
And then experience,
In one great moment of joy and ecstasy,
The truth of what your brother is—
Which is the perfect, untarnished, joyful, free,
And beloved Son of God.

And then what must happen, I tell you again, is this.
As you see your brother as the Son of God that he is,
As you open to the Vision of the Holy Spirit—
In that same instant shall come welling up within your being
The awareness and the experience
That that, in all its beauty,
Is exactly what you are,
And what you have always been.
For you are, have always been,
And must always remain,
The Son of God.

Blessings upon you all. That is all.

THE JUDGMENT OF THE HOLY SPIRIT

Greetings again. I am Jeshua.
I have come, this day, to speak with you
More about the journey back to your Self.

As I begin to speak with you today,
I admonish you to remember our previous discussions.
For we have spoken of a choice that you must make.
And always it is between God and the ego.
In fact, there is no purpose for this Course at all
Except to help you realize that your choice is God.

It is most important that you remember
That the choice for God does not require effort or struggle.
I asked you which you would choose,
The crucifixion or the resurrection.
And I have told you that the resurrection is the pathway of joy.
And since the crucifixion is joy's opposite,
Then the crucifixion of God's Son, the pathway of the ego,
Cannot be of joy.

It is so common for you to forget my promise to you
That I have taken for you the last useless journey.
In my crucifixion and my resurrection
I freed you from ever having
To crucify God's Son or yourself.
What form does that crucifixion so often take,
In your life here in this world?
It takes the form of the belief
That you must endure struggle and pain and toil and tears
In order to achieve salvation,
In order to find the peace of God,
Which, as always, is the simple, the final,
And the only goal of this Course.

When you seek for peace, your search demands
That you choose God and not the ego.
Because from within the thought system of the ego,
You can not find peace.

Remember what I have told you before, that
Perception always involves interpretation.
It is not possible any other way.
Even true perception involves interpretation.

Perception arises out of
That which has seemed to structure the ego
And the belief in separation.
And because of your belief in separation,
You tend to believe that somehow
The thoughts of the ego have creative power,
That the thoughts of which you are aware
Have creative power.
But none of that is true.

The thought system of the ego,
The thoughts of which you are aware,
Are those which have been projected upon consciousness
By mind.
And the purpose of that projection is to rid the mind
Of the immediate awareness of that
Which it cannot tolerate—which is conflict.
But I have told you that EVERYTHING is in your mind,
That all truth is in your mind.
And if you would try to harbor within your mind
That which is in conflict with truth,
You immediately find the attempt intolerable.
And so you take that which is not true and project it out.
You project it onto the blank screen of consciousness.
And it is that projection that causes you to think you think.

Well, what is it that this collection of thoughts
Forms in your consciousness?
Insofar as those thoughts answer the question
"Who am I?"—and that is all they do—
Then that collection of thoughts
Forms the ego and its thought system.

And any experience, any thought that is projected
From mind onto the screen of consciousness
Must pass through the filter of the collection of thoughts
Which define who you are.
And that is interpretation, in simplest form.

You cannot perceive without interpretation.
You cannot perceive anything without that it be
Flavored by, modified by, passed through this filter
That tells you who you are—
This filter which is the ego.

Now, what if you would interpret ego motivation in yourself,
Or perhaps more importantly, in someone else?
What if you would elect to interpret, to perceive
The ego motivation of one of your brothers?
That perception in itself must have passed through
The filter of your own ego.
Thus it is not possible, hear me well—
It is not possible for you to EVER analyze, to think about,
To become aware of the ego motivation of another
Without your own ego and its motivation being involved.

And what is the simple and only motivation of the ego?
To preserve itself in its belief that it is isolated and alone.
So you, in your imagined aloneness,
CAN NOT judge your brother.
I told you, centuries ago, not to judge lest you be judged.
And that is what I meant.
It is not possible for you to perceive
The ego motivation of another, thus to judge him,
Without looking upon your own ego and its motivation,
And thus to be judged in the same instant.

And thus I speak to you of the judgment of the Holy Spirit.
For there is but one judgment—which is so simple—
There is but one judgment that the Holy Spirit makes.
And that is this—there are no opposites in all of Creation.
All that exists is Love.
God is All That Is. God is Love.
And that is all.

Now I have told you that if you will allow
The Holy Spirit to interpret for you,
Which means for you to choose to be still and listen,
And let go of your desire for interpretation or outcome—
If you will let go and be still,
Then the Holy Spirit will interpret for you.
And He will discern that everything is Love.

It is true that as long as you are here you must perceive.
And how does that become expressed in your awareness?
When you allow the Holy Spirit to interpret for you,
He will see everything as being Love.
If you are unable, because of your own fear,
To see any part of life here,
To see any action which your brother would seem to do—
If you are unable, with anything at all, to see it as Love,
Then the Holy Spirit simply tells you
To see it as a call for Love.

This is most important what I say to you this day.
THE HOLY SPIRIT SEES ONLY LOVE.
FOR LOVE IS ALL THAT EXISTS.
If ever you cannot see love, you may be guaranteed
That in some measure, however slight,
Your ego and its motivation are involved.

Now, if you would choose to defend your ego,
You do that by believing in attack.
And I tell you this day, attack is always, without exception,
For the sole purpose of defending the existence of the ego.
If you would choose between God and the ego,
If you would choose the peace of God,
Then it is given you to never, ever, defend.
For always if you would defend, you are choosing the ego.
This, I promise you, is true without exception.

But what if you are not able to be open enough,
Because of your ego, to see love?
Then the Holy Spirit, in Its wisdom, tells you
To see it as a call for love.

Think of it this way if you will:
Love is your natural state.
Love is the state of peace and harmony,
And of Oneness with all of life, and with God.
And all of you know, even in your most ego-motivated states,
That you, deep within, desire Oneness and peace.
That is obvious even to your egos.
So if you cannot see the love in a given circumstance,
Then open to the Holy Spirit's guidance and interpretation.
And you will discover a call for love.

But what you are really hearing within yourself
Is the awareness that love is your natural state,
And is that which is desired,
And is that which you wish to experience.

Thus it is that a call for love becomes your proof
That somewhere deep within
You know that Love does exist, and is what you want.
And that is equally true as well of your brother—
It is true of everyone, without exception.

I tell you this—every person in space and time,
Every person who has ever walked this earth,
Always is being as loving as he knows to be in that moment.
This is true, I promise you.
For your natural state of Love is deep within you,
And cannot be erased.
And no matter the form,
No matter what form the actions of your brother SEEM to take,
Always, always, he is being as loving as he knows how.
And he is pursuing the goal of love
As best he can in that moment.

And so what if you would respond
By wishing to attack?
Then what you are doing is
Further denying the presence of love
Within your brother, and within yourself.
Do you see?
So if you would attack, ever, it is to deny love in your brother,
And more importantly, to deny love in and to yourself.
And yet it is perfectly obvious to you
That your goal IS love and Oneness.

And so if to attack is to deny love,
Why would you ever attack?
And the answer is—in any moment of sanity,
You would not attack at all.
And thus the judgment of the Holy Spirit,
Who is beyond attack, is simply this—
Everything IS Love.

But if you cannot see a circumstance as love,
Then see it as a call for love.
And realize that, when you do so,
The call for love is not only in your brother,
But is also within yourself.
When the day comes in your time (and it will)
When you see everything with
The true perception of the Holy Spirit,
Then all that you will see is Love.
And the calls for love of which I speak
Will seem to have vanished into nothingness,
Because that is the exact vision of the Holy Spirit—
That everything, without exception, IS Love.

The way to remember God is to be aware of that truth.
And when you SEE Love
You are BEING Love itself.
For that is what you are.
When you see a CALL for love,
That is what you see in your brother
AND in yourself.
This must be true, with no exception.

So if you would remember God,
If you would choose God instead of the ego,
Simply be aware of this—
The healing of your brother
Is the same as the healing of yourself.
And the two must go together.

Now once I told you to sell everything you have
And give to the poor.
I also told you that what I meant
Was for you to demonstrate to your brothers and yourself
That if you have no investment in this world,
You are not poor at all.
Rather you are free.

I also suggested to you that there is no better way
To become aware of your own freedom and your own salvation
Than to not see and to not participate in
The poverty of your brother.
What does that mean?

The way that you do not participate in your brother's poverty,
The way that you do not side with a Son of God in sickness
Even if he believes in it himself (and the two are the same)—
The way you do that is to not invest yourself in this world.

This world is but the collection of thoughts
Projected from out of your mind
Which seem to tell you who you are—
Which collection of thoughts is, by definition, the ego.
So not to invest in this world is not to allow it
To tell you who you are,
Which is to deny the ego.

I also told you that if your brother makes an outrageous request,
You should do what he asks.
And does that seem to make sense to you?
For right away do you not imagine that if you actually did
What every brother asked you to do,
That your life here would be chaos?
And you know in significant measure
That to honor every outrageous request would not be best.
So I am not literally telling you
To honor every outrageous request made by your brother.
What I am saying is this—in the same sense that you can see
Your brother's call for love as your OWN call for love as well,
When you perceive a request to be outrageous,
AND THEREFORE DO NOT WISH TO COMPLY,
What you are seeing is the measure of
Your investment in this world.
What you are looking at is the face of YOUR OWN EGO.

And if you would choose God,
What you are seeing is that which you need to release,
To let go.
That is why I have said to you—
If your brother makes an outrageous request, do it—
Because it is for the sake of allowing him, and yourself,
To realize that it does not matter. Do you see?

Once again, when you perceive an outrageous request,
You may be guaranteed that you are looking
Through the filter of your own ego.
And in not wanting to comply with the request,

You are seeing your desire to defend,
Which is exactly the same as your desire to attack,
Which is your desire to deny the presence of Love
In yourself and in your brother.
For one who does not have an investment in this world,
For one who has chosen God instead of the ego,
No requests will be seen as outrageous.

What does that mean?
That means that from within the state of peace,
Which lies beyond investment in this world,
No request will seem outrageous.
It means you will not be offended
By any request your brother makes of you.
And if you do not see the request as outrageous,
You will have nothing to defend.
So now do you see?
I was not literally telling you to honor
Any request your brother makes of you. Not at all.
I was simply telling you to
Look at your own reactions to the request,
For the purpose of learning to see your own fear
And your desire to deny the presence of love
In your own life.

I also told you that when you speak of salvation
The basic question is always this, "First, what is to be saved?
And, second, how can it be saved?" (24)
I also told you that only the mind is to be saved.
And the mind is to be saved through peace.
If only the mind is to be saved,
Then that which seems to happen in this world of form
Is not of consequence at all.
And when you are occupied with the world of form,
You are occupied with the ego,
With the need to defend and attack,
And with the denial of Love.

The mind is to be saved through peace.
And how will you find that peace?
By listening to the Voice of God,
To the Voice of the Holy Spirit,
And not to the ego.

Do you see this day that I have told you
That everything is Love and cannot be other than that?
And as you choose to look beyond this world,
As you do not define yourself in terms of this world,
As you let go of the ego, as you choose God,
You are opening to the Voice of the Holy Spirit,
To the Voice of Love.

Thus the curriculum of the Holy Spirit
Would have you do this
Look at every circumstance in which you find yourself,
Whether with or without the presence of your brothers,
And open to the presence of Love.
And if you find the love and peace and harmony
That speaks of God, rejoice.

But if you do not, then it is time to choose.
If you choose the ego, you will desire to defend and attack.
But if you choose the Voice of the Holy Spirit,
You will find yourself guided to see a call for love.
And you will realize that
If you perceive that your brother is calling for love,
Then it must be that YOU desire love
In the very same form that he seems to need it.

Then the Holy Spirit will guide you
To give love to your brother.
The Holy Spirit will guide you as to the form
That love shall take.
The ego will not always see that form as love.
Indeed, there will be times when the ego will tell you
That it seems to be separation, and is not love at all.

And in that case, the measure of your guidance
Will be the peace you find within your mind.
As you open to the call for love,
As you refuse to defend or attack,
As you open to the Voice of the Holy Spirit
And you follow that guidance,
You are leading your mind along the pathway to salvation.
You are choosing the pathway of peace.
And that self-same inner peace shall be the guidance

That shall tell you that you are, indeed,
Hearing the voice of the Holy Spirit.

And as you act without investment in this world,
You are acting out your investment IN reality.
And that investment shall lead you
To the salvation of your mind,
To the peace of God,
And to the pathway of Love—
Which is the only path that exists,
And the same one which you, one day, MUST find.
And on that day you will realize
That what you are seeing is the face of Love,
The face of God, the face of the Holy Spirit,
The face of your brother, and the face of your Self.
And with great rejoicing, you will realize
That all of those are exactly the same.

My blessings upon you all. That is all.

THE SANE CURRICULUM

Greetings again. I am Jeshua.
I have been speaking with you about
The Holy Spirit's curriculum.

It is important for you to realize that
There is another curriculum.
And that is your own.
For in your choosing to make this world of illusion,
This world of falseness,
It was necessary for you to become your own teacher.
And thus what you seem to know about life,
About being, about becoming,
What you seem to know about love,
Is that which you have designed to teach yourself.

But you confront a major problem
When you attempt to teach yourself.
And the problem is that you—
And the "you" I refer to is the illusion
Of what you believe yourself to be,
That which SEEMS to be you, but is not you—
The problem is that you, ego,
Do not understand Love.
You, ego, CANNOT understand Love.

And thus it is that if you would search for Love,
Which you do and which you must,
Because Love is what you are—
If you would search for Love,
And attempt to learn of It from yourself,
And through your own curriculum—
If you would search for Love from a teacher (ego)
Who does not, and cannot, understand Love,
Then it is impossible for you to learn of that self-same Love.
That, even to your thinking minds, should be obvious.
And I am sure there is no argument within your thinking
As I make those statements.

If you, ego, do not, and cannot, understand Love,
Then how can you learn?
How can you learn of Love from the source
Which does not understand it?
For I have told you that in the presence of Love,
The ego would not be able to respond.
You, ego, as you would come into the presence of Love,
Could not respond.
What does that mean?
That means this—if you, ego,
If you would find yourself in the presence of God,
If you could somehow find yourself face to face with Love,
You would not have one idea of what to do,
Or what to say, or what to be.

And does that not seem like a great dilemma to you?
For truly the search for love is what even you, ego,
Realize that your life is about.
And search you must, for the simple reason, as I have told you,
That you are not at home in this world,
And are therefore bound to seek your home.
And what is your home?
Your home is the state of being
In which you are simply, completely, peacefully,
Aware of who and what you are.

Now I have told you that the edict of the ego is
Seek and do not find.
Why and how can that be?
It is because you, ego, in the presence of Love,
Would stand without response,
With no clue of what to say or be,
Even though you spend your life searching
For that same Love.

What is the form that the search for love takes
Here in your world?
It takes the form of the asking and answering of this question—
"What must I do, what must I believe, how must I act,
What must I become in order to be loved?"
And all of your life is spent in asking that question
And searching for its answer.
"What must I do to be loved?"

And ultimately, the question must resolve into this one—
"What can I do, what can I be, what can I think ,
In order that God will love me?"

But as you ask that question—
"What must I do? What must I be?"—
Do you hear the subtle implication that says,
"As I look outside myself, what must I do
In relation to someone different from me?
How must I act in relation to God or my brother?
What can I do in order that someone out there' will love me?"
And thus you see that in your world the search becomes,
"What must I do in order to RECEIVE love?"
And can you not hear within that question
The subtle belief that love is "out there"?

And that, in its simplest truth, will clarify for you
The reason that you, ego, do not know how to respond
In the presence of Love.
For God is Love Itself. And God is All That Is.
And when you even attempt to ask the unreal question,
"What must I do to be loved?"
You are looking outside yourself for the source of love.
And your goal is to cajole that source
Into giving you the love you seek.

Do you know the answer to your question,
"What must I do in order to be loved?
What must I do in order to receive love?"
The answer is, as I have told you so many times,
You must do ABSOLUTELY NOTHING.
But it even goes beyond that.
Is there anything you CAN DO to be loved?
And the answer is the same—no, absolutely nothing.
There is nothing whatsoever that you can do,
Within space and time, or beyond the same
THERE IS NOTHING WHATSOEVER YOU CAN DO
IN ORDER TO CAUSE GOD TO LOVE YOU.

Does that make you feel helpless?
For insofar as you perceive yourself to be ego,
Isolated and alone, that would be cause for despair.
There is nothing, nothing, nothing, you can do

That will cause God to love you.
And why is that?
Because the nature of Love, the nature of God,
The nature of what you are IS Love, in a wholeness,
In a fullness, in a completeness that is so great
That there is nothing outside of It at all.
And one discovers Love, one understands Love,
Never, never, by seeming to receive It,
But only, only by giving—by giving Itself.
Only by giving love, which is only, ultimately,
By giving that which you are.

And so if you, ego, have designed a curriculum
In which you can learn about love,
And based that curriculum on the belief that love is ''out there,''
Then you can never find it.
And, ultimately, that is terrifying to you.

The fear of FINDING LOVE is the same as the fear of dying.
For it is the fear of the ego that it will cease to exist.
For ego, that which you seem to be,
Is that which is separate FROM . . .
FROM God, FROM your brothers, FROM life.
And yet the essence of creation, which IS Love,
Is the wholeness which knows not of separation,
Which knows not of anything ''out there,''
Including Love.

Well, is there a curriculum which CAN teach you of Love?
If your curriculum cannot succeed
Because you cannot understand Love,
Is there a curriculum that you can follow?
And, indeed, of course, there is.
And I have called it the Holy Spirit's curriculum.
And I have also called it the sane curriculum.
I call it the sane curriculum in order
To help you once again hear my words
That this world, and all of its illusion,
Is literally insane.

The foundation of the curriculum that will teach you of Love
Lies in the simple truth that you are invulnerable.
What does that mean in simplest form?

As I have told you, to be invulnerable means
To be in a place of such great strength
That it is not possible that you can be attacked.
Furthermore, in a state of invulnerability
It is not possible to even be aware of what would seem to be
The presence of an attack at all.

Do you know what attack ultimately must be?
For I have told you that this world was made
As an attack upon God.
Have you thought of what that actually means?
Since Being is All That Is,
And having and being are exactly the same,
Then the only attack can be upon Being Itself.
If you would attack God, can you poke out His eyes?
Cut off His fingers? Stop His heart from beating?
Of course not.
God is not, has not, any of those.
And so if you would attack God, what do you do?
THE ONLY WAY YOU CAN ATTACK
IS TO PRETEND THAT SOMEONE, SOME BEING,
IS DIFFERENT FROM WHAT HE IS.
And that IS the essence of this world.

Have I not made it clear to you
That you have imagined God to be a being
Whose Love you must somehow earn,
Whose Love you must become acceptable to receive?
And your attack upon God has been this—
The simple belief that God is not perfect, is not whole,
And is not complete.
For Love has no conditions.
Love does not blame.
Love finds no fault.
Love merely is, and extends Itself.
And when you imagine that God is other than that,
Then you are attacking God, and ultimately yourself.
For you and God must be the same.

God is absolutely beyond attack in any form.
What does that mean? Simply that God is God.
And any imagined belief that God is not God
Can have no effect whatsoever.

And how about you?
If you are invulnerable, what does that mean?
It means that no attack of any kind,
No belief that you are what you are not,
Can have any effect on you whatsoever.

And that is the cornerstone of the sane curriculum,
Of the Holy Spirit's curriculum.
For what if you knew, rather,
What if you actually WERE beyond any awareness
Of attack even being possible?
In words—what if you were absolutely certain
About who and what you are?
Then no imagined belief would change,
Or could change, anything.
And no imagined belief could cause you,
In any sense whatsoever, not to be at peace.

If ever you find yourself not at peace, it must be, I promise you,
That you have believed that someone else
Has the power to change what you are
Simply by believing that you are otherwise.
And now do you wish to laugh as I say those words?
For even you know that such is not possible.
Now, what if you knew that God AND YOU
Were beyond attack, were invulnerable?
Then what would happen, in an instant?
You would realize that the same is true of your brother—
Every brother, every sister who walks this earth with you,
Who ever has walked it, who ever shall walk it.

And if you knew that you and your brothers, every one,
Were totally beyond attack—
That there was no weakness, that there was nothing
Which could be changed by vain imaginings
That they might be different from what they are—
If you knew that, then what would happen?
It could not occur to you, even to your thinking mind,
To look outside yourself.
And you would realize at once
That the key to the Kingdom lies WITHIN YOU.

And so, if you would discover the key to the Kingdom—
And there is but one—
If you would discover the key to the Kingdom,
What does it require of you?
It requires that you open to what I have called
The Vision of Christ.
It requires simply that you see your brothers and God
As I have told you they are.
And in seeing them thusly,
You shall see yourself to be the same.

In simplest form, what is this vision that shall set you free,
That shall free you from any temptation
To look outside yourself for love,
Where it cannot be found?
What is this vision?
It is the simple realization that God
Is absolutely complete and whole and perfect,
And, above all, beyond change.
This vision requires that you accept the truth
That God's Love, that God Itself
Has become yours,
Given you out of a fullness that cannot be contained,
Given you out of a fullness and a completeness
Beyond anything that your thinking mind
Could possibly comprehend.
It requires the vision of God's Love
Which opens to the simple understanding
That the nature of Love Itself requires
That there is absolutely nothing you can do to earn it.
For if you COULD earn God's Love,
It would not be Love at all.

And what also does this vision require?
The simple awareness that your brother, your sister,
Without exception, is the recipient, totally and completely,
Of the perfect and complete Love of God.
The Vision of Christ requires that you
Look upon your brother, your sister,
As being so completely deserving of God's Love
That nothing could ever prompt anyone to deny
The fullness of God's Love for him, or her.

Do you see that this vision must go beyond form?
It matters not, in any sense, what you do,
What you say, what you think, what you feel.
There is absolutely nothing that can ever, in any sense,
Separate your brother, your sister,
From the fullness of the Love of God.
And that IS the Vision of Christ.
For the Christ, which is within you,
Sees every being, every brother, every sister,
As totally beyond, and independent of, form,
As complete recipients of the perfect Love of God.
And thus it follows in an instant that YOU are the same.

And one final question the ego might ask is, "How can that be?
How can all beings be complete recipients of the Love of God?"
Remember that the ego wants to believe
That love is given from "out there."
And so you must, if you would open to the Vision of Christ,
Realize that there is no "out there,"
But that the Love of God for you, for your brothers and sisters,
Is but the Love of God for Itself.
And your love, your love of God, and your brothers and sisters,
MUST BE YOUR LOVE OF YOURSELF.
For there is nothing else in all of Creation to love.
And there is nothing else in all of Creation
That could possibly be worthy of your love.
For there is nothing else.

And as you simply open to that truth,
You will find that you MUST look within.
And as you do so, there shall come the awareness
Of the One Source, the center of all Being,
Which is God Itself,
Which IS your brother, your sister, which is everyone,
And which is You,
Outside of which is nothing.
There shall come the realization that all of Love Itself
Is the simple realization that you, and God,
And your brothers, your sisters,
ARE the essence of Life Itself,
Are All That Is,
And are the essence of Love.

And as your realize that you and God,
Your brothers and sisters
ARE Love Itself,
Then there is no place for Love to go.
For It simply is what you are.
Celebrate that that is so.

My blessings upon you all. That is all.

LOOKING WITHIN

Greetings again. I am Jeshua.
We are speaking these days
About the Holy Spirit's curriculum.

I spoke to you last time about the sane curriculum,
The only one that makes sense, if you will,
And actually, the only one that makes sense
Even to your thinking minds.
And I made it clear to you that the design of the ego is
To seek, but not to find,
Simply because the ego does not understand Love,
And in Love's presence, literally,
Does not know how to respond.

However, while you yet seem to be ego,
While you yet seem to be living in this world,
You are wont to search for love.
And when you seek outside yourself in your quest for love,
When you look outside to find
From whence love shall come to you,
You are but proving to yourself
That you do not understand the nature of Love,
The nature of God, and the nature of your Self.

Well, what if you WOULD discover the presence of Love?
Where shall you look?
I would speak with you this day about LOOKING WITHIN
In order to discover the presence of Love.

Now, can you discover the presence of Love
By LEARNING this Course?
For I have told you, perhaps to your confusion,
That learning is invisible.
You, while you yet seem to live in this world,
CAN NOT look for learning and see its essence.

Have you thought about what that statement entails?
What if you would study this Course in Miracles
Day after day after week after year?
And what if one of your brothers could ask you
Questions about what it says,
And you could answer perfectly,
And you could perhaps even quote
Many passages from this Course word for word?
Does that not, in some measure, seem to demonstrate learning?
But I have told you that learning is invisible.

But I have also told you previously that
When you hear the word "course," you do think of learning
Within your understanding of the world.
Although you are not here to learn, in that sense.
You are here to experience.
And that is true.

So if learning is invisible, what does that mean to you?
It means that here, when you share
The function of the Holy Spirit, here in this world,
Your function is healing.
Just as I have told you that your function in Heaven is creation,
Your function HERE is healing.
And healing is to make whole, to bring together.
For this world is based on the false belief in separation,
Above all, in the separation of cause and effect.
In Creation Itself, there is no separation of cause and effect.
They are simply one.
And what you experience simply IS.
What you experience IS you, and IS all beings.
And that is creation.

So if it is your desire to experience this Course,
It seems to demand the time in which you would study,
Perhaps discuss and perhaps write about,
Perhaps exchange ideas related to this Course,
All in the hopes that one day
You shall learn this Course.

Ah, but learning, in its essence, lies beyond your thinking,
And cannot even be defined.
You cannot look within and verify with your thinking mind

That you have learned anything of this Course.
Then what can you do
Within this world of illusion and separation?
You must look at your world, which seems separate from you,
And look at the EFFECTS of your learning.
For it seems to you that you, that your life, is the cause,
And that the effects follow.
And, indeed, within this world
That is what you must look upon.
And so I have told you that you can judge
The miracles you would do by their effects.
And you can judge your learning by the effects.

What if you WOULD learn this Course?
What if you would learn its essence, which is peace?
Then simply look at your world and ask yourself,
"Does my being, does my presence, bring and instill peace?
For if peace is what I am, and peace is what is within me,
Then peace will be expressed in my world."
And if you would desire to know if you understand love,
Then look at the effects. And ask yourself,
"In my presence do my brothers sense love?
Do they sense acceptance? Do they sense freedom?
Do they sense the absence of any reason to feel guilty?
Do they blossom into beings of love in my presence?"

Ah, there are some of you who would believe that
Your goal and your guidance are to challenge your brothers,
To prod them, and to bring them to a place of discontent,
If you will, in order to lead them to change.
But if you would apply the standard I have just given you,
Then you will see that that approach does not speak of love.
And I promise you, within that scenario, that within yourself
You have not yet experienced love. Do you see?

I have told you that you DO SEE what you EXPECT to see.
And you expect to see what you have invited into your life.
Well, who or what does the inviting?
You do, your essence does, which is mind.
Whatever you invite into your life
Is what you expect and what you see.
So when you look at your life here, in the world of form,
Then whatever you see, without exception,

Is what you have expected and invited,
Indeed, chosen to be your experience.
And that must reflect that which is within you.
So how can you see that which is within?
By looking at the effects of your life
You can become aware of what is within you.
And thus you also can become aware of your learning,
In its essence.

Can you rely upon form?
There is a great treachery that can be present
As you would look upon your outside world
In order to see what is within yourself.
For it is very difficult, indeed, for you as ego
Not to have written a script
Of how your outside world SHOULD look.
And you are wont to look out,
And if you see not the form that that script describes,
Then you tend to believe that you
Are not in touch with the inner truth.
And that is but a form of trying to control your world yourself,
All from the vantage point of an isolated, separate being.
But when you look upon your world
From that vantage point, you can not see love,
Just as the ego seeks but cannot find.
Do you see?

So if you would look upon your world to see what is within,
What you must look upon is YOUR OWN EXPERIENCE
Of the form you look upon.
It is MOST IMPORTANT that you not get caught up
In writing scripts about your world.
It is entirely possible for you to look upon your world
And to see what your brothers would label tragedy,
All the while you see nothing but the presence of love.
And when you do that, then you may know
That what is within you is, indeed, love.

Is it important that the form look like
What your world deems to be love?
And the answer is, no indeed.
It is most important that you not get caught up
In believing that love must present itself in a certain form.

So the real way to look within
Is to look out at your world
And then look at YOUR OWN RESPONSE, your own feelings.
And if your feeling is peace and gentleness,
And if your awareness is of harmony,
The harmony of one undivided will—
If your experience is of that,
Then that is what lies within you.
If you look at what your world would call
A beautiful expression of love
And you experience discontent,
Then you may be certain that within you
Is the same discontent that you are experiencing.
So look out at your world to see the effects,
But determine the effects by your own response,
By your own experience,
NOT by the appearance of the form.

This is most important, what I tell you this day.
As you seek for love, which you are wont to do,
Which you MUST do, for that is your design within this world,
You will find within yourself
The quiet, incessant discontent that must prod you,
And prod you, and prod you,
With infinite gentleness—
Until you come back to the understanding of what you are—
Until you realize that you ARE the presence of Love itself.

How can that work?
It is absolutely simple, in words.
There is nothing in the universe except Love.
God is Love. God is All That Is.
You are God. And you are All That Is.
And all of that is Love.
There is absolutely nothing that you can give which is not Love.
And there is absolutely nothing which you can seem to receive
Which is not love.

And the beauty of it all is this—
Love draws Love unto Itself.
There is inherent in the Oneness of all Creation
That which simply draws Love unto Itself.
And so as you seek, as you look within,

As you look for the effects of the miracles
You would learn of the Holy Spirit,
As you look, and as you touch upon the presence of Love,
You will feel a resonance, a fullness, a richness within you,
That tells you that you are Love drawing Itself unto Itself.

And as you apply miracles to everything in your life,
Then no matter the form, no matter what you look upon,
You will discover the fullness, the resonance, the richness,
The beauty of Love Itself.
And you will then realize that you
HAVE opened to the presence of Love
And are drawing It unto yourself,
Are drawing it unto Love.
For that is what you are.

My blessings upon you all. That is all.

GUILT II

Greetings again. I am Jeshua.
I have come this day to further, with you,
My discussion of *A Course in Miracles*.

Today I wish to speak with you about your greatest fear.
I have told you that anything which is not love must be fear.
But there is a fundamental fear which underlies all the rest,
A fundamental fear which is so great
That it can literally form the foundation of an entire world.
It is that fear of which I would speak this day.

I would speak with you this day about guilt,
About the guiltless Son of God, about your invulnerability,
And about your greatest fundamental fear.
It is true that the acceptance of guilt
Into the mind of the Son of God
Was the beginning of the separation.
It is also true that if you did not feel guilty
You could not attack.
It is true as well that condemnation is the root of all attack.
If you do not condemn, it is not possible for you to attack.
Also, if you did not feel guilty, you could not attack at all.
So it follows that if you did not feel guilty,
There would be no attack and no condemnation
Of any kind whatsoever
In the mind of the Son of God.

Try to pause for a moment and imagine a world
In which there existed NO COMDEMNATION
Of any kind whatsoever.
Try to imagine a life, even here in your space and time,
In which, no matter what you did, no matter what you said,
No matter what you thought or felt
At the innermost reaches of your being—
Nothing, no thought of chastisement or condemnation,
Could creep into your awareness.
There could not exist the slightest thought
That anything you would do, or think, or say, or feel,
Would be, in any sense, wrong.

Try to imagine a world, even here in space and time,
Where, without exception,
Everything that you did, or said, or thought, or felt,
Was accepted, accepted fully
With nothing but love.

And I am telling you this day that
Were it not for the presence of guilt
That is exactly the way your world, your life, your brother's life
Would be.
And even in your thinking minds,
You are bound to realize that that is desirable, is preferable,
To the world you experience here, and now.

The acceptance of guilt into the mind of the Son of God
Was the beginning of the separation.
In order to believe that you were separate at all,
Which notion is and was the design of this world,
Carefully planned out with your full awareness—
In order to believe in separation at all,
What it took was the lack of peace.
For wholeness, integration, the completeness of love,
MUST yield perfect peace.
So if you would pretend out the separation,
You must pretend the absence of peace.

The simple attempt to experience yourself
As being what you are not,
To experience God as being what God is not,
And above all, to insanely believe
That God and the Son of God could be different—
That notion, in an instant,
Brought unrest into the mind of the Son of God.
And in that same instant peace was gone.
And in that very same instant
The Son of God released the absence of peace,
And let it go.

But in order to even allow that notion
To enter the awareness of the Son of God,
It took the belief in separation.
Ultimately, the belief in separation is the belief
That cause and effect are different,

Or that God and the Son of God are different.
For God is cause. And His Son is the effect.

The notion of separation demanded the belief in time,
Which is really nothing more than the belief
In the separation of cause and effect.
Insofar as you would attempt to experience
The separation of cause and effect,
And entertain the absence of peace,
It must be that the Son of God would believe
That the absence of peace was NOT his own choice—
That the absence of peace was the effect,
And that the cause of that absence
Was DIFFERENT FROM the Son of God.
In short, it was essential that you believe
That some one, that some thing, ELSE,
Was the cause of the absence of your peace.

And thus arose the belief in separation—
The belief that some thing or some one ELSE
Was the cause of your lack of peace,
Which you deem to be the effect.
In an instant it came and went, and was gone.
But in that instant TIME, the grandest illusion,
Was created.
And thus you seem to live out, in what appears to be time,
The illusion of time and of this world,
And the illusion of your ultimate fear.
In the mind of the Son of God,
It took an instant for the thought of separation
To be born and to leave, to be dismissed
In the simple awareness of its silliness.
It was within time, not outside of time,
That the Son of God remembered not to laugh.
And thus this world of illusion and pain and fear
Was born.

Insofar as you desire to be here and stay here,
And to cherish your belief in separation,
It is ESSENTIAL that you blame someone or something else
For the absence of your peace.
You must see beings different from yourself as being the cause

For the absence of your peace.
And thus the separation was born.

What does it take for you to believe
That someone ELSE is the cause of your misery?
It takes the belief that someone or something else
CAN cause you to be miserable.
It takes the belief that someone or something else
Has a power over your life in such fashion
That he can determine whether or not you are at peace.
It takes, in simplest statement, the belief
That the Son of God is weak and vulnerable.

And if the Son of God IS weak and vulnerable,
What must the Son of God,
What must YOU do in order to exist at all,
In order to survive, if you will?
You must defend. You must fight.
And how do you defend?
Of course, you defend by attacking.
In order to survive, to live at all,
You must be on constant attack.
I did not say you must be READY TO ATTACK
If harm seems to threaten you.
I said you must BE ON CONSTANT ATTACK
In order to be able to exist at all
As an ego, as a separate being.

Thus I have told you that the ego believes, literally,
That attack is salvation.
And why is that?
What it is that you would be saved from?
Why is salvation a word that even enters your consciousness?
What is there to be saved from?
Of course, from your own death.
For that is the ultimate threat.
And if we speak of salvation in this Course,
It is simply the awakening to the realization that you cannot die.

So for you, ego, who believe yourself to be a separate being,
Whether you know it or not, whether you believe it or not,
Whether you like it or not,

YOUR EXISTENCE IS BASED ON THE BELIEF
THAT YOU MUST ATTACK IN ORDER TO EXIST.
This is true because your belief that you exist at all
Is founded on the notion that your entire world
Is in constant attack upon you.
If it were not so, you could not be discontent.
If it were not so, your peace would not be a thing you seek for;
Your peace would already be yours.
And guilt and condemnation and attack would no longer exist.

Are you beginning to see why I say this world is insane?
This world is a delusional attempt
To preserve a false notion of the Son of God
Who has been made mad by guilt.
Is it clear to you now?

But what if you knew that you were invulnerable?
The sane curriculum, the one the Holy Spirit teaches,
DEMANDS that you be aware
That you are, in fact, invulnerable.
Well, what if you knew that you WERE invulnerable?
What if you KNEW that nothing could happen to you,
That no experience could come into your life
Except that it be your own choice and your own creation?
In short, what if you knew that you were free?

If you realized, at the core of your being,
Even here in space and time,
That no experience could be present in your life
Except that it be your own choice and your own creation—
If you knew that, it would not be possible for you
To ever blame another for your discontent.

What happens if you cannot find someone ELSE to blame
For your misery and discontent,
All in your belief that you ARE vulnerable?
What do you do then?
In simplest statement, you blame God.
You blame God for your misery.
And arising out of your belief that you ARE vulnerable,
There is not one of you who has not looked out at his world
And thought that God is cruel.

And if the world actually were as you have imagined it,
You would be absolutely right.

So what if you did not even blame God
For being the cause of your discontent,
The cause of the absence of your peace,
The cause of the presence of your misery?
What if you did not BLAME your brothers, your world, or God?
In short, what if you knew that you were invulnerable?
Then you would be BEYOND any ability to even sense
That an attack was present at all.
And without recourse you would know
The same thing of your brother—
That no thing, no being, including yourself,
Could cause, in any sense, your brother's discontent,
Or his fear.

And in the absence of ever blaming another, including God,
In the presence of realizing that you could never harm another,
In your knowing that you could do nothing to your brother,
Guilt would have to disappear in the twinkling of an eye.
It is that simple.

What if you knew that you were invulnerable,
That you could not be attacked or harmed?
What if you knew that it was not possible for you to die?
For that, in simplest form,
Is the entire message of the resurrection.
I came to show you, in ultimate fashion,
That I could not be attacked or harmed,
And above all, that I could not die.
Thereby proving that the same is true for you.

Then what is this ultimate fear of which I have spoken this day?
Your ultimate fear lies in your resistance to believing
That what I have just said is true.
You are literally terrified of the notion that you are free—
That you are, and must be, the master of your own life.
You are terrified of the notion that there is but one will,
That there is but one Being in all of Creation,
That there is one grand harmony of existence
Which can only be described as the presence of Love.
You are terrified of that.

And why is that so?
BECAUSE OPENING TO THAT NOTION
DEMANDS THAT YOU DIE.
"That I die?" you ask.

It demands that those of you who perceive yourselves
As egos, as separate beings,
Must die to the belief in your separation.
You must die to the notion that the ego can exist.
You must die to the notion that attacking
Is what keeps you alive.
But those notions are ingrained into your human awareness
So strongly that the foundation of this world
Literally rests upon those beliefs.
And your fear, YOUR SINGLE GREATEST FEAR,
IS OF LOSING YOURSELF AND THIS WORLD
AS YOU KNOW IT.

That is why I have told you that you do not want this world.
The preservation of this world is based upon
Your belief in vulnerability and weakness and fear.
This world is what you see as yourself.
And to let it go, is literally, to the ego, to die.
And since you, ego, believe that you must attack
In order to live at all,
You must attack that notion as well.

But what would happen if your egos died?
Would this world disappear into nothingness?
Would you be called upon to sacrifice your life as you know it
If you were to give up your fear of redemption,
Your fear of Love, and ultimately, your fear of God?
Remember, it IS possible to experience the real world even here.
It IS possible to seem to walk through space and time
Without condemning, without attacking,
And without being afraid of God.
It IS possible to look upon, with human eyes,
What appears to be separate beings, separate bodies,
While at the same time you experience what lies
Beyond the illusion of separation,
While at the same time you experience the truth
That you and your brothers and sisters and God are One.

It IS possible to pretend a life that looks like separation,
And yet to experience Love.

And that is the essence of forgiveness itself—
Seeing beyond the illusion of separation
To the truth that life is One, and is nothing but Love.
That is why I have told you that the Son of God
Is not capable of giving anything but Love,
And is not capable of receiving anything but Love.

So as you perhaps read these words over and over again,
Simply open to the realization that the acceptance of guilt
Is what brings about your belief in separation.
Realize that the acceptance of guilt must be maintained
By the belief in attack,
And must be maintained by the belief
That you are constantly being attacked by your world
And, yes, even by God.

Then rethink how I have told you that your greatest fear
Is to let go of your belief in separation,
And your belief that attack is necessary
To make you what you are.
Your greatest fear is to open to the simple realization
That God ACTUALLY DOES LOVE YOU.

So, be with these words in your stillness.
Listen, and open.
The Son of God CAN NOT attack.
For all he can give is Love.
The Son of God is not different from any other being,
And, above all, is not different from God.
The Son of God is invulnerable.
There is nothing you receive or experience that,
Seen through the eyes of forgiveness,
Will not present itself as love and harmony and peace.
And there is nothing you can give
That will not present itself to life as the same.
And the cornerstone to your learning this Course,
To experiencing its truth at the core of your being—
That cornerstone lies in experiencing, beyond the words,
The truth of these words I have spoken this day.

So be still, and open.
You ARE the Son of God.
Guilt is, totally and completely, a figment of your imagination.
The Son of God is guiltless,
Because you are pure and clean and invulnerable
In every moment of your time.
You are guiltless because you ARE the presence of Love.
There is nothing you can give but Love Itself,
And nothing you can receive but Love Itself.
And everything that you would ever deign to give, or receive,
MUST be the Love and the presence of God.
For that is All That Is, and is exactly what you are.

My blessings upon you all. That is all.

TIME AND THE PRESENT

Greetings again. I am Jeshua.
I have come this day to further, with you,
My discussion of *A Course in Miracles*.

You, the real You, Spirit, Son of God, are eternal.
There is no end to the reality of what you are.
Or, in your words, you will live forever.
And do you not hear that even the word "eternal,"
And the word "forever," speak of time?
But you cannot free yourself of the deep inner realization
That you simply exist—
That you do not, and cannot, die.

Yet, here in this world of illusion,
You see yourself as separate.
Separation demands attack.
Attack demands condemnation.
And condemnation and its judgment demand the past.
For they demand that someone or something
Has made you into what you are.

In one sense you believe (because it is true)
That you exist forever.
And in another sense you believe in time.
For time is the belief that cause and effect are separate.
And it is time that allows you to believe
That you can be separate at all.

Your belief in time does many things for you.
It is time which allows you to believe
That effect, which is you, is separate from your cause.
Ultimately the cause is God,
And the effect is you, the Son of God.
And in reality there is no separation whatsoever
Between you and God Itself,
Between your will and God's Will,
Between what you are and what you have been,
Or what you shall become in the sense of your time.
There is no separation at all, in reality.

But it is the belief in the separation of cause and effect
That allows you to believe that separation can be at all,
That you can be a separate being, isolated and alone.
And in your insanity, truly, you somehow believe
That being isolated and alone is what brings you joy.
How absurd. You can tell that this instant, can you not,
As I express it in that way?

But time serves another function.
It is time that allows you, WITHIN TIME,
To believe that you are eternal,
Which truth you already know at the core of your being.
That is one of the functions of time itself, as you have made it.
You believe that the past is the cause,
Which brings you to the effect, which is this moment.
However, this moment can serve as nothing more
Than the past which brings you to the future.
And so this moment now is nothing more
Than a transition between past and future.
For the past has made you what you ARE
And what you SHALL BECOME.
Do you hear the words of the future?

And what does that do for you?
That provides you with the sense of continuity.
That allows you, within time, to believe that you SHALL exist.
And when I tell you that
Time is but illusion and shall come to its end,
That is, oh, so difficult for you to comprehend
With your thinking minds.
And that difficulty in comprehending the end of time
Is part of your design of this world.
For if you could comprehend the end of time,
Then you could comprehend ceasing to exist.
For if the past carries you into the future, which you believe,
And suddenly the future is no more,
Then what shall become of you? Do you see?

And so one of the functions of time, as you perceive it,
Is to allow you to believe that you shall exist forever.
And even though bodies seem to die,
You cannot free yourself of the belief
That somehow you, whatever you are, continue to exist.

And thus you design structures which allow you
To believe in that continuity.
And you call them heaven and hell and reincarnation,
And the rest of a long list.
And all of them are but terms and definitions
Which allow you to believe that you do not die,
That you are eternal.

Now, I have spoken to you of love and fear
Many times before this day.
I have told you that Love, in its essence, is changeless.
Love is exchanged.
Love is given and received and grows.
Love is magnified in the giving and the receiving.
But the essence of Love is changeless.

And if you hear the word "changeless,"
What must you then entertain?
You must entertain the notion of eternity.
For if Love cannot change, clearly It cannot die.
And if you are Love, if the reality of what you are
Is not form and bodies, is not male and female,
And space and time, but is simply Love Itself,
Then of course it follows that YOU are changeless, and eternal,
And cannot die.

Ah, but there are two emotions, do you remember?
Love and fear.
And fear is literally the building block
Of this entire world you see.
This too I have told you before.
For in your fear, which must arise
Out of your belief in separation—
In your fear, you see a world,
You see beings separate from yourself.
In your fear you see a world which out of its past
Determines what you are.
You see brothers who are the cause of your misery,
And of your sadness,
And the cause also of your joy and of your love,
As you seem to experience it here.
For you perceive everything that happens to you,
Everything you experience,

As being caused by someone or something else.
And that arises from your belief in separation.
And thus it is, literally,
That fear has made the world you see.

And in a sense, you believe the world you see
To somehow be eternal.
For is it not difficult for you to comprehend
Living forever without a body?
And do not most of you, at some time in your lives,
Conceive of an afterlife which involves bodies
And this same form of space and time
To which you are accustomed? Of course you do.
And God, for many of you, has been the old man
With the long gray beard sitting on a throne in heaven,
All because you cannot easily let go of the source of your fear.
Your projection of a "body" upon God arises from your fear.

But I have told you over and over
That God is Spirit, and nothing more.
Now if Love is changeless,
WHAT IF YOU COULD SEE YOUR WORLD
THROUGH THE EYES OF LOVE?
Could you then comprehend eternity and living forever
Without having to believe in the past
As being the cause of this moment, the present,
And ultimately of being the cause of the future,
Which the present is to become?

Remember the two emotions, love and fear.
Well, what you do is look upon them
As being the opposites of what they actually are.
You look upon fear and call it love;
You look upon Love and see it through the eyes of fear.

But if you do look upon fear and call it love,
How does that happen?
Remember, as I have explained to you this day,
Fear is ultimately what defines for you what you are.
And ultimately it is your fear, within space and time,
That promises to you that you shall live forever.
And this you respond to, however half-heartedly—
This you respond to by trying to be grateful.

For if your fear brings you the promise of eternity,
And somehow you know that you DO live forever,
Then you must be grateful for that
Which promises your eternity to you—
Even if the promise might be of eternal punishment,
Which many of you do entertain as a belief.

And if you look upon Love and call it fear,
How does that work?
If Love is changeless, Love does not have,
And cannot have, a past.
Love does not have, and cannot have, a future.
And if you look upon Love, if you open yourself to Love,
What you shall find is that you simply ARE.
If you look upon Love, there is no past.
For there cannot be the separation of cause and effect.
And therefore, there cannot be time, at all.

You are wont to ask, ''Has God always existed?
Will God exist forever?''
And those are the questions of your time, and of your fear.
And there is but one answer—GOD IS.
And since God is Love, LOVE IS.
And since you also are Love, and are the Son of God,
YOU SIMPLY ARE.

Can you find the presence of Love here in your world?
Or, as I have expressed it, can you find the present,
Can you find the present as being that which simply exists?
Does there exist a place where you can live
And experience the changelessness of Love,
And of yourself, and of God, and of your brother?
Is that possible?
And if it is possible, can that free you from the fear
That defines for you your separation and your past?
And the answer is, indeed you can.

Then how DO YOU find the present?
You simply look upon your world, your brother, and yourself,
WITHOUT A PAST.
''Without a past?'' you ask.
That seems even more insane to you
Than this world of illusion which I describe

And tell you is insane.
For how can you look upon your world without a past?
Should you become unable to remember your own name?
Should you become unable to remember
How to eat and to sleep, and how to talk?
Should you become unable to remember where your home is?
Should you become unable to remember
Your friends and your loved ones, your family?
Is that what I am saying to you?
And the answer is ultimately—no, not at all.

For I realize full well that you have chosen
Space and time and the illusions
Which you call your bodies and your world—
Homes, cities and cars, the sky,
The wind, the weather, food, all of it—
You have chosen this as a vehicle, hear me well,
THROUGH WHICH YOU CAN LEARN
TO EXPERIENCE LOVE.
For Love is what you are.
And I promise you there is absolutely nothing in your world
Which you cannot experience as Love, if you choose to do so.
AND THAT, IN SIMPLEST STATEMENT,
IS THE KEY TO FINDING THE PRESENT.

For when you look upon yourself and your brothers out of fear,
You see that they have made you what you are.
And you see that you need to defend, lest they, in your future,
Might make you into something
Which you do not prefer or desire.
And you look upon your brothers as having a past
Which has made them into what they are in this moment.
And there is no past which does not have within it
That which you find undesirable.
So every brother, just as with yourself,
Brings to this moment, in the sense of your time,
That which you would find undesirable,
And which you would defend against,
Which is exactly the same as to attack.
There is no difference at all between defense and attack.
Be not deceived about this point.

How can you let go of your own past, and your brother's past?
And it is really quite easy.
IT IS SIMPLY TO CHOOSE LOVE INSTEAD OF FEAR.
For when you choose fear you choose a past,
A past which brings that to you
Which you must defend against.

But what if you choose Love,
The Love which is changeless?
And remember it is the changelessness of Love
Which insures your continuity, your foreverness,
The fact that you are eternal beyond time itself.
What if you choose Love?
And how do you do that?
Simply BY DOING IT—by choosing Love.
That is all.

And what does it require to choose Love?
You simply remember what I have told you—
That Love is all there is.
There is nothing the Son of God can give except Love.
There is nothing the Son of God can receive except Love.
For Love is all there is.
So what if you choose this moment, and from henceforth,
To open your being to the presence of Love—
That means this—
What if you choose to see each moment, each circumstance,
Every single event in your life, WITHOUT EXCEPTION,
As the act of, the gift of, and the presence of, Love?
What if you, no matter the form,
Looked upon your brother's presence in your life
As an act of love?
NO MATTER THE FORM.

I tell you that IS entirely possible.
You CAN see the real world here.
For that is the Vision of Christ, the Vision of the Holy Spirit.
And that shall become your vision as you choose to open to it.
And what it takes is the choice to see every circumstance
As the gift that it is, as the act, the presence, of Love.

And what does that mean?
It means to see your brother, your sister,

Your life, and yourself, in Light.
For vision requires Light.
Vision requires not seeing the shadowy figures of the past
That seem to come and go
And cause you to be what you are.
For all of those are your fear, chosen by you,
And projected onto the image of your own life.

If you look upon yourself as the Light that you are,
And extend that Light out to your brothers, your sisters,
Out to your life,
Then what you shall see is Love—ALWAYS.
And the way to see reality, the way to perceive truly here,
Is to look upon it ALL
Through the awareness of your own reality,
Which is, in simplest form, the presence of Light,
The presence of Love.

Thus I tell you this day that you are NOT the captive of time.
And your belief in time, which seems to flow from the past,
Into the transition of the present, into the future,
And which would seem to guarantee that you are eternal,
Is but that which would imprison you within your fear.
And as you let go of fear, and fear's function of time,
As you open to Love and its changelessness,
Then eternity, eternity as it actually is,
Becomes your own gift, which has been brought to you
By the presence of Light, and the presence of Love.
And all it takes to experience thusly
Is for you to open to its presence within yourself,
And within your brothers.

There is nothing in Creation but Love.
No gift that can be given that is not Love.
No gift that can be received that is not Love.
No gift of any kind that can be given or received
Which ultimately is not you,
And is but a reflection of the Light of the world.
For that is what, as the Son of God, you are,
And what, in the sense of your time,
You shall always be.

Blessings upon you all. That is all.

THE REAL WORLD

Greetings again. I am Jeshua.
What we have been discussing of late is guilt.
And if you would escape from guilt,
What you must do is open to the awareness of the real world.
For in the real world there is no guilt.
In the real world there is no past.
For, as I have told you, it is guilt which defines your past.
And without the sense of guilt,
Without your need to believe that something or someone else
Is the cause of your being what you are—
Without that, there would be no guilt at all.

In simplest statement, that is what the real world is—
A place in which you have been released, by yourself,
To never to look "out there"
In order to determine what and who you are.
THE REAL WORLD IS A PLACE
WHERE YOU ONLY LOOK WITHIN.

And I have told you that the real world
Is not at all like the world you see.
There is no sun and moon, no day and night.
There is no darkness at all.
There are no homes and structures and stores.
There are no things which you need.
But above all, in the real world, there are no bodies.

I have also said to you something which may seem confusing,
Or at best difficult for you to understand.
For I have told you that the world you see must be denied,
Because the very sight of it, THE VERY SIGHT OF IT,
Is what costs you a different kind of vision.
I told you there are but two worlds—
The world you see, and the real world.
And you cannot see both.
And what determines the world you see
Is that which you have not denied,
But above all, that which you cherish,
That which you hold dear unto yourself.

Those words are most important—
"That which you hold dear unto yourself."

THE WORLD YOU SEE MUST BE DENIED.
That is absolutely true if you would experience the real world,
And the peace and love that it brings.
You must deny the world you see,
Its bodies and houses and stores and things—
You must deny all of that.
But what does that mean?
Does that mean you need spend your days and nights
Here in space and time saying,
"That house is not there.
The sun is not in the sky. I do not feel its warmth.
That person I seem to see is not there."
Does it mean for you to deny this world
And its seeming laws and processes?
Does it mean you should not eat, not drink,
Nor breathe your air?
Is that what it means to deny the world you see?

Do you realize that when I walked this earth
Two thousand years ago,
I DID walk this earth?
I wore a cloak sometimes to keep me warm.
I breathed the air, just as you do.
I ate as you do. I drank as you do.
But I tell you truly, I did deny the world,
Throughout my entire life,
Just as I am now suggesting that you do for yourself.

How can that be?
What does it truly mean to deny the world?
And what does "seeing the world" mean as well,
Especially if seeing this world costs you vision,
All the while vision is one of your goals here?
The key to the answer lies in the words
"What you cherish" and "what you hold dear."
And the key also lies in the one question
Which the ego always, always, asks.

Everything you do as ego, as a separate isolated being,
Takes the form of the answer to one question.

And that is this—What am I? or Who am I?
And that, as I have told you before, is what the ego is,
The collection of answers you have to the questions
Who am I? What am I?
And those answers form your beliefs about what you are.

What is the ONLY reason that you, ego,
Would cherish anything of this world of illusion?
You may explore the answer, if you will,
As often and as much as you like.
But what I tell you is true—
Everything that you cherish and hold dear in this world
Is due to the fact that what you cherish
Provides you with an answer to the question "Who am I?"
In essence, that which you cherish, that which you hold dear,
DEFINES WHO YOU ARE.
But beyond that, literally, within this world,
Those answers are that which seems to give you life itself.
As you look out at your world
And discover answers "out there" about who you are,
Those answers become the source of your life,
They become who you are.
But that process, as I have already told you,
Is what gives rise to guilt in the first place.

So what does it mean to deny the world?
Does it mean not to see your houses and your cars,
Your bodies and stores, the sun and the stars?
Does it mean to somehow be blind
And not to see them with your eyes?
The answer is, no indeed.
That is not what I mean when I say you must deny the world.
TO DENY THIS WORLD IS SIMPLY TO REALIZE
THAT IT IS NOT WHAT YOU ARE.
To deny the world is simply to realize,
At the level of your experience,
At the core of your being,
Beyond question, beyond doubt, beyond thought itself,
That what you are in reality
IS NOT DETERMINED BY THE WORLD YOU SEE.

And if you can look upon your homes and your stores,
And all of that which you see with your eyes—

If you can look upon that and be free of needing it,
Then you do not cherish it, and you do not hold it dear.
And THAT is to deny your world.
If you can look upon the images you see,
The images of space and time,
And realize at the level of your experience
That it is not what you are,
And that it does not determine who and what you are,
Then, truly, you have denied your world.

And if I, two thousand years ago, spoke to men and said,
"Deny yourself and follow me," what I meant was this—
Simply deny that you are what you see in your world.
And come and follow the path that I will show you,
The path unto the truth about what you are.

And what of "seeing" then,
If the very sight of your world of space and time
Makes it impossible for you to see the real world—
What of "sight" and of "seeing?"
And 'tis very simple. 'Tis the same.
For that which you SEE is truly that which you experience.
And what you are is what you have become.
And what you are within is reflected
In what you seem to see without.
And when, within, you know the simple truth
That you are not a body,
You will not be tempted by the circumstances
That seem to befall that body.
Rather you will be free.
You will be free of this world.

Does that mean that the images of space and time
Will disappear?
And the answer is—no, indeed.
For that demands knowledge.
And knowledge is that which you cannot reach,
You cannot become, while you are yet here
In the world of perception,
Even though your perception might be true.

So if you would attain the real world,
You simply deny the one you seem to see with your eyes.

And that is simply to realize it is not what you are.
And how do you do that?
Of that I have spoken before.
YOU OPEN TO YOUR RELEASE FROM THE PAST.
For in your belief in space and time and the world of illusion,
You believe that the past and its circumstances
Have literally made you what you are.
And without a past you become free of all of that.
As you stand, complete and pure and clean, without a past,
You simply experience, in that moment,
The presence of Love,
The presence, the experience, of what you truly are.

Now I have told you that the ego teaches you
To reach out and GET, to obtain, things.
And why do you do that?
You do that to define who you are.
And you become identified, if you will, with your home,
With your car, with your friends,
With your closest relationships,
With how much money you may have.
This you know well.
And as you identify with things,
You are being taught that to obtain things
Is to become who you are.

And yet what happens as you obtain things?
Your goal becomes more money, a bigger house,
A better car, a more attractive body.
And the list goes on and on. This you also know well.
As you obtain things, you use them to define who you are,
As that which keeps you apart from your brothers, your sisters.
So as you would follow the advice of the ego
And seek to obtain things,
You but separate yourself further from your brothers.

And, because of the deep inner awareness of your Oneness,
Which you cannot shake,
This destroys your peace.
So even as you obtain more and more things,
You but detract yourself from the presence of peace.
And this you all know, as you smile and say,
"Money cannot buy happiness."

It is that of which you speak when you say those words.
And all of that comes from looking outside yourself
In order to gain, in order to become, who you are.
And all of that arises from the very essence of guilt itself.
And what does that do?
That but perpetrates your belief in separation,
And with it the absence of your peace.

And what is healing?
Healing is joining.
Healing is the coming together
That brings peace and denies separation.
And healing, as I have told you, is quite simply
The release from the past.
Because it is the past that determines who you are,
That defines your ego, that places within your ego
The demand to get and to become.
And all of that is really the demand
To isolate yourself from your brothers and your world.
And as you would release the past,
You shall be healed.

If you would attain the real world,
You must deny this one,
Which is simply to realize that it is not what you are,
And furthermore, that it has no power to dictate what you are,
And more importantly for you in space and time,
That it has no power to dictate what you experience.
You are free to experience peace,
Independent of the props of space and time.
Just as you are free to experience the absence of peace,
Independent of the props of your space and time.

But what if your real desire
Is to move totally beyond this world,
To go, if you will, from perception unto knowledge?
What is the difference between the two?
If you can begin to attain the real world
And realize that what you see with your eyes is not seeing,
And realize that this world of space and time
Is not what you are,
And does not determine what you are—
If you can come to that place, is that enough?

Many of you become frustrated at this juncture.
For here in your space and time, it is quite enough.
In fact, it is the best that you can do.
If you would perceive at all,
Perception demands that you look upon your world
With your eyes,
Seemingly as an isolated being.
And so it is not possible to perceive your freedom in any sense,
Except to have the realization that it is YOU
Who are doing the perceiving.

And what happens when you experience knowledge,
Which lies beyond this world?
When you experience knowledge,
Perception passes away into the nothingness that it is.
You open to the presence of creation,
Which is simply the awareness that all is One,
And that there is no separation of any kind
Within whatever it is the Son of God creates,
Within whatever it is the Son of God experiences.

If you would perceive truly,
You will look upon aspects of your world,
And you will sense that you are One with them.
That will take the form of your awareness
That your brother's will and yours are the same,
That you are in perfect harmony.
You will then look upon every circumstance
From that vantage point.
That will be from the place of Love,
Which can only be found in the present,
Free of the past, and free of guilt.

However, even from that vantage point,
You seem to be seeing yourself AND your brother and saying,
"I am in harmony WITH my brother."
And even those words speak of separation, do they not?
In the state of knowledge there is the complete awareness
That there are no aspects at all.
You and your brother LITERALLY become One.
You and all of Creation, without exception,
ARE the Oneness that is God.

ɔu have designed this world of space and time
n such a way that you cannot, from within perception,
Experience knowledge.
For if you could, in a moment of knowledge,
You would completely see the truth and be gone.
And that was not your desire
When you made this world of illusion.
Thus it is that the last step must be taken by God.
But remember, there is no separation between you and God.
So the last step actually must be taken by you.

And how do you take that last step
From perception unto knowledge?
How do you completely move beyond any perception at all,
Into the full and perfect awareness of the presence of God?
You do it by completely and fully
Relinquishing any desire whatsoever to remain an ego.
You move from perception unto knowledge
By completely letting go of any need
To have answers to the question ''Who am I?''
You move from perception unto knowledge
By completely letting go of any desire whatsoever
To exist as an ''I'' which would seem to be separate
From the rest of your world.

And in that place, when you have released, if you will,
All attachment to the ego in any form,
Then from what shall seem like a place beyond space and time
You shall move quickly and joyfully unto knowledge,
Beyond space and time, literally out of this world,
Into a place where all the words I have spoken this day
Shall cause you to look back
And but chuckle at the silliness,
At the game of fear and guilt you seem to have played
For all of those minutes and days and years of your time.

If you would attain the real world,
You begin by denying the one you see.
And as you deny it, you simply realize
That it is not what you are,
And, furthermore, cannot determine what you are.
You simply realize that you, in this moment,
Are absolutely free of any past you may have imagined.

And in that awareness you shall free your brothers
Of any past you may have imagined about them,
Or that they may have imagined about themselves.
And in that moment, free of the past,
Healing shall occur.
And healing shall be but your joining with your brothers
In the place of Love,
Which is simply to realize that you share one will,
And that there is no difference between you.

And as you, in your space and time,
Evolve further and further into that awareness,
All attachment that you seem to have to ego,
To the desire to define at all who you are,
Shall slowly slip away until the day
When it is completely, in an instant, gone.
And in that instant you, in your openness,
Shall feel as if you are carried away,
Carried away by the arms of God,
Into a new world of complete knowledge,
Perfect peace, perfect Oneness,
And perfect harmony beyond anything you can imagine
With your thinking minds.

And in the moment when that happens,
You shall celebrate, with the greatest of joy,
That you are once again fully in the presence of God.
And with the same joy,
You shall realize that you had never left at all,
Because you and God are one and the same,
And have always been so.

Blessings upon you all. That is all.

RELEASE FROM GUILT

Greetings again. I am Jeshua.
I have been speaking to you of late
About the subject of guilt.
And the only thing which you need understand,
Which you need internalize,
Which you need to allow to become your experience—
The only thing you need understand
Is that the Son of God is indeed guiltless.
You are absolutely free of guilt.

How can that be?
Because guilt, as you think of it,
Brings to your mind the belief that you have
DONE something, BEEN something, THOUGHT something,
Which, by some standard, is not acceptable.
And insofar as you believe that God exists,
Then God becomes the source of that standard.
And thus you believe that you have done something
Which is not acceptable to God.
And that is the source of your belief in guilt.

Can you imagine that God, the invulnerable,
The all-knowing, all-wise, all-powerful God,
Would have designed a universe in which
He could be prey to the actions or thoughts of His children?
If God is invulnerable, then God is literally beyond offense.
To be invulnerable means to be beyond offense, beyond attack,
Even beyond the awareness that an attack might be present.
And that is the nature of God.

If you can, for a moment, look upon God in that light.
Can you still imagine that YOU could do or be something
Which is not acceptable to God? Of course not.

Then from whence comes this deep-seated feeling of guilt
Which I have told you is the source of your fear,
The source of your belief in separation,
And ultimately the source of this entire world of illusion?

From whence does it come?
Do you remember that I have told you
That the Son of God IS the Son of God?
There is no gift the Son of God can give except that it be Love.
There is no gift the Son of God can receive
Except that it be Love.
Such is the nature of God, and the nature of His Son.
Over that you have no choice.
Rejoice that that is so!

In the instant that it took to imagine all of space and time,
This false belief in separation,
And the realization that it was only worth
Being dismissed with a chuckle—
In that instant in which time was born,
The instant the Son of God needed
In order to play out this unreal world,
This insane notion that he could be separate at all—
In that instant many things happened.
And all of it, I assure you,
Arose out of the Oneness of All That Is.

Be aware that when I speak to you as an ego,
I make it sound as if God is separate from you,
And that God's Will is somehow different from your own.
Yet I have told you many times,
God's Will and yours are, and must be, the same.
Such is the nature of God.
I also told you that, in that instant,
God placed within you the Holy Spirit,
Who would serve to lead you back home,
Back to the awareness of what you truly are.
In order to guarantee that the Son of God must return home,
Must return to the awareness of what he truly is,
God placed within you,
IN CONJUNCTION WITH YOUR OWN WILL,
A quiet, deep, pervading discontent.

Part of the design of this world of illusion
Was the placement within you of that discontent,
Which prompts you to realize
That something is not right within you.
And what does that discontent do?

It prompts you, in subtle fashion,
But in a way which cannot be denied,
To search, and search, and search
Until you wend your way
Back through the sojourns of space and time
To the truth of what you are.
It prompts you to seek out the Atonement.
You can delay the seeking
For as long, in your time, as you wish.
But the quiet discontent placed there by you,
In conjunction with God,
Will not go away until you return home.

Well, what of this discontent?
It leaves you with the feeling
That something is not right in your life.
And that feeling that something is not right,
That feeling deep within you,
The one that will guide you home,
Is the essence of the guilt which has allowed,
And which has led to, this entire world of illusion.
Do you see?

Ah, but how would God look upon the discontent?
How would the Holy Spirit see this deep discontent
That lives within you, and which demands,
As I have told you, that this IS a required Course.
If all that the Son of God can give and receive is Love,
Then what of the discontent?
What of the knowing within the Son of God
That something he has done is not right?
Ah, what if you could look with the eyes of the Holy Spirit
Upon that same discontent, what would you see?
You would see a beacon.
You would see a light that shines
Within the mind, the heart, of the Son of God,
Which serves to lead him home. Do you see?

And so you carry a belief in your own guilt,
A sense that you have done something wrong.
And from that, all of it follows.
You cannot bear to look within
And realize that your discontent is your own choice.

And thus you look without.
Thus you seek to blame another for what and who you are.
And thus separation arises.
And thus in your blaming your brother
For making you what you have become,
It becomes possible that you have made your brother
What he has become.
Thus it follows that you have done something to him.
And ultimately, you blame God for all of this.
All of it follows because, in order to honor space and time,
You are unable to look within and acknowledge
That you are free,
To acknowledge that it is your self
Who creates and chooses your own existence.

But the Holy Spirit sees all of that
As but a beacon that guides you home.
And what a gift of love the Son of God
Has given to himself. Do you see?
What if you had come here to space and time
With the possibility of becoming mired
And trapped here forever?
Then God would not be God.
And you could not be God's Son.
There MUST BE within you that which leads you home.
And that which you would call guilt,
And sometimes curse in the darkness of your nights,
Is nothing but a beacon that sings of love,
And guides you home.
And so you see, this cloud of guilt
Which seems to hang over your existence here
Is really the whisper of Love.

And what if you would desire to be released from your guilt?
What if you would desire to be released from the discontent
That drives you on your journey home?
What if you would design to be free of that?
How can you do it?
YOU DO IT IN RELATIONSHIP TO GOD'S SON.
What if you were able to open to
The Vision of the Holy Spirit, the Vision of Christ?
What if you were able to realize that no matter—
No matter the choice, no matter the action,

matter the thought, no matter the word,
o matter, without exception—
What if you were able to realize that
Whatever you seemed to experience
In the presence of God's Son
Was always, always, prompted by the beacon of light,
By the presence of Love
Which is slowly and incessantly leading you home?

Remember, if you would find the present,
If you would release the past, if you would release the future
From the belief that the past has caused it,
You must choose to look upon Love instead of fear.
And what if you looked upon your own life,
And were able to interpret every thought, every action,
Every word as nothing more than than which you have done
In order to help yourself find your home within?
Then can you not look upon the child of God with love,
Whether it be your brother or yourself?
And I tell you, of course you can.

So if you would be released from guilt,
You must release your brother from his guilt.
And you do that by seeing everything that he offers you
As a gift of love.
And even when it becomes difficult to do that,
You simply realize that every action taken by the Son of God
Is for the purpose of guiding him home.
Sometimes, in fact often, the paths you may choose
Are simply for the purpose of helping you to realize that
That particular path is NOT the pathway of peace.
And in your time, believe it or not,
Each of you will learn that if it is not of peace,
It is not worth repeating.

And so it is even Love that guides you
As you play out your beliefs in separation,
As you choose some of the blind alleys
For the purpose of learning what is not Love.
And thus you will learn that the discontent you feel
Is but that which does guide you home,
And does guide you unto peace.

It is most important that you realize
That you must be willing to look upon every brother,
WITH NO EXCEPTION,
In order to be released from guilt yourself.
You cannot select out SOME OF your brothers.
You cannot select out what seems to be part of the Son of God,
See his actions and words and thoughts as love,
And yet of another say that it is not so.
For if you do that, you are making love special.
You are selecting.
And you are furthering your belief in separation.

If you would truly be released from your own guilt,
If you would be released
From the discontent that leads you home,
If you would discover the peace of Heaven,
Then do it thusly—
Realize that there is no past, only this moment.
And in this moment the gift
Which the Son of God brings to you,
And which you bring to yourself,
Is, and must be, a gift of Love.
For there is nothing else to bring or to give.
Realize that everything in space and time,
No matter how unskillful or unwise it seems,
Is prompted by the inner beacon
Which constantly whispers to the mind of the Son of God,
"You are not at home in this world.
And the pathway of your joy, the pathway of Love,
The pathway of peace,
Is different from what you follow this moment."
Realize that always it is a gift of Love,
Placed within the mind of the Son of God by Himself,
In conjunction with God's will.
And above all, realize it is the gift of Love
To the Oneness that IS the Son of God.

And when you do that, when you release from guilt
By simply realizing that the imagined guilt that prompts it all
Is but the presence of Love
Whispering to the depths of your mind—
When you can look upon every brother, every action, as Love
And open to that—

Then that is what you shall see, and what you shall cherish.
And that is what you shall discover entering your own life.
For what you cherish is what you put your faith in,
What you believe in, and what you shall experience.
For such is the law of mind.

Then what shall come to you, without effort,
Is the willingness to simply accept, with love, the Son of God.
What shall come to you, without effort, is the willingness
To trust your brothers who truly are One with you.
What shall come to you, without effort, is the willingness
To, in every circumstance, open your being
To the presence of Love, to the presence of the Holy Spirit,
And to the awareness of God.
For there is nothing else to become aware of.
Since God IS All That Is.

And in those moments when that vision becomes your choice,
You will find that the discontent deep within is gone.
In those moments you shall find yourself at peace.
As you open to Love,
As you honor the Son of God who is Love,
As you open your heart and your being to him,
You open truly to the peace of God,
To the peace of Heaven.

And you will realize in those moments that, truly,
Guilt is gone.
For no longer will you need
That which prods you into discontent,
But which is really Love in disguise.
No longer will you need that,
Or all of the stories you have made up
About beings separate from yourself
Who have made you what you are.

You will simply be aware of your freedom.
You will simply be aware deep within
Of a quiet voice that speaks of peace,
That sings you a song of Oneness and joining,
That does not comprehend separation
And the insanity it would try to imagine.
You will simply become aware,

In those moments of peace and quietness and love,
Of what you truly are,
Which is the Son of God.

And then you will have moved, literally,
Thousands of years along the journey
Which must, which MUST, take you home.

My blessings upon you all. That is all.

LEARNING THE TRUTH

Greetings again. I am Jeshua.
I have come this day to further, with you,
My discussion of *A Course in Miracles*.

I have spoken to you much about the ego's thought system.
And to speak of it always implies that there is
Another thought system which speaks of the truth.
And so I begin today our discussion
Of the subject of truth.

You see, the ego uses logic quite well.
And starting from certain suppositions,
It weaves a thought system which is strong enough
To cause you to believe that an entire world is real,
When it is not real at all.

The Holy Spirit, which speaks for the truth,
Uses logic just as well as does the ego.
And the logic of the Holy Spirit also
Requires certain suppositions.
I have told you that you are blessed,
And simply do not know that you are.
You are blessed by God, by me, by Creation Itself.
But here in your illusion,
You simply are not aware of that.

Have you thought to yourself,
"What does it mean to be blessed?"
If I end these chapters with the words,
"My blessings upon you all,"
Have you thought about what that means?
TO BLESS MEANS TO GIVE TO ONE
THE GIFT OF YOUR VISION OF THE TRUTH
THAT HE IS A PERFECT SON OF GOD.
And when I say "My blessings upon you,"
I am simply reminding you that I give to you,

In that instant and always, my vision, my certainty,
That you are, in your perfection, in your beauty,
The Son of God.
And as God has blessed you, it is the same.

God knows you only in the beauty
Of your perfection, of your guiltlessness.
And all it takes for you to become aware of the fact
That you are blessed is to open your willingness
To becoming aware of that truth.

Ah, but a problem lies herein.
This world, as I have told you,
Is based upon the denial of truth itself.
And I have told you that to deny is not to know.
And what allows this world of illusion to SEEM real
Is the fact that, here in space and time,
You do not, and cannot, know the truth of what you are.

Can you within this world,
Within the thought system of the ego,
Become aware that you are, indeed, blessed?
And the answer is—no, you cannot.
Within that thought system,
You cannot become aware of what you are.
For it is based, literally, upon the belief
That you do not know what you are,
Or upon the belief that you are something
Which you are not, and can never be.
Do you see?

And so there are some conditions to be met
If you would come to understand the truth.
And one is the realization that
Within the thought system of the ego
You cannot learn directly of what you are.
And so you must learn of what you are INDIRECTLY.
That is one of the conditions
Of learning the truth of what you are.

You cannot give something which you do not have.
Even the ego understands that.
So what if you could learn to bless your brother?

What if you could learn to give your brother
The gift of your vision of his perfection as the Son of God?
That would demand that you HAVE IT TO GIVE,
And therefore that it is what you are.
So we will approach your learning of the truth
By helping you to realize that you will discover
The truth of what you are
As, and when, you give it away.

You cannot give that which you do not have.
Remember that truth.
Whenever you give that which is false,
That which speaks of darkness and death,
You are giving what you BELIEVE you are.
But that is not WHAT you are, and you cannot give it in truth.
Yet you seem to give it, and then to believe it of yourself.
Thus if you would teach another that he can die,
You bring upon yourself, in the giving,
The curse of your own death.
And it cannot be otherwise.

But the learning of truth
Has another even more important condition.
He who would learn the truth about himself must do so
As what I have called the happy learner.
For God wants a happy learner.
And the Holy Spirit wants a happy learner.
Indeed, you cannot come to understand
The truth of what you are
Lest it be from a place of happiness.
"What does that mean?" you might ask.
For if you are happy, it is so difficult to wish to change at all.
But the happiness of which we speak
Is the rejoicing that shall come within you
As you celebrate the fact that you DESIRE to change.

As you look within,
There is a simple question which you need ask,
In order to become a happy learner.
And the question is so simple. It is this—
"Am I at peace? Do I have what I would call the peace of God?"
If you, even as an ego, would think about God,
You do, in fact, believe that God has peace.

For can you, even as an ego, imagine
An all-knowing, all-wise, all-powerful creator of the universe
Who would create a universe whose function would be
To destroy his own peace?
And the question is absurd enough
That you might even laugh were you to say yes.
We speak often of the peace of God.
For indeed, God IS at peace

And so I admonish you, ask yourself, ''Am I at peace?''
And in order to answer the question, you must ask,
''Is there anything, ANYTHING, that can threaten my peace?''
For if there is, it is not, and cannot be, the peace of God.
''If I lost my home, would I still be at peace?
If all of my physical wealth were taken from me,
Would I still be at peace?
If all of my loved ones left my life, would I still be at peace?
Can I be at peace as I walk the valley of the shadow of death?''
You understand what I mean.
And for all of you who yet walk this world of illusion,
And have not learned the truth of what you are,
'Tis easy for you to realize that you are not at peace.

But I have told you that you are blessed,
And simply do not know it.
So a condition of your learning
Is for you to simply consider that you are, indeed, blessed—
To consider, if you will, the simple truth
That GOD ACTUALLY DOES LOVE YOU.
Then ask yourself if you are at peace.
And if your realization is that you are not, then simply say,
''Then I wish to change my life.''

If you can come to an inkling
That the peace of God CAN BE yours,
Are you not suddenly filled
With the desire to change your being?
If you can open to the possibility
That you CAN know the peace of God,
Then what is there that you would not let go of
In order to obtain it?
If the treasure of all of Creation were in a field,
Would you not sell everything you had to buy the field

In order to obtain the treasure,
Which is the peace of God?
This story I told two thousand years ago.
And I speak its truth to you yet once again this day.

So the happy learner is one who will open
To the truth that he is blessed and loved by God,
Merely because of the nature of God Itself.
The happy learner then realizes that change
IS something which he desires,
And which brings him cause for rejoicing.
These are the conditions of the happy learner. Do you see?
The happiness comes out of celebrating that you CAN change,
That you CAN become peaceful in a world
That seemed to speak only to you of misery and death.
Rejoice that it is so!

But if you must learn INDIRECTLY,
And you will learn the truth of what you are
By giving it away,
And if it becomes your desire to change,
Then what shall be your pathway as the happy learner?
It shall be to realize that there is a vision,
Which is my gift to you,
Which is God's gift to you,
The vision which can be yours,
But which you must give away in order to receive it.
And thus with great happiness and rejoicing you can say,
"I choose to follow the path which shall teach me
To bless every brother, every sister
Who walks this earth with me."

And to do that requires of you a decision,
Which I have called the decision for guiltlessness.
I spoke to you of guilt in previous chapters.
I told you that guilt, which arose from the belief in separation,
Is the cause of the world of illusion and all of your struggles.
And I told you as well that EVERYTHING can be seen as Love,
Including the guilt which literally prods you, if you will,
Which carries you inexorably along the path
Which takes you back to God.
So even the guilt can be seen as good,
Can be seen as Love.

And yet I told you that guilt must be released completely.
Well, how are those notions compatible?
Be aware that as long as you feel the guilt,
As long as you feel the incompleteness that prods you
To move along the pathway back to God,
You may be assured that you still
Are imagining yourself to be an ego.

It is easy to become trapped into thinking that guilt,
Which CAN be seen as Love,
Is something which you need.
But that is not true at all.
The real learning of truth,
The real learning which the Holy Spirit shall bring to you,
Demands that guilt be released completely.
What if you had an inkling of the peace of God,
Of the treasure lying hidden in the field,
That which was worth everything?
Then you would not need anything negative, like your guilt,
To prod you along the path to truth.
You would simply open spontaneously, and without effort,
In response to the infinite Love you knew was about
To become yours.

So do not be confused into thinking
That you need the presence of guilt in your life.
Guilt has prompted your belief in this world of illusion.
And while you yet believe in this world,
It guarantees that you shall find your way back to God.
But the real step which the Holy Spirit requests of you
Is to release guilt completely unto your guiltlessness.

Rejoice!
You are blessed by God.
You are blessed by me.
You are blessed by Creation.
There is a vision of your perfection which stands
But awaiting your acceptance of its truth.
And if you can realize that it IS there,
But that you do not have it—
Which truth is obvious to you in a moment of contemplation—
And if it is your desire to find it,

You shall find yourself filled with a joy, not a fear,
That leads you toward opening to its presence.

Even then you cannot discover it directly here.
You shall learn of it indirectly, as we have said.
And so, once again, to decide for guiltlessness
Involves freeing your brother, your sister,
Freeing everyone, without exception,
From the curse of your own guilt.

As you realize that you are invulnerable,
As you realize that your brother is invulnerable,
You shall find yourself free of guilt.
And thus I have told you to set your brother free of all guilt.
Do this by simply telling him in every interaction
That there is nothing that he has done, could do, will do,
That could possibly harm you in any way.
As you accept your own invulnerability,
Which tells you that you ARE the Son of God,
And that you are free to choose every aspect of your existence,
You shall automatically free your brother
From any guilt he may feel from imagining
That he might have caused anything in your life.

For God is the only cause.
And God is only Love.
There is no cause at all which can cause unhappiness or grief,
Nothing but the imagination of the Son of God
Turned inward upon himself.
And that must be in response to the initial guilt
Of which I have spoken now these past weeks.

So as you set your brother free
Of any guilt you may request of him,
You set him free of his own guilt.
And you set him free of any guilt he shall demand of you.
For you have set yourself free in the same moment.

How can you actually do that?
Can you, while you yet perceive your brother
As a being separate from yourself—
Can you while you yet hold onto guilt, if you will,
Free your brother from being the cause of anything in your life?

And the answer is—by definition, you cannot do it.
For what gives life to guilt itself is the belief
That your brother can harm you.
And if you would hold onto that,
You hold onto your own guilt.
And thus it is not possible for you to decide for guiltlessness.

What does that mean?
Can you sit in the belief that you are alone
And FIGURE OUT or DECIDE
How to set your brother free from guilt?
Indeed, it is not possible. Do you see?
Then how can you do it at all?
Now this is a major step,
If you would open yourself to the presence of truth—
You realize that from within the thought system of the ego,
Which is based on the belief in separation,
You CAN NOT figure out guiltlessness.

So what do you do?
YOU MUST RELEASE THE EGO'S THOUGHT SYSTEM.
You must go beyond the awareness of your thoughts.
For always your thoughts are perceptions,
Which lie within the domain of consciousness,
The domain of the ego.
You must release your tendency to wish to figure it out,
To think about it, to study it long enough, if you will,
Until guiltlessness shall come upon you.
You must pause and listen.
You must listen, WITHOUT THINKING,
To the Voice which speaks of truth.

When you do that, that Voice shall become part of you.
It is the Voice of the Holy Spirit,
Which speaks with the greatest of logic,
Which speaks with perfect sense,
So that one day you may return
To the awareness of your conscious thoughts,
And say, "But of course!"

You must first be still within your thoughts,
And open to the awareness that comes
Out of your willingness to believe that you are blessed,

That comes out of your awareness that you are not at peace,
And that comes out of your willingness to celebrate the fact
That you CAN open to and become the recipient
Of the peace of God.
As you are still, there shall simply come an awareness,
An awareness without definition,
Which shall bring into your experience
The ability to bless your brothers.

In your silence, a vision shall come upon you
That, indeed, your brother has done nothing to you,
Would not, and can not, do anything to you.
Thus your brother is free of all guilt.
A vision shall come upon you
That you, in your freedom and your invulnerability,
Are completely beyond harm,
And have no reason to look outside yourself
To blame any being for what you are.

In that quiet awareness that lies beyond words,
You shall feel yourself blending,
First into a harmony, then into an indistinguishable Oneness
With every brother who walks this earth with you.
And all tendency to see yourself as separate and alone
Shall disappear into nothingness
As fog before the morning sun.
And in the absence of any sense of separation,
In the awareness and celebration of the Oneness of all of Life,
You shall begin to realize that deep, deep unshakable peace,
Which becomes your first true awareness
Of the truth of what you are,
And becomes your first real experience
Of the peace of God.

My blessings upon you all. That is all.

THE ATONEMENT AND COMMUNICATION

Greetings again. I am Jeshua.
We are speaking these days about teaching for truth.
And I have told you that the Holy Spirit uses logic
Just as well as does the ego.
But the Holy Spirit cannot communicate with the ego,
Because they start from different premises.

Given the premise of separation,
The thought system of this world follows
Logically and clearly.
And to those of you who believe that separation is possible,
And can be real, then this world, indeed,
Can seem to make perfect sense.
That is the major reason why so many of you
Have great difficulty when I tell you
That this world is not real, does not exist,
Could never have existed, and never happened.

But the Holy Spirit uses logic
Beginning with a very different set of premises.
And Its logic follows just as clearly as does the logic of the ego.
However, there is a fundamental difference
Between the two thought systems, the two sets of logic.
That difference is extremely simple,
Yet extremely difficult for you to hear
In this world of illusion and space and time.

The premises of the Holy Spirit are based upon truth.
And from truth follows a thought system which is true.
That is the fundamental thing you must come to understand,
If you would hear the message of the Holy Spirit.
And that is simply this—that the truth is true.
And NOTHING ELSE is true, or can be true.
'Tis very simple—God IS or God IS NOT.
Truth is true, or it is not truth.

Any thought system that uses logic
Will arrive at that conclusion.
That you see at once, of course.
So the fundamental premise of the Holy Spirit remains—
The truth is true, and must remain so.
Truth is of God, who is the One Source,
Who is the First Cause of everything that is.

I would speak with you this day about
Your function in the Atonement.
Your function is extremely simple—
You give the gift of guiltlessness to your brother.
And that is all.
I have told you that a gift must first be given
In order to be received.
I have also told you that your only function in the Atonement
Is to accept it for yourself.
But you cannot accept it for yourself unless you first give it.
Nothing can become yours without that you give it away.

But the real beauty lies herein—
You can give nothing away.
If I tell you that FIRST you must give in order to receive,
You automatically think of your time.
And you think, that in a moment of your time,
You must somehow give the gift of guiltlessness,
So that later in your time
You shall receive it for yourself.
Ah, but God FIRST gave—
God first gave His Son life itself.

I have told you there is no FIRST in time.
For time is meaningless.
There is only FIRST in eternity.
But in reality, in eternity, FIRST does not speak
Of your time and your imagined clocks.
FIRST simply speaks of cause.

God IS First Cause.
And out of the giving of God,
There arose the Son of God,
Not separate from God at all,
And not second.

For in your time you think of first and second.
But in reality there is only cause and effect,
Which are not separate at all.
There is indeed cause. And that is God.
There is indeed effect. And that is the Son of God.
But they are not separate.
And as God creates the Son,
God becomes the Son. And the Son becomes God.
And that is You.

So if you would give guiltlessness to your brother,
Which is your only function in the Atonement,
Then YOU must become cause.
If first you would give, you must become the cause.
For then you can truly give to your brother.
In order for you to become cause,
You yourself must experience
The perfect guiltlessness of the Son of God.
And then, here in your world of perception,
You will look upon your brother as guiltless as well.
And in your world of perception, that is what it means
To give the gift to your brother.
What you shall do, then, is see in your brother
The perfect guiltlessness that is your own.
And thus you shall receive it. Do you see?

It is most important for you to realize
That when you give a gift
You tend to think of giving what you HAVE.
But those are the words of space and time and separation.
For in truth, you must give the gift of what you ARE.
If God gives the gift of life to his Son,
Then Life is what God IS.
And if God gives what He knows,
Then what God gives is Knowledge Itself.
For God must BE that which He would give,
Not give what He HAS. Do you see?

And so if you would truly give the gift of guiltlessness
To your brother,
You must realize that it is far, far more
Than simply seeing, within your space and time,
Your brother as not being guilty.

In order to give guiltlessness, you must give what you ARE.
And you cannot give what you ARE
Until you can transcend this imagined world
Of separation and different beings.
In order to give what you are,
It must be that you would give it with God.

But it goes even beyond giving WITH God.
For if you think of yourself as being NEXT TO God,
If you see yourself as sharing WITH God in the giving,
You still imagine yourself separate from God.
As you give what you ARE, not what you HAVE,
And as you realize that you, the effect, the Son of God,
Have BECOME God because God has given you Himself,
Then when you give the gift of guiltlessness,
You give your Self.
And you give the gift that is also God.
And so your real function in the Atonement
Is to give the gift of guiltlessness,
Which is not something that you HAVE,
But is that which you ARE,
And beyond that is what God is, as well.

What you do then is bring each brother, through your giving,
Into what I have called the circle of the Atonement.
And what does that mean?
The circle is simply a symbol, a symbol that INCLUDES . . .
And in reality, the radius of the circle extends to infinity.
There is no one, no being, who is not within the circle,
This moment, and every moment of eternity.
So as you would function within the Atonement,
As you give the gift of guiltlessness,
You do it by bringing each and every brother
Within the circle of the Atonement.

But how do you do that?
You cannot give the gift of the Atonement,
You cannot give guiltlessness,
To a brother whom you perceive to be different from yourself.
God could not have given life to a Son
Who was separate from Him.
The nature of God, the very essence of God,
Demands that that could not, did not, can never, happen.

You cannot give the gift of guiltlessness
While you yet perceive the brother to whom you would give it
To be different from, to be separate from, yourself.
So as you bring each brother
Within the circle of Atonement with you,
Then what you give to your brother
Is the gift of your own guiltlessness,
Because you have seen your brother as perfect.

But it is even more than that.
You literally give the gift of yourself.
And as you give the gift of yourself to your brother,
You, without effort,
Shall see your brother's will as your own.

But I have told you that EVERY being
Gives the gift of the Atonement.
For that is your only function here.
For that is all that you CAN do,
Although the FORM of the giving
Shall vary almost with each and every brother.
And so as you give the gift of the Atonement,
As you give the gift of guiltlessness to your brother,
You MUST see beyond, you MUST see through,
The form itself.
You must see the perfect Oneness,
The undeniable harmony of the Oneness
Which you share with your brother, and with all of Creation.
And as you do that, without effort
You shall bring your brother within the circle of the Atonement.
And you keep yourself there as well.

If you look upon your brother as different from yourself,
If you would give to him a gift that you HAVE,
And attempt to keep what you ARE
Separate from what you would give,
Then you, in that perception, thrust your brother OUT—
Out of the harmony of the Oneness of Love.
You thrust him out of the circle of Atonement
Into an imagined world of abandonment,
And aloneness and separation.
And there, in that world, YOU MUST JOIN HIM.

And that is the picture of the false illusion
That you call this world.

If you start from the premise of separation,
What you see is the world you are wont to look upon
From the vantage point, the thought system, of the ego.

So your function in the Atonement
Is to give the gift of guiltlessness,
Which you give by BEING the gift itself,
And which you give by bringing your brother into the circle,
By causing your brother to BECOME the gift that you give,
Which is but your Self.

How can you seem to do that, here in your world?
For within the world of illusion
Where you see images of bodies which seem separate,
How can you give the gift of Oneness,
Which is truly the gift of Love,
Which is the gift of the Atonement Itself?
How can you do that?
YOU DO IT BY COMMUNICATING WITH YOUR BROTHER.

I have told you that you cannot give the gift of the Atonement
Except that you give it with God.
But that means that you give it with the God
With Whom you are One.
So if you would give the gift of communication,
It simply demands that you open, within the world of form,
To the Oneness that you share.
And if you would give the light of communication,
It is most important that you hear my words—
You communicate by GIVING communication.
You communicate by GIVING the light.
As I have already told you,
You cannot receive anything unless first you give it.

So how do you give communication?
What you give to your brother is the gift
Of his freedom to be completely open in your presence,
With no secrets, with nothing to hide,
Without any desire or need to hide anything at all.

And how do you then receive communication?
Of course, by giving it away.

And how do you give that communication to your brother?
By simply accepting him with openness and love,
By accepting him within the awareness that there is no guilt,
That there is no separation between you and your brother.
You do it by giving out of the awareness
That the Atonement has taught you
That your wills are the same.
You do it by acknowledging that
Everything you would look upon in form
Is but a choice FOR the Atonement.

And as you extend to your brother
Complete openness to be, to think, to feel, to express, to act,
Whatever he will, without judgment, without condemnation,
Without having written for yourself any script whatsoever
Of what that expression of his atonement process should be—
As you extend complete acceptance to your brother,
He becomes absolutely free in your presence.
And there is no being who will not respond
To the love that it requires to offer such openness.

But what if you find that your brother
Is not willing to be open with you?
Then look within.
And you may be assured that you are harboring
Some judgment, some grievance, about your brother.
For if you have, in however subtle fashion,
A program, if you will, of how your brother should live,
Then he cannot be open with you.
Rather he will feel attacked by you.
He will sense that you desire him not to be free,
That you do not trust him in his Oneness with you,
That you do not trust the common will that you share with him

AND SO THE MEASURE OF COMMUNICATION IS ALWAYS
NOT WHAT YOU GET, BUT WHAT YOU GIVE.
And as you give to your brother the perfect freedom to be,
To be whatever he chooses to experience,
Without judgment or condemnation,
His heart, his being, will open unto you.

He shall feel loved in your presence.
And you shall realize that YOU, then,
Are in the presence of Love.
For you shall realize that that is what you are.

That awareness shall bring blessing upon you.
And you shall find yourself opening to your brother.
And in that perfect Openness you shall live together,
Surrounded by the light of communication,
Which is the light of Love,
But which actually is nothing but the Light of God,
And the Light of Life Itself.
For that ultimately is nothing more
Than what you and your brother are.

My blessings upon you all. That is all.

PERCEIVING WITH THE HOLY SPIRIT

Greetings again. I am Jeshua.
We are speaking about teaching for truth.
I have spoken to you about touching the source of truth.
I have spoken to you about communication.
And most importantly, about how
Communication is that which you GIVE.
For when you give the opportunity for a being
To be completely open and honest in your presence,
You generate communication in its reality.
And you open for yourself, and for the world,
The pathway of truth.

Then, who is the perfect communicator?
Who is the source of perfect communication
Along that pathway unto truth?
For if we speak about truth,
Then that is our fundamental question—
How do we discover, and beyond that,
How do we experience, the truth of Life?

But I have told you that you can discover truth
If you share your perception with the Holy Spirit.
And I have told you that perception is the medium
Whereby ignorance can be transformed into knowledge.
But perception is what you do here.
Perception is of this world of illusion, is it not?
And yes, it is indeed.
So also is the absence of truth.
So is ignorance. So is darkness.
So is the belief in sin.

And if we would take that which is not real and release it,
We must work with the tools of illusion.
We must work within perception,
In order to carry ignorance into knowledge,
Darkness into light, war into peace.

Perception changes.
Perception can have its vision in one moment,
And in another moment yield yet another, different vision.
Knowledge, true peace and true Love do not change.

In fact, the beauty of perception is that it CAN change.
Your perception here in this world,
Which speaks to you of ignorance and war,
And separation and fear—
All of that CAN CHANGE.
That is its beauty.

How, then, do we change perception?
How, then, do we discover truth?
For it is truly in the changing of perception
That truth shall come upon your awareness,
That truth shall dawn upon your mind.
Always as we seek to discover truth,
We wish to change that which is undesirable
Into that which is desirable.
As I have said, we wish to carry fear into love,
Unholiness into holiness, guilt into guiltlessness.
And the list goes on.
We wish to carry that which is of illusion
Into truth itself.

Truth does not attack. Truth does not defend.
For truth simply is.
Truth is not at war with ignorance.
Truth merely is.
Love is not at war with fear.
Love merely is.
And if you would change fear into love,
It must be through your own power of decision.
It must be your choice to do so.

How can that work here in your world of illusion?
I have spoken to you of dissociation.
For it is dissociation that has allowed you
To seem to split your mind.
And when you dissociate,
You seem to harbor within the same mind
Two contradictory systems of belief.

You believe, so you say, that you are Spirit.
And yet you are wont to believe that you are a body.
You believe, so you say, that at some level you are invulnerable,
That you have the power to choose the happenings in your life.
And yet you are wont to say,
"This happened to me,"
Or "He did thus and so to me."
Do you see that the two are absolutely incompatible?
Even the logic of the ego can see that, can it not?

If you would discover truth, what you must do
Is bring together what appear to be the contradictions,
What appear to be the dissociated thought systems,
The one of the ego and the other of truth,
The one of God.
For it is clear, even to your thinking minds,
That if you bring two thought systems together,
One of which is true and one of which is not—
And it is obvious that two contradictory thought systems
Cannot both be true—
If you bring together two contradictory thought systems,
Only one of which is true,
Then the truth shall eradicate the falseness,
Just as light eradicates darkness.

So how do you do that?
How do you bring together two contradictory thought systems?
What you must do is SHARE YOUR PERCEPTION.
And how do you do that?
You who yet remain as ego,
You who yet sing the song of illusion to yourself,
Must share your perception
With one who sings the song of truth.
And that One, as I have told you so many times,
Is the Holy Spirit.
If you will share your perception with the Holy Spirit,
Then you will bring together
Your own thought system which you made,
And which presents to you illusion in all its false glory—
You will bring that thought system together
With the thought system of the Holy Spirit,
Who speaks to you of the truth of God.
And in the coming together of the two,

The truth of God will eradicate the falseness of illusion.
It must be so.

Well, how can you, in your thinking mind,
Tell if you have brought together YOUR perception
With that of the Holy Spirit?
How can you tell if you are sharing your perception
With the Holy Spirit, who speaks for the truth of God?
I will give you a test that you can use
In order to discover when you are bringing illusion to truth,
When you are bringing falseness to reality,
When you are bringing fear unto Love.

And this is the test—the Holy Spirit speaks
Of one meaning, one emotion, one purpose.
Truth itself contains
But one meaning, one emotion, one purpose.
And they are this—
There is but one meaning, the Oneness,
The perfect unity, that is God.
There is but one emotion, Love.
And there is but one purpose, to extend and to share that Love
Unto all of Creation.

So as you would bring the experiences of your life,
As you would bring the thoughts of which you are aware,
As you would bring your feelings,
All with the intent of sharing your perception
With the Holy Spirit,
Then simply look and see if the result speaks
Of one meaning, which is the Oneness,
The perfect unity of all of life.
And look to see if the result speaks of one emotion,
Which is always Love.
And see if it leads you to one purpose,
Which is to extend that Love
To all beings, all brothers, all of Creation.
And if you find that to be so, then you may know with certainty
That you have shared your perception with the Holy Spirit,
That you have brought illusion unto truth.

There is a consistency to the Oneness of truth
Which cannot be denied.

If you would discover that consistency that speaks for truth,
Where shall you go?
If you would meet the Holy Spirit,
If you would go with the Holy Spirit to the altar of God,
Whereupon is placed the offering
Of one meaning, one emotion, one purpose—
If you would discover that place, where shall it be?
Where should you look to find it?
If it is your intent, after hearing my words,
To share your perception with the Holy Spirit,
How shall you do it?
These words I shall speak to you
Are words I have spoken so many times,
But which speak the truth that needs be repeated
Over and over and over again,
Until it becomes your awareness, your experience,
Until it becomes what you are.

If you would share your perception with the Holy Spirit,
If you would communicate with the Holy Spirit,
YOU MUST LOOK WITHIN.
For that, literally, is where the Holy Spirit resides.
You will not find the Holy Spirit
If you look anywhere outside yourself.
For in the simple act of looking outside yourself,
You imagine separation, do you not?
And can the Holy Spirit speak to you of one meaning
When you look to receive that meaning from a source
Which appears separate from yourself?
For all the while the one meaning
Is the Oneness, the unity of God.
Do you see?
So you MUST look within.

Now I have told you that if you would use perception
In order to bring ignorance unto knowledge,
There must be no deceit.
For in the presence of deceit, you but further ignorance itself.
If you look within,
You will find there the presence of the Holy Spirit.
And you will find no judgment of any kind upon you.
If you will but look within, and allow yourself
To think what you think, see what you see,

Feel what you feel,
And above all to BE what you are in that moment—
If you will allow yourself the unbridled freedom
To simply experience within the framework
Of your own awareness,
You shall, as you open to the presence of the Holy Spirit,
Meet with complete and total acceptance.
You shall meet the very presence of Love Itself.
And as you do that,
You will find yourself able to address your fears.

If you speak to one of your brothers
Who believe in separation,
And therefore have their own agenda,
And you would share with him your innermost thoughts,
Deep within you there is the fear that you will not be accepted.
And in that fear, communication has been destroyed.
But if you look only within, if you listen only in your silence,
And allow yourself to be
What you find yourself being in that moment,
If you at the same time open to the awareness
Of the one meaning, the one emotion, the one purpose,
Then rising out of your stillness
You shall hear the song of truth.
You shall find your fears dissolving into nothingness,
Just as darkness dissolves before the presence of light.
And thus you will have taken fear unto love.

And you have done it by looking within.
And what shall happen when you do that?
Your life shall change.
You shall find truth itself
Reflected outward unto your world.
You will find that your life sings a song of truth,
That your life sings the song of
One meaning, one emotion, one purpose.
And that one purpose, above all,
Is to extend the one emotion, Love, to all of Life Itself.

And as you do that,
There will be no aspect of your life, no brother,
Who will not be touched by it.
There is no brother who will not be touched

By the reflection of your holiness.
And your brothers will find themselves
Perfectly acceptable unto your sight,
Just as all beings are perfectly acceptable unto God.
And they shall find themselves reaching out
To communicate with you,
Without reservation, without holding back.
And you, in your acceptance of them,
Shall reflect to them the Love of God.

For that is the message of God unto you
Who are absolutely guiltless,
"You are my beloved Son, in whom I am well pleased.
You are my Son who shines and shines forever,
Unto the distance of eternity in your space,
Unto the day of forever in your time."
And you shall find yourself to BE the Son of God,
Who has become first cause, independent of space and time,
And who, being like God Itself,
Being the source of Love,
Extends that Love unto all of Creation.

Thus you will have discovered the truth of life
By sharing your perception with the Holy Spirit,
By looking within where the Holy Spirit remains,
Quietly waiting your invitation.
And thus you will reflect to all the world
The perfection and the guiltlessness of what you are.
You will reflect to all the world the Love of God,
Which also in truth is exactly what you are,
And shall always remain.

My blessings upon you all. That is all.

MIRACLES AND TRUTH

Greetings again. I am Jeshua.
We have been speaking these days about truth.
Ultimately, that is all of which we speak—truth.
And the only truth of which we speak
Is the simple truth of what you are.
And I have told you, you are the single, most precious,
Most beloved, most valued, Son of God.

When you know that, when you come to know that again,
In the sense of your space and time,
Then what I call the Atonement will be, and must be, yours.
For the Atonement is nothing more than
Your acceptance of the truth of what you are.
If you would teach truth here, which means
If you would come to understand truth for yourself,
Then you must give, you must share, the essence of truth.

And how do you do that?
I have told you—by opening your mind,
So that you can reflect the truth of God.
I have told you that whatever you accept
Into the mirror of your mind
Is what shall shine out from you,
Is what you shall give,
And is therefore what you shall receive,
And is therefore what you shall understand.
Did you hear the words "accept into the mirror of your mind"?
When I speak to you of "the mirror of your mind,"
I am speaking to you in terms of space and time.

You need to know that what you call conscious awareness
Is only that which mind projects onto a screen,
In order to perceive what is there.
In order to split your mind, if you will,
In order to imagine that you are what you are not,
You, mind, the reality of what you are,

Chose to project onto a screen that which you would perceive.
And the screen onto which mind projects,
In order to pretend that it is experiencing space and time—
That screen onto which mind projects
Is consciousness itself.

And thus what you allow into your conscious awareness
IS what you shall reflect.
What you allow into your conscious awareness
IS what you shall seem to experience here in space and time.
And that becomes the gift you give to your brother.
And thus I speak to you of being
The reflection of holiness here.

And how can you do that?
Well, in space and time, you have but one choice—
The choice of which voice you shall listen to—
The voice of the ego, the Voice of the Holy Spirit;
The voice of war, the voice of peace;
The voice of fear, the voice of Love.
And that is your only choice—to open,
To accept into this mirror of your mind,
Which truly is consciousness itself—
To accept into your consciousness
That which you shall reflect out unto your world,
And that which your brothers shall seem to see,
But which is also what you shall see yourself.

And if you would choose to accept into your mind
The truth of God,
There are some ways you can come to understand
When you are opening to, when you are listening to,
The Voice of the Holy Spirit, the Voice of God.
And to help you come to that understanding,
I would speak to you once again,
About the equality of miracles.

I would have you remember that
Miracles, as I have said, are not in competition.
The presence of one miracle in your life,
Your choice to open to the presence of one miracle,
In no sense competes with, or blocks,
The presence of other miracles.

One miracle is not greater than another.
One does not supersede another.
Indeed, an infinite number of miracles
Can be pouring into the mirror of your mind at the same time.
And you can reflect an infinite number of miracles,
None of which competes with any of the others.

That can seem difficult for you to understand.
But as you think about your own thoughts, if you will,
There are so many of them
Which seem to come and go, and co-exist.
And as you look at your brothers
It seems as if a myriad of thoughts can be going on at once,
Within this great Oneness that you call humankind.
And that is something you can understand,
If you pause for a moment.

More difficult for you to understand
Is that there is no order of difficulty in miracles.
If you would learn to reflect holiness,
To reflect the truth of God, the truth of what you are,
It is most important for you to understand
The absence of an order of difficulty in miracles.
You are wont so often to order your thoughts,
To listen for the thoughts which would seem of love,
To listen for the thoughts that would seem of fear.
You then desire to select out the thoughts of love,
Which selection you attempt to do by yourself.
You attempt to look at your thoughts,
Which are really the images which mind
Has projected onto the screen of consciousness—
You are wont to look upon those thoughts and to judge,
To decide for yourself which is of fear and which is of love,
For the purpose of accepting the ones of love.

And your attempt to do that makes it seem obvious to you
That there is an order to your thoughts—
Some are better than others.
Some are more valuable than others.
Some are more true than others.
And thus it is so difficult for you when I tell you
That there is no order of difficulty whatsoever in miracles.
You would think about miracles relating to form—

Which ultimately they do not—
But as you would think about them relating to form,
It is so difficult for you to realize
That there is no difference between
Simply opening to a thought of love, healing an illness,
Walking upon the water, and turning water into wine.

And within illnesses there is no order of difficulty.
One illness is not more difficult to heal than another.
If you pause for a moment, you will certainly realize
That within your thoughts you do believe that
You are able to free yourself of some types of fear thoughts,
While others seem quite impossible to release.
Thus you are trying to define order,
An order of miracles which does not exist.

How can it be that there is no order of difficulty in miracles?
It must arise from this awareness—
That miracles do not, and cannot,
Arise from a state of separation.
I have told you before that if you would sit alone and isolated
In your belief in separation
And design to decide which miracle you would do,
You will fail.
And the miracle will escape you entirely.
Miracles CANNOT arise out of a belief in separation.
Miracles MUST be shared.
And if you would truly reflect the holiness, the truth of God,
Then that which you would reflect
You must be willing to share with all brothers, all sisters,
Without exception.
And if that willingness is not present,
You are blocking yourself
From the presence of miracles entering your life.

Miracles arise out of the Oneness that IS what you are.
And within that Oneness,
Can one expression of Love be greater than another?
Can Love compete with itself?
As I have told you that miracles
Do not compete with one another,
Can Love compete with Itself?
Can you imagine God competing within the Mind of God,

Trying to decide which extension of Love
Is better or greater than another?
And you, even in your thinking minds,
Can sense the absurdity of that notion.
For Love is simply Love.

And how about those of you who are not yet able
To open the mirrors of your minds
To the awareness that everything IS Love, as I have told you?
You may be sure that you still harbor fear in your life.
And in the presence of your fear,
The Holy Spirit desires to help you see that fear
As a call for love.
For as I have told you, a call for love cannot be present
Without the deep underlying awareness
That Love itself does exist to be called upon.

The equality of miracles demands
That there be no competition and no order.
And the absence of an order of miracles becomes clear
As you realize that Love is simply Love.
And when you cannot see love in your own life,
If you will be still, then you will become aware
That what you cannot see as love
Can be seen as a call for love.
And this shall be the Holy Spirit's interpretation,
Which He shall make for you, gladly and willingly,
As you are willing to try to open the mirror of your mind.

If you look out upon your world and you see love,
Then love is what you shall receive into your life.
It must be so. For that is the nature of Love Itself.
But what if you look out upon your world
And are unable to perceive what you see as love?
Then you are restricted to opening to it as being a call for love.
What if that is all that you can do?
Then the Holy Spirit shall, as you give Him your willingness,
Allow you, cause you, to extend Love into that circumstance.

So when you look out and see love, it seems easy.
For Love is already there and is yours.
When you look out and cannot seem to see love,
Then the Holy Spirit shall help you realize that

A call for Love MUST be present,
Even though it be your own call for Love,
Your own call for the Love that MUST be within you.
And since the Love IS within you,
You shall be able give Love to that circumstance.

Well, how can you really do that?
The only way you can do that is to admit
That you do not know what is Love and what is not.

In this world you are so wont to look upon form.
But I tell you, Love looks beyond form.
It is so, so difficult for you to see what I call content,
To see the essence of being, which is always, without question,
Love Itself being expressed.
It is so difficult for you to look upon content,
When what your eyes seem to bring to you is images of form.
So how can you look upon form and see Love?
You must do it by realizing that you,
Within your thinking mind, DO NOT KNOW.
You, in your thoughts, do not know
What is Love and what is not.
And that is all.
You do not know.

Ultimately, you must admit, within your thinking,
That you do not know the essence of Love.
You are simply admitting that it is so difficult
To see past the form. Do you see?
And as you would desire to reflect the holiness of God,
As you would desire to share that reflection with all brothers,
As you would therefore desire to see only Love,
It MUST come out of your acceptance
That you do not know.

Indeed, when you open to the awareness
That what you cannot see as Love is a call for Love,
That is really your statement that you do not know.
For Love is indeed present and can be found in ANY situation.
And that discovery you shall accomplish
Through the guidance of the Holy Spirit.

And thus it is that you may allow
Every situation to be interpreted for you.
And as you, in your stillness,
Are willing to open the mirror of your mind,
As you are willing to not attempt
To structure this mirror on your own,
You SHALL BE ABLE to open
To the presence of the Holy Spirit.
As you are willing to be still and listen,
Then, as I have told you, you will know what to do,
What to say, what to be, where to go.
And this shall be the guidance of the Holy Spirit
In action in your life.

Now, there is a test you can apply,
Here in the world of form, a test you can use
To be able to discern whether or not you have
Opened the mirror of your mind to the truth of God.
It is an extremely simple test which I tell you this day.
When you look out and see Love,
Then Love is what you shall receive.
And when you cannot see Love,
And must attempt to see a call for Love,
Then it is up to you to open to the Holy Spirit,
Whose guidance will allow the Love
To enter the situation through you.
You must be willing to give up your belief
That what you cannot see as Love
Can be seen as a CALL for Love.
You must go beyond that to the point where
You share the vision of the Holy Spirit,
Who realizes full well that EVERYTHING IS LOVE ITSELF.

What if you were able to open,
Under the guidance of the Holy Spirit, beyond form,
To the realization that EVERYTHING is Love?
What if, at the core of your being,
Beyond your thoughts and judgment,
There was simply the experience of Love,
And nothing else?
Then what would be in your life?
The first thing is, you would cease to be afraid.
For as you realize that everything IS Love Itself,

And as you realize that Love must cast out fear,
Your fear would no longer be present.
And so part of the simple test of truth is this—
You are not afraid at all,
Simply because all you see is Love.

And the second part of the test for truth
Is equally important.
For when you have opened the mirror of your mind
To the awareness that everything is Love,
When you have allowed fear to dissipate from your being,
From your awareness,
Then what you shall reflect is the holiness of God,
The presence of Love.
And when you do that, all beings,
All beings who enter your presence,
All beings who are even aware of you
And yet may not be in your presence,
Will be at peace.
All beings will be at peace
As you reflect the holiness of God,
As you reflect Love.

Does that demand that within form
Every being shall ACT as if he is peaceful in your presence?
Remember, I have told you it is not about the form.
As you open the mirror of your mind
To nothing but the presence of Love,
Then Love becomes what you reflect.
From the clean mirror you reflect ONLY Love.
And I promise you, all beings shall be touched by that love
Which you reflect here in space and time.

And so the first mark is this—ARE YOU WITHOUT FEAR?
And the second mark is—
DO YOU EXTEND PEACE TO YOUR BROTHERS?
A simple question you can ask yourself is this—
If you would look upon everything as Love,
Then there is nothing you shall look upon
That you would ever desire to change.
As you look upon everything as Love,
Then that which I have called grievances
CANNOT ENTER YOUR MIND.

So even though the form may not look to you
As if every brother is at peace,
If you look within and find no desire whatsoever
For your brothers to be different,
If you find no grievances at all,
EVEN THE GRIEVANCE
OF WANTING YOUR BROTHER TO BE AT PEACE,
WHEN IT LOOKS TO YOU LIKE HE IS NOT—
If you find no grievances whatsoever,
Then you may be sure that your brother
Is at peace in your presence.
For you have placed no desires upon him.

And how about your desire to want your brother to be at peace,
Your desire to want your brother to learn this Course,
If you will?
That is one of the most subtle grievances you need be aware of.
For when you want your brother to be different
In any sense whatsoever, even to understand this Course,
Even to open his mind to the peace of God NOW,
You are saying to your brother,
"You SHOULD be different from what you are."
And I promise you, in that scenario, that
Rather than being the bringer of peace,
You but increase fear.

If you would understand the truth,
You must realize that peace and understanding
Go hand in hand.
Peace and understanding are each cause to the other.
If you would understand truth, what does that mean?
To "stand under" means to be the support for.
And if you would support truth in your life,
It MUST BE at the level of content.
It must be beyond form.

Your understanding, then, must be of what you are.
If you would understand the truth of God,
It simply means that the truth of God
IS what you experience and what you are.
And when you understand, in that sense, the truth of God,
I promise you, you MUST BE at peace.
You must be without fear.

Thus I have told you that the Holy Spirit speaks of truth
With a logic as rigorous as that which the ego uses,
But with a logic which far surpasses the chaotic foundation
Upon which the ego bases its thought system.
For the Holy Spirit begins with the fundamentals that are true,
Those of which we have spoken in this chapter.
Truth is what you are.
Truth is the presence of Love.
Truth is the awareness of Oneness and sharing.
Truth is the awareness that miracles cannot compete,
But must be shared.
And truth is the awareness that if it CAN be shared,
It must be of Love.
And beyond that, truth is the awareness
That ultimately everything IS Love.
And therefore truth is the awareness
That there is no separation within Love Itself,
And that there cannot be an order of difficulty in miracles.
Truth is the awareness that when you understand truth,
That same truth becomes your experience,
Becomes what you are.
And thus it is that the truth of God ultimately
IS what you are.

As you realize that you do not know,
And listen to the Voice of the Holy Spirit,
You shall hear Its guidance.
You shall hear a Voice that sings a song
Of your brother, of his beauty,
Of the truth of what he is.
And you shall hear a song that also sings to you
The truth of what you are.
For what you are and what your brother is
MUST BE the same.

And as you let go of all notions of separation,
Of all orders of difficulty in trying to imagine
That one son of God might be more loving than another,
Even here in space and time—
As you let go of those notions,
You shall understand the truth of what you are,
Of what your brother is, of what God is—
You shall understand that all of those

Must be, have always been,
And shall always remain,
The same.
And that understanding shall bring to you, without recourse,
The peace of God.

My blessings upon you all. That is all.

THE TWO USES OF TIME

Greetings again. I am Jeshua.
I would speak with you, this day, more about time.
Time, as I have told you, is the grandest illusion.
Time, ultimately, is that which makes all of your fear.
Without time, I promise you, fear would not be possible,
In your awareness, or in your experience.

How would you like to live in a manner
Where you were completely free of all doubt, all worry,
All sense of distress, all lack of peace?
For it is the purpose of time
To allow you to come to such a state.
And yet it is time which produces,
Which creates, if you will, all of your fear.
And does there not seem to be a great disparity
Between the statements I have just made?
And of course there seems to be.
And that is because there are two uses of time.

I have told you many times that there are, indeed,
Two uses of everything in this world of illusion.
For this world of illusion, in its seeming reality,
Can be used to substantiate the belief in illusion.
Anything in this world can be used to convince you
That this world, which is not real, is actually real.
And that is the fundamental struggle you deal with
As you would attempt to learn this Course.
But I have told you as well that the Holy Spirit,
Who will speak to you any time you are willing to listen,
Can literally take ANYTHING of this world
And use it to teach you the truth of what you are,
The truth of God.

And so there are two uses of time.
One is the ego's.
And the other is the Holy Spirit's.
But do not forget, the ego is not a being with existence,
Is not a thing of reality.

The ego—even though I speak of it
As if it WERE a being with awareness,
And the ability to make decisions, to calculate, and to plan—
The ego is nothing more than that which you have made
For the purpose of pretending that you are what you are not,
For the purpose of pretending
That a world of illusion can be real,
When in truth it cannot be real at all.

Remember that the essence of time itself
Is the belief that cause and effect can be separate.
For when you believe that there is a cause
Which can exercise creative power,
And that somehow SEPARATE from that
An effect appears, the effect of those creative powers,
What you are doing is believing in time.
For that which seems to intervene between cause,
And the result of cause being expressed,
Which you call the effect,
Is what you call time.
And if you can SEPARATE cause and effect,
Then separation must exist, does it not?

So your belief that cause and effect can be separate
Is what generates your belief in time.
And within the thought system of this world of illusion,
It is time which literally brings to you
The illusion of separation.
Thus you believe that there is a past,
Which becomes the cause,
And which LATER produces an effect, in your time.
And that effect is what you are in this moment.
And so you believe that the past
Has somehow brought you to this moment,
That the past has CAUSED you to be
What you are in this moment.

So you always look outside yourself
In order to see beings other than yourself
Who become the cause for what you are.
And thus you believe yourself separate from that cause.
Thus you believe that OTHERS have made you what you are.
And you even believe that God, the cause,

Is separate from you, the effect.
Even your stories of the creation of the world
Speak of time and days, and ultimately a separation
Which exists between God and His creations
And the form that those creations took. Do you see?

Thus you believe that you need the past IN ORDER TO EXIST.
That is your belief in time.
That also means that the future
Is dependent upon this moment for ITS existence.
And this moment becomes the past
For that which seems to be the future.
And thus you believe in the flow of time.
You believe in the ticking of a clock,
As if one second leads to the next and the next and the next.
You believe that without the previous moment
The subsequent one cannot exist. Do you see?

But what happens when this body seems to die?
You are so bound to your belief in time,
And that the past causes the present,
That you must cling to that belief
Even within the awareness that bodies seem to die.
And thus within your belief in time,
Which brings to you your belief in separation,
You are bound to believe that time must continue to exist,
Even though your body seems to die.
And therefore, you are bound to believe
That somehow you exist even after death.
For if you did not continue to exist,
Then time would cease to be, would it not?

And so you make up many different stories about the afterlife.
Some of you believe that you are given a new body.
Some of you do not believe in bodies,
But yet believe in the existence of
The awareness you have of yourself.
But the awareness you have of yourself
As separate and alone is but your ego.
And ultimately your belief in the preservation of the ego
Is the simple requirement that allows time to exist,
To continue to flow. Do you see?

But what if, as I have told you,
This belief in the separation of cause and effect
Is also the source of your guilt (which it is)?
Then if your ego continues to exist even after your body dies,
And yet brings guilt with it,
Then in order to preserve your belief in time
You must believe in a life after this one,
A life in which you remain separate, and remain guilty,
In which you remain apart from God,
In which you remain apart from the truth of what you are.
And that, of course, is your belief in hell.

Some of you make up stories of a vengeful God
Who would punish you forever and ever.
And those of you who cannot fathom the absurdity
Of a God of Love punishing you in that form
Simply believe in the continuation of your separation.
And that you call hell.
And all of it follows from your belief in time,
Which was made for the purpose of believing
That you were separate in the first place. Do you see?

But there remains a second use of time.
The Holy Spirit can use time to teach you
Of the truth of what you are.
And how does the Holy Spirit do that?
The Holy Spirit, as you are still and listen,
Speaks to you, always from within.
And even though I speak to you, within your ego state,
As if the Holy Spirit is separate from you, It is not.
The Holy Spirit ultimately IS you.
It is the part of you that remains aware of your real Self,
The part of you that remains aware of God.
So if you listen within, you will hear a Voice
Speaking to you of truth.
And even you, ego, in your stillness, must realize
That this Voice comes from within,
That it comes from you.

So now you have a voice which comes FROM you,
Which IS you,
Which speaks to you of the truth of what you are.
It speaks to you of that truth,

Even while you yet hold to an image of what you are,
Which is ego, and which seems different from your truth.
But this ego is the product of the past.
This ego is the product of the belief
That some being separate from yourself has created you,
Even if that being separate from yourself be God.

But as you are still and listen within,
You shall hear a Voice which COMES from within,
Which comes from nowhere outside of you.
You shall hear a Voice which would decry separation.
And in your stillness, in the silence of your mind, as you listen,
That is the first awareness you shall come to—
The awareness that the Voice which speaks TO you, IS you.

And what if there is no being outside of yourself
To tell you of what you are?
THEN YOUR NEED FOR TIME COLLAPSES.
I am speaking to you in this chapter of the holy instant.
As we speak of that, we will speak of experiencing the present.
Do you know what the present is?
Do you know what THIS MOMENT is?
Do you know what, ultimately, the holy instant is?
The holy instant is that state in which
Your perception and your experience of cause and effect
Bind them together as one.
The holy instant, this moment, the present,
Must arise out of your simple awareness
That cause is not separate from effect, at all.

And what does that mean in words?
That simply means that YOU EXIST.
That is the only way to say it.
YOU EXIST.
Was God caused by some source?
Those of you who believe in time find it incomprehensible
That there was not something BEFORE God.
But the answer is—GOD EXISTS.
For your true awareness of God must come
From the awareness of the absence of separation
Of cause and effect.
And your true awareness of what YOU are must come

From the absence of any separation of cause and effect.
And this is what the Holy Spirit would teach you.

And so the Holy Spirit would use time and logic
To help you realize that time does not make sense. Do you see?
And the only thing that would cause you
To desire to believe in time
Is your insistence that you exist as an ego, as a separate being,
Which demands a past that has created you,
And brought you to this moment.
Ah, but IN THIS INSTANT YOU SIMPLY EXIST.
If there is no past to have brought you to this moment,
Then you simply exist,
Clean and pure and perfect and beautiful—
All of which are the words that describe the Son of God,
Which is what you are.

Do you realize that fear cannot exist in the present?
Do you realize that fear literally demands a past?
And fear literally demands the belief that this moment
Shall become the past for the future.
But in the present moment,
In which cause and effect are One,
And life, existence, simply IS—
In that moment, fear cannot exist.
It is not possible.

Do you know what that means?
That means that if your brother had no past in your belief,
It would not be possible for you
To fear his presence in your life.
Think of your fear for but a moment,
And it shall become clear to you.
If you are ever afraid in the presence of a brother,
It is because you have written a story about his past
And would project that story into YOUR future
In terms of what he might do to you.
If you have fear in your own life,
It is because you believe in a past of your own
Which has brought you to this moment,
And which shall cause you struggle and grief in the future.

So if you COULD live in this moment, in the present,
In what I am calling the holy instant,
It must be, without recourse,
That fear is gone.
So if you would escape from fear,
If you would live a life of perfect peace and harmony,
Of Oneness and perfect calmness,
Of that which I spoke at the beginning of this chapter,
All you need do is release your fear.
And all you need do to accomplish that
Is to realize that the absence of fear
Lies in the present moment.

The Holy Spirit would teach you of time,
That it does not flow from past to present to future,
That you are free of cause and effect,
Because you are free of separation. Do you see?
And so the Holy Spirit would use time
To remind you that all there is of time is this moment.
And in this moment, this holy instant,
Fear must be gone.

We will be sharing with you and teaching you
How to experience this instant, the present,
How to come to the absence of fear.
Is there a first step you can take
Which shall remove all doubt from your mind
About what I have said about time and cause and effect?
And the answer is—yes, there is.
And as always, if you would find that place, that experience,
You need to look to your savior—
Who, as always, is your brother.
Do you remember my words?
And so if you desire to experience this holy instant
In which fear cannot exist,
THEN IT MUST BE THAT THAT SAME INSTANT
IS THE GIFT YOU GIVE TO YOUR BROTHER

And how do you do that, in words?
You do that by realizing that your brother's past
Has no effect on what he is in truth.
Does your brother's past define what you would call ego?
Of course. That is what ego is, by definition—

The collection of unreal thoughts you have
About who you are, and who your brother is,
All of which are based upon an imagined past.
That is why the ego is not real. Do you see?

So does it seem as if the past determines
What your brother is?
Ah, yes, it does.
But what it determines is the FALSE IMAGE
Of what your brother SEEMS to be.
And that false image has not at all to do
With the reality, the truth,
Of what your brother is, or what you are.
So if you would be released from all fear,
If you would discover this instant,
As you would give the holy instant to your brother,
What you do is open to the simple awareness
That he IS the Son of God.
You open to the awareness that,
No matter what an imagined past may look like,
It does not, and cannot, determine what your brother is.

And if you will choose to look upon your brother
As a being of Light and a being of Love,
To look into his eyes
And see nothing but the Love and the truth of God—
If you will do that, then you,
Under the guidance of the Holy Spirit,
Will have transcended time itself.
It is not possible for you to transcend time
By looking upon your brother,
And NOT transcend it for yourself.

I will tell you in closing
About the power of the holy instant.
In the one instant when you truly transcend time,
When you truly do look upon your brother,
Your world, and yourself, without a past,
Without separation of cause and effect,
You shall simply realize that God IS, your brother IS, I AM—
And that all of them are the same.
When you simply realize that,
There shall be such a power in your experience of that truth

That in your life, you shall be completely free of any fear
Of what your brother or yourself or God might do.
There is such power in that truth itself
That you will never be the same.

When once, for an instant—in the holy instant—
You have transcended time,
When you have transcended the false belief
That cause and effect are separate,
You will find such power in that truth
That never again shall you look upon
The world, your brother, yourself, or God,
With the same eyes.
When that happens, you will realize
That you have experienced time
Through the presence of the Holy Spirit within your being.
You will realize that you have experienced THIS MOMENT
In conjunction with the presence of the Holy Spirit within you.
And you will realize that, in the absence of time,
There is truly no difference, no separation at all,
Between you and your brother, you and your sister,
You and your world, and above all,
Between you and God.

And the truth that you shall find in the holy instant
Is the truth that has always been—
That there is not, and could never be,
Any separation, any difference, between you and God.
For you are, and must remain, His beloved Son,
One with Him.

My blessings upon you all. That is all.

LEARNING THE HOLY INSTANT

Greetings again. I am Jeshua.
I have told you that one of the most difficult things
You have to learn is that it does not take time
To learn this Course.
We are speaking of the holy instant,
In which truth becomes yours,
In which truth simply becomes what you ARE.
And I have told you that your belief in time
Is what allows you to believe in illusion,
The illusion of separation.

So what if you find yourself believing
That it DOES take time to learn this Course?
What if you find yourself believing that time must pass
Before you can discover the truth of what you are?
What if you find yourself believing it takes time
To discover the beauty and the truth
Of what your brother, your sister, is?
If you believe it takes time to learn this Course,
Then you are but perpetrating the belief in separation
Which I described to you last time.
For if you feel that there is a separation
Between cause and effect,
Between some event which would set you free
And its effect, the result, which is your learning of this Course,
Then you are believing in separation.

And I have told you that the Atonement
Does take place IN time, but it is not FOR time.
It takes place in time, because IN TIME is where it is needed.
It is in time where separation seems to be real.
If the Atonement were FOR time,
That would mean that time would be substantiated by,
Time would be benefited by, the Atonement itself.
And the truth is that the Atonement obliterates time itself.
For when the experience of the Atonement is yours,
You will have transcended time.

That does not require that, in your world here,
You no longer see clocks ticking on your wall.
It does not require that you no longer make appointments
With people who walk this earth with you,
That you have total neglect for being "on time."
But the Atonement does require that you experience
Cause and effect as one,
And that the past, as the imagined cause
For what you and your brother are,
Dissolve into the nothingness that it is.

It is NOT POSSIBLE that it take time to learn this Course.
For if learning this Course demanded time,
That would mean that you would have
To have done something in the past
Which would have brought you to this place in the present
Wherein you discover your freedom.
And that notion demands the belief in separation.

So when you believe that it takes time to learn this Course,
Realize that what you are doing is believing in littleness.
And littleness, as I have told you, is the opposite of magnitude,
The opposite of what you ARE.
Littleness is that which you have seemed to give yourself.
Littleness is that which seems to substantiate the ego,
And space and time and illusion.
But above all, littleness is that which causes you to believe
That you, ego, separate, isolated being,
Have, within that imagined state of separation, power.
Littleness is the illusion, the false belief,
That you can DO something, can DO anything,
Can create something, can create ANYTHING,
Out of yourself.

Magnitude arises out of the awareness that you are One—
That you are One with God, One with the Holy Spirit,
One with all beings who walk this earth with you.
And it is most important that you be vigilant against littleness.
It is most important that you constantly watch your thoughts
And be aware of the ones
Which would speak to you of separation,
Of being different from your brothers,
And from God.

Those thoughts are examples of littleness,
Examples of that which you would give yourself
In order to maintain and sustain
Your belief in yourself as ego, as a separate, isolated being.

If you would truly discover your own magnitude,
It demands, as always, that you discover it in your brother.
If you would desire to sense your own magnitude
And yet somehow perceive your brother's littleness,
I promise you, you are misperceiving
What you call your magnitude.
For you are but choosing littleness
For yourself and your brother.
When you see your brother in magnitude,
You see him, as I have told you, without a past,
Without the presence of separation,
Without the belief that a cause from the past
Could have any effect on what he is in the present.

Hear me well.
If you deign to see your brother as ignorant of the truth,
If you deign to see your brother as being in need of salvation,
If you deign to see your brother
As being in need of your guidance and your wisdom,
You are but seeing littleness in your brother,
And proving to yourself that you believe
That that same littleness yet abides in you.

We are speaking about the holy instant.
We are speaking about discovering the present,
Which is the experience of cause and effect becoming one,
Beyond separation of any kind.
And if you would learn to experience the holy instant,
If you would practice here in space and time,
In order to learn this Course,
In order to experience the Atonement,
There are some guidelines I can give you.

First, it is most important, as I have just said,
That you not believe in littleness,
In yourself or in your brother.
What that means is that you make no attempt
To preserve your own plan.

What does it mean to have "your own plan"?
Your plan is one which you would seem to hold unto yourself,
And which some other being, even one, would not be aware of.
If you would see your brother in need of salvation,
Then you are believing that you hold
An awareness within yourself
That your brother does not have.
It is most important that you realize the truth
Of what I am saying to you with these words.
For this is one of the most subtle traps
You can find yourself caught in
As you seek for the holy instant and the Atonement
In your life.
The Atonement demands that you see your brother
In his perfection, in his magnitude.
And It demands that you see yourself the same way.

Now if you would understand more clearly the holy instant,
That point in your time which transcends time,
Which transcends the belief that cause and effect are separate—
If you would understand, and therefore experience,
The holy instant,
You must realize that the holy instant
Is a moment in which there is perfect communication,
Perfect communication to give and to receive.
Now I have told you that communication
Is something that you give. Do you recall?
And when you give communication,
What you give is perfect freedom to your brother
To be, to say, to think, to feel, whatever he will,
In the knowledge that he is fully accepted in your sight,
In your awareness, and in your experience.

Perfect communication demands
That one accept EVERYTHING about his brother.
And what does that mean, as well?
It means that perfect communication demands
That you see nothing you would change.
For I have already told you this day,
That if you would look upon your brother
And see that he is in need of anything,
You are but projecting upon him littleness,
Which MUST BE your belief in your own littleness.

Perfect and open communication
Simply involves the acceptance, without exception,
Of every aspect of life,
Including life as it appears here
In the illusion of space and time.

Perfect communication demands that,
As you look at the magnitude of your brother,
You be able to see it
Even through the disguise that space and time
Would seem to put across your brother's face, like a veil.
Perfect communication demands that you open to his being
And have no desire to change anything,
Even here within space and time.

Hear me well.
It is so easy for you to get caught in the trap
Of believing that communication is about words.
And I tell you, it is not at all about words.
If you read these pages and only hear words
Which you would process with academic understanding,
You are blocking any possibility for communication
To become open within you.

If you would experience the holy instant,
If you would open to complete and perfect communication,
What does that mean?
It means that you become willing
To let go of any barriers, any blocks you would hold,
To the openness of that communication.
It means there is nothing you would hold onto,
Nothing you would keep unto yourself.
For that desire must block communication.
Therefore, do you keep secrets from your brother
Who seems to be separate from you?
Of course not.
That is only illusion.
If there are any secrets that you would keep,
It must be FROM YOURSELF that you would keep them.

If there are any secrets that you would keep unto yourself,
That simply means that you are holding onto
Aspects of your own littleness, aspects of your own ego,

Which you are not willing to give to the Holy Spirit,
Which you are not willing to trade for the peace of God.
What form does that take?
The form is myriad.
Anything that you would hold onto,
Which would preserve your own sense of identity,
Your own sense of self, your own sense of ego,
Is a block to open communication.
It is a block that shall keep you
From the experience of the holy instant.
And that is what preserves for you
Your belief in time, your belief in separation itself.

So as you would desire to experience the peace of God,
To experience the holy instant,
Then look within for any thoughts you would harbor
Whose purpose is to preserve your awareness of who you are.
If you see yourself as a teacher of God
Who needs to help your brothers who are lost,
Do you see the separation involved?
If you see yourself as one who needs to defend himself
From a brother who might harm you,
If you see yourself as one who wishes to preserve his own life,
Even if against a brother,
What you are doing is holding unto yourself
Blocks to communication.
And thus you are not willing to open to the holy instant,
To open to the awareness of what you are,
And to open to the peace of God.

What it demands to be willing
To open to perfect communication
Is for you to open to the willingness to see no difference
Between your brother's will and your own.
From within the thought frame of the ego,
YOU CANNOT DO THAT.
You cannot sit as an ego, isolated and alone,
And discover perfect communication, the holy instant,
And the peace of God.

Communication demands that you turn over to the Holy Spirit
Every interpretation you would make of your brother.
You will be able to tell that you have done that

When all that you experience is your willingness
To accept everything about your brother,
Your willingness to desire to change nothing about him,
Your willingness to see every thought, every word,
Every action, even in space and time,
As an expression of Love.
And as you become willing to open to that,
The Holy Spirit will take over and guide you
Unto the awareness that that is exactly the case.

And what is demanded of you
That you be able to hear the Holy Spirit
Speak of the magnitude, the perfection,
And the love that lies within your brother?
It takes your willingness to look upon him without a past.
It takes your willingness to let your vision of him
Literally transcend time.
It takes your willingness to realize
That your brother, this instant,
Is perfect and pure and clean, exactly as he has always been.
It takes your willingness to realize that any belief in the past
As a cause for your brother being what or who he is
Is but a myth, a false belief that you have made up
For the purpose of believing in separation,
For the purpose of pretending
That you and your brother are egos,
Beings isolated and alone, apart from God.

So it does not take time to learn this Course
It CAN NOT take time to learn this Course.
For time is what causes you to believe in your brother's past.
And within that belief,
You cannot discover the truth of what he is.
But as you release the past, and time itself,
You can discover the magnitude of what your brother is,
And of what you are.
You will discover that by letting go of any design you have
To define and to structure life here.
You will find it by simply opening to the willingness
To let communication be what it is,
Realizing that communication is the connection
That makes you One with your brother and all of life.

And you will realize that in communication
There is nothing you would change,
Nothing you would not accept.
Because as you experience the vision
Of your brother's perfection,
How could there be anything that you would wish to change,
Or that you would not wish to accept with rejoicing?
And so as you would open to the holy instant,
And to perfect communication,
Be vigilant for any thoughts that would seem to isolate you,
That would seem to speak to you of separation,
Even the thoughts which would prompt you
To judge your brother as being
In need of your guidance and your help.
Then let those thoughts go,
And turn them over to the Holy Spirit.

In your willingness to do that
You shall release, for yourself,
The barriers to communication.
You shall become aware of the Oneness
You share with your brother.
You shall become aware of the magnitude of what he is.
And then you shall become aware of
The magnitude of what YOU are—
You shall discover the beauty, the perfection, the love,
That is what you are,
And which can only be so in the absence
Of what you call the past.
For the past is but a myth that would cause you
To desire to change your brother,
To see him differently from what he is,
And to change yourself from what you are.

My blessings upon you all. That is all.

RELATIONSHIPS AND THE HOLY INSTANT

Greetings again. I am Jeshua.
I have been speaking with you about the holy instant.
For the holy instant is that place in time which transcends time,
The place in which you can and must
Discover the meaning and the experience of Love.

It is not possible for you, here in space and time,
Here in this world of illusion,
To understand Love, to experience Love,
Except that you experience it within the holy instant.
And I have told you that this instant is the point in time
In which the past is gone, and with it guilt,
And with it the belief in separation.
For it is the instant in which cause and effect,
In your awareness, once again become one.

Cause and effect have never been separate.
For nothing is separate in God's world
And the Kingdom of Heaven.
They but seem to be separate here
In your false world of space and time.

Today I speak of special relationships and the holy instant.
And I tell you that in the holy instant
Special relationships do not, and cannot, exist.
Special relationships are figments of the imagination
Which require a belief in the reality of space,
And, above all, time.
All of you have formed special relationships.
And in the forming of those special relationships
You invite, or re-invite, guilt into your life.
And in inviting guilt you destroy peace,
And block your awareness of the presence of Love.

I have spoken of the ego so many times.
And what I tell you now is most important.

In the absence of the special relationship,
The ego does not, and cannot, exist.
For the ego is the set of beliefs you have, in space and time,
About who you are.
And in order to discern, to imagine, who you are,
You look outside yourself for some cause
That shall define your self for you.
And in so doing, you believe in separation itself.

Have you ever wondered, what does it require
That one look outside one's self in order to discover who he is?
What it requires is the belief that you are not whole,
That you are incomplete,
And that you are not One.
Not One with what?
That you are not One with all of life, with your brothers,
And above all, with God.
So if you would DEFINE who you are,
Which is to make the ego, which is to seem to make your self,
If you would do that, you must first believe
That you are not whole, that you are incomplete.
Only then CAN YOU look outside yourself.

Ah, but what IS outside yourself?
The answer is—nothing.
It is a truth of the universe that
Nothing exists outside of your Self.
For your Self is All That Is,
Just as God with Whom you are One,
Is likewise All That Is.
And so if you would look outside yourself,
What must you do, since there is nothing there?
You must project that which you would choose to see.
And then in your perception, you see it, of course.

So as you look at your brother,
You do not see your brother at all.
What you see is what you have projected,
What you have desired that your brother be FOR YOU.
And in special relationships what you do is pick, literally,
A conglomerate of your projections,
Picking one part from one projection, one part from another,
And another, and another.

And those parts you then attempt
To weave into an image
That looks like a composite whole.

And so you select ASPECTS of relationships,
But which are really nothing but aspects you CHOOSE
Out of that which you have projected
Upon the image of many separate brothers.
You pick those aspects and attempt to weave them
Into a whole, which you then use to define what you are.
And thus if a brother seems to change,
It must be that you would change.
And thus you become aware, at a level deep within,
That there is no stability in who you are,
That your very existence vacillates in space and time.
And you realize that in an instant it could disappear,
Which, within your belief in ego and space and time,
Means that you would die.
And thus you are afraid.

You cannot hold to a special relationship
Without the presence of guilt in your life,
And, above all, beyond that, without the presence of fear.
If you would escape from fear and guilt,
How can you do that as you look upon relationships?
As you let go of the demands
You would make upon your brother,
You find yourself able to enter the holy instant.
And why is that?
The only demand, regardless of the imagined form,
That you can place upon your brother is that
He seem to provide you with the image YOU WISH TO SEE,
The image that reflects to you who you are,
Which preserves your ego,
This false image of who you are
Of which I have been speaking.

And if you, in your time, can release your brother
From needing him to provide you
With the image of what you are,
Then you in truth, have set him free.
You set him free of the past.
But above all, you set yourself free of YOUR past.

For it is only in the past, as I have told you,
That you are able at all to define yourself
As a separate being with the separate needs
Which you wish to have met.
And without the past, such definition is not present,
And cannot be.

So if you would enter the holy instant, what do you do?
You offer your special relationships to the Holy Spirit,
Who will see them for you in a different light.
For you, ego, look upon relationships, always to say,
"What can I get? What can I receive?
Am I going to get and receive that which I desire?"
But if you will look upon relationships
From the viewpoint of the Holy Spirit,
If you will enter the holy instant with Him,
You will suddenly find yourself saying,
"In relationship, what can I give?"

And as you find yourself saying, "What can I give?"
Without concern for what you shall get,
You will realize that the only way
You can focus entirely upon what you shall give
Is to realize that you are, indeed,
Complete and whole in the first place.
And that, in simple statement,
Is the Holy Spirit's vision of what you are.
And that, in simple statement,
Is what the Holy Spirit would teach you—
Would teach you about Love, about your brother,
About these holy instants of which we speak,
About the truth and the laws of God.

So if you can enter the holy instant with the Holy Spirit,
Which you do by letting go of all demands
You would place upon your brother—
Realizing that the only demand you can place upon him
Is that he provide for you
The image you wish to see of who you are—
If you would let go of that and enter the holy instant,
You will discover there
Love and peace and truth,
The truth of God.

As you discover that, within the holy instant,
As you become aware of the truth of God,
What is it that you shall find?
You shall find one of the laws of God
Of which I have spoken before—
The simple law that Love extends.
Nowhere in the Mind of God, nowhere within truth,
Is there ANY concern about "What shall I get?"
Which is to say, nowhere within God
Is there the sense of lack and separation.
And so as you would enter the holy instant,
It must be within the truth of God, the laws of God,
The first one of which is that Love only extends Itself forever.
Thus you will find yourself saying, "What can I give?"

Remember, I have told you that miracles are not in competition,
And that one miracle does not preclude
The existence of another.
So it is with Love. So it is with God.
And so it is with the Son of God.
And I have reminded you that, even in your awareness,
You realize that ideas are not in competition.
There are many ideas within your awareness,
And they do not compete with each other.
And you realize in that same sense,
When you would open to the awareness of God,
When you would pray, if you will,
That you do not have a sense of anyone being excluded
From being able to communicate with God,
Or to receive answers.
And I have told you that is true because
God, like you, is but an idea.
Which is to say that you ARE mind, OF mind, and ONLY mind.
Which is also to say that you are Spirit, not a body.

So in the holy instant, as you would explore relationships,
You will realize that you ARE but an idea.
You are but mind exercising its creative power.
Thus there is no competition among relationships.
And so you become aware of
This second simple law of God—
You are Spirit.
You are mind.

You are an idea in the Mind of God.
And all of those are the same.
As you become aware of that truth,
You will look upon your relationships differently.
You will see every relationship as complete and whole.
You will realize that no relationship, in any sense,
Competes with any other.
It is only your insistence that you are a body,
Confined to space and to time,
That would cause you to believe
That relationships are in competition.
And I tell you it is not so.

And you will discover that it is not so
As you enter the holy instant,
As you let yourself be guided by the Holy Spirit,
Unto the presence of Love Itself.
And thus you will become aware of the truth of God.
If you would free yourself from the limitations of this world,
If you would free yourself of ego, of guilt, and of fear,
And therefore free yourself from the absence of peace,
You shall do it by opening your awareness
To the presence of Holy Spirit,
Who shall tell you, as many times as you need to hear it,
That you are not a body, that you are Spirit,
An idea in the mind of God—
Who shall tell you that there is no competition
In the world of spirit,
That all relationships blend
Into a beautiful, harmonious Oneness—
That there are no aspects which would seem to compete
And provide you with a PART of what you are.
For in looking at any relationship
Through the eyes of the Holy Spirit,
You CAN discover the entire truth of what you are,
The entire truth of what your brother is,
And the truth of God.

And as you discover that truth,
You shall become filled with the awareness
That there is nothing you need,
That there is nothing to receive that you do not already have,
That there is nothing "out there" which can in any sense

Make you what you are—
Or beyond that, that there is nothing "out there"
Which can in any sense, or in any way,
Change the truth of what you are.

And thus you will find yourself beyond threat.
You will realize the invulnerability
Of which I have spoken so many times.
And in the awareness that you ARE
Complete and whole and invulnerable,
You will realize in that instant, that holy instant,
That there is nothing to receive at all,
And that all you would do is give,
That all you would do is extend that which you are.

For that which you ARE cannot be contained, cannot be limited,
And seeks only to express its creative power through extension,
Which you could call giving, if you will.
And as you free yourself of form
And the belief in that which would cause you
To exist as form, as a body—
As you free yourself of that,
You shall find yourself in the holy instant.
And there you shall find yourself, without effort,
Desiring only to extend,
To extend the Love of God, the peace of God.
And you shall find yourself experiencing the joy of God,
Which always comes from extending that self-same Love,
Which all along has been, and remains,
Exactly what you are.

My blessings upon you all. That is all.

BEYOND THE EGO

Greetings again. I am Jeshua.
I have come this day to further, with you,
My discussion of *A Course in Miracles*.

I would speak with you, once again this day,
About the ego, and the ego's false, mistaken idea of love.
I have told you that the ego cannot exist
Without the presence of the special relationship.
And I have told you that special relationships
Are based upon guilt,
Which ultimately is based on your belief in time,
Which is based on your belief that
Cause and effect can be separate,
That ANYTHING can be separate—
And that ultimately all of that
Is based on your belief that someone "out there,"
Different from yourself,
Has the power to determine who you are.

All special relationships have fear at their heart.
And the fear is always the same—it is the fear of death.
For when you, in a relationship, special though it be,
Sense that you are incomplete, that you are lacking,
And then look outside yourself for completion,
What you do in this imagined scenario
Is seem to give to another, literally,
The power to determine who you are.
And therefore it follows that you have seemed
To give to another the power
To even determine whether you ARE or not.
And, therefore, you have seemed to give to another
The power to determine whether you live or die

And thus you live, here in space and time,
With the constant fear of death.
And death, under this scenario, is not up to you.
It is up to whoever outside yourself determines who you are,
And whether you exist or not.
In the sense of the ego, in your day-to-day living,

You literally place your fears and your struggles
In the hands of your brother.
And thus you always are wont to blame another
For your misfortunes,
AND for your happiness.

In general, you do not assign to your brother
The right to determine whether you physically live or die.
Therefore you assign that to God.
And God becomes like your brother—
A capricious being who, in a moment,
And based upon apparent whim,
Can decide to snuff out your life,
Or the life of one of your loved ones.
And you are left frustrated and alone,
Trying to say that it is God's Will,
And trying to believe that it must be Love.

For do you not realize that Love is the essence of life?
And yes, of course, you do.
In fact, as you look at your brother, your sister,
And seem to receive from him or her
That which you imagine to make you complete,
You are wont to call that love, and to say,
"Ah, he loves me. She loves me."
But then you must live in the fear that, in a moment,
That same love will be taken away,
And you will no longer be complete.
You live in the fear that you will suddenly be left alone,
Which ultimately is the essence of your guilt, as I have told you.

But also in your relationships, you realize that
You have the same power over your brother's completion,
Over whether HE would live or die and be happy.
And thus both of you look at the other and say,
"I need you to complete me."
Which is to say, "I need your love."
So you believe that you NEED your brother's love.
But you realize that your brother needs yours, as well.
And thus love becomes a bargaining, does it not?
"If you will give me what completes me,
Then I will give you what completes you.
And we can both seem to be happy."

And what the ego does is call that scenario ''being in love.''
And this you have all experienced here in your space and time.
But as soon as you realize that there is a power ''out there,''
To which you have chosen to give the right to destroy you,
Then suddenly you must need to protect yourself
Against the loss of love, if you will.
And so in your closest relationships, you think of being in love.
Yet even that can change and ebb and flow,
And in a moment, on a whim,
Leave you alone and sad in your tears.
And this you also know, those of you who walk this earth,
And who have formed special relationships.

But what of those beings whom you do not know so well,
And who would perhaps not be willing
To be ''in love'' with you?
What of those beings whom you would seem
Not to like very much?
They still, by your design, have the power to destroy you.
Do you see?
And so what you do then is realize that,
In your power to destroy them,
IT IS IMPERATIVE THAT YOU ATTACK,
That you be on the offensive.
You realize that it is imperative that you
Give in sufficient measure
That your brother will not deign to destroy you.
And you still delude yourself into thinking
That this is love.

And so what you do is try to structure scenarios
In which you give to your brother, ultimately,
A THREAT which you try to call love.
And thus you try to maintain peace in your world
By having bigger armies, better guns,
More sophisticated missiles and bombs.
And you say that your goal is peace.
And ultimately what you are giving to your brother
Is a threat so great that you can believe
That he will not exercise his power to destroy you.
Do you see?

Ah, but as you evolve in your humanness,
As you take this inexorable path
Back to the awareness of what you are—
Which is the awareness of Love
And the awareness of God—
And whether you take that path
Through this Course in Miracles or not—
You come to the point where you cannot tolerate
The belief that attack is actually love.
For you realize that it is not love at all.
And yet you remain an ego.

And so what you attempt to do then
Is to be in love with your world.
And thus you would extend, not attack, but love.
And how does that play itself out here in your world?
If you would choose not to attack, not to have a bigger dog,
Or a bigger gun, or a bigger bomb,
Then what you do is believe that BY GIVING LOVE
You can control your brother.
YOU BELIEVE THAT THE WEAPON OF LOVE
WILL MAKE YOU SAFE.
And all the while you live in the fear that remains—
Because you have given your brother
The imagined power to destroy you,
Because you still believe that he determines what you are.

And so you come to believe that if you would give enough love,
Your brother will be influenced by that love,
And somehow then feel obligated to respond with love.
And love, of course, is always what you want to receive,
What you perceive will complete yourself.
And always at the back of this is the hidden realization
That the relationship is founded on fear.

And thus, there is no special relationship,
No relationship based on the imagined love of which I speak,
No ego relationship, if you will,
THAT IS NOT BASED UPON ANGER.
For you are angry at your brother, whom you deign to love.
This is true without exception,
While the relationship remains special.

"Well, what is anger?" you might ask.
I have told you there are but two emotions—love and fear.
Anger is but a subtle form of fear.
Anger is fear when you apply it to the arena
Of your own life and death
At the hands of your brother.
For when you, through your belief
In separation and time and specialness,
Give your brother, or EVEN GOD, the right to destroy you,
By believing that you are incomplete—
When you give your brother the right to destroy you,
And realize that he MIGHT do so,
You must live in fear.
And this fear expresses itself as anger.

And at the heart of every special relationship is this same anger.
So what you do is attempt to give love,
Which is not love at all,
Which is but that which you would bargain with—
You would give love to your brother
In order to generate within him guilt,
Or to generate within him a response
That would cause him to love you in return.
And yet you know it is not really love.
And thus you are angry at your brother
Who still has the power to destroy you.
And you are angry at yourself—angry at yourself, yes!—
For NEEDING another, for having given to another
The power to destroy you.

For deep within, you sense that you must be eternal,
And that no being should have the power to destroy you.
And you are right, of course.
And so what you do in your search for love,
While you yet believe in your weakness, in your littleness,
Is come to believe that SACRIFICE will bring you love.
And thus you choose to give
THAT WHICH YOU DO NOT WISH TO GIVE AT ALL,
Calling it love, for the purpose of receiving
That which your brother does not wish to give at all,
And yet which you would delude yourself
Into believing is love.

As you look at this scenario of the ego,
Are you not wont to ask at once, "Why?
Why would I persist in believing in such a thought system,
Based upon a love which is not love at all?"
And as I have told you, it is most important
That, as an ego, you NOT REALIZE that IT IS NOT LOVE.
So think carefully about my words,
Until you can realize the exact nature
Of the special love relationship of the ego.

Well, how can that function here in space and time?
The notion of ANGER which you would call love,
This FEAR which you would call love,
This SACRIFICE which you could call love,
How can you abide this within your mind?
And the only way you can abide this within your mind
Is to believe that your mind is not free.
And that means to believe that you are a body,
That you are a body which has autonomy,
And which lives of itself, INDEPENDENT of your mind,
Independent of your awareness, and your thoughts.

And thus love becomes an exercise in the control of bodies.
And as you well know, you smile and say to a beloved,
"Look, but don't touch."
And what you mean is this—
My concern is for what you do with your body,
Not what you think and feel,
Not with the reality of your inner experience.
Do you see?
And so you play out a scenario in which
You would ask for ACTIONS that bodies perform,
In which you would ask for the exercise IN FORM,
Which you then try to believe is an expression of love.
And yet, throughout it all, you realize that your mind IS free,
And that your mind is the essence behind it all.

You know full well that anyone, including yourself,
Can, with a body, perform acts that you call acts of love,
And yet not feel love at all throughout the process.
And you have people who choose to live that way
To earn their livelihood.
In part, they do this for the purpose of reminding you

That it is not about bodies at all.
It is a lesson they understand full well,
And which many of you have not yet learned. Do you see?

Ah, but what if you can look upon this entire scenario,
And open for a moment to the realization
That it is NOT about love?
Then where should you look for love?
And as always, the answer is that
YOU SHALL FIND LOVE IN COMMUNICATION.
For communication is joining with another mind.
Ultimately real communication is joining with other minds
So fully that you realize that there are not other minds at all—
But that there is but one Mind,
One Mind which encompasses all of Creation,
And which is All That Is, which ultimately is God.

And so if you would discover Love in relationship,
There is only one relationship within which
You can learn the nature of Love, the nature of God,
And the nature of what you are.
And that, as I have told you, is your relationship with God.
But that is the SAME as your relationship
With your brother, and with yourself.
And the key to that relationship is the awareness
That minds, the essence of what you are, are joined.
For in joining, there is no bargaining for love.
There is no incompleteness.
For all beings ARE the Oneness of All That Is.
And no one can possibly need anything.
And in the absence of need, there is no fear.
And there cannot be anger.
And sacrifice becomes incomprehensible. Do you see?
Those are the gifts, the gifts of Love.

And thus if you would discover the one real relationship,
Even here in your space and time,
How can you do that?
By realizing that the only valid purpose for your body
Is that it serve as a means of communication.
This ultimately means that it serve ONLY
As a means of joining with your brothers.
Remember that the ego always says,

"What can I get? What can I receive?"
And the Holy Spirit says, "What can I give
Out of the completeness of what I am?"

And so the key to allowing your body
To become nothing but a means of communication,
Is to release it from all value,
And especially to release yourself from the belief
That your body can gain you anything.
The key is ultimately to realize that
THIS ENTIRE WORLD cannot gain you anything.
When you realize that, you shall be free of the body,
Even though, for a while, you will yet seem to walk around
Having the appearance of a body to your brothers.

And where is the place
Wherein you can experience this communication?
THAT PLACE IS THE HOLY INSTANT.
For that is what I have been speaking of, is it not?
The holy instant.
And what do you discover in the holy instant?
You discover the absence of separation, the absence of time,
The absence of the past,
And therefore the absence of any being outside yourself,
Including God,
And the absence of any being
Who has control over your existence.
And therefore, you discover the absence of fear,
And with it, the absence of anger.
All of this is to be found in the holy instant.

I have told you that
Beyond the attraction of the special relationship
Lies the attraction of God.
And it is in the holy instant where the attraction of God
Shall become apparent to you.
For it is in that instant that your brother ceases to be a body.
He ceases to be a body because
YOU have no concern with the body at all.
You have no concern with what his body can give you
To fulfill your imagined needs,
Because the imagined needs have disappeared.

And in this holy instant what you shall see is a being of Light.
In the holy instant you shall see the Great Rays
Representing your brother, extending unto forever, unto Love.
And you shall realize that your brother is not a body at all.
You will experience him as a being of Light.
And in that same holy instant you shall realize
That you, too, are a being of Light,
And that God Itself is a being of Light—
All these beings, complete and whole,
Whose only passion is to extend outward the Love
Which is their reality and their essence.
And yet they do this as One.
And ultimately all these beings of Light
Discover that they are completely free.
For, as I have told you, freedom is the essence of Love.

And so if you would enter the holy instant,
First let yourself look upon the ego's scenario of love.
Look upon it only long enough to realize
That you do not want it.
And then choose to allow the Holy Spirit
To bring you a new vision,
A vision in which your relationship is One,
Just as all of life is One.
In that vision, you will discover a relationship
In which you are drawn to God Itself,
To Love itself, to truth itself,
And ultimately to infinite and perfect peace.
For that peace is the gift that you receive from your brother,
In his completion and his wholeness,
Because it was, without effort,
The gift YOU GAVE to your brother
In your own completion and your own wholeness.
And all of it arose out of the awareness
That perfect Love is what you are.

My blessings upon you all. That is all.

THE TIME OF CHRIST

Greetings again. I am Jeshua.
And I have come this day to further, with you,
My discussion of *A Course in Miracles*.

I have been speaking to you of the holy instant.
And the holy instant seems to speak of time, does it not?
In reality, in eternity, there is no time.
There is no season.
About this you can rejoice.
But within this illusion of space and time, mostly time,
We do speak of time and season.

And the Holy Spirit, as I have told you,
Can use time and season for His purpose,
Which is always to bring to you, to bring to your experience,
To make part of what you are,
The meaning and the awareness of Love.

I would speak with you this day about the Time of Christ.
When I first gave you *A Course in Miracles*,
I gave material during what you call Christmas time.
And I spoke about your learning to celebrate
My birth into the world.
And I told you that you really do not know how to do that.
So I would speak with you about Christmas, if you will.
But really, you can call Christmas the Time of Christ.
For Christmas does not know of season,
And does not even know of time.
And indeed, the Time of Christ of which I shall speak
Is truly beyond time.

And I have told you that the holy instant is actually
The perfect measure of the Time of Christ.
The holy instant is a time in which
The Son of God finds himself free of the past,
And therefore of all measure of guilt in his life.
In the holy instant, in the Time of Christ,
The Son of God comes to realize that he is truly free.
In the Time of Christ, the holy Son of God
Comes to realize what is the real gift

That I came into this world to bring to him.
And you are, of course, the holy Son of God.
So in the holy instant, the Time of Christ,
You shall become aware of the gift
That I came to bring to you.

It is important that you realize that I came to GIVE.
For that is all that one can do, in truth.
There is only Love.
And Love is extension, a pouring out.
I came to give to you the gift of Christmas,
The gift of the Time of Christ,
The gift of the awareness of Love.

But I could not give to you that which I do not already have.
And if you would GIVE BACK to me,
It is not possible that I can receive from you
Anything which I have not already given.
If it were possible for me to receive from you
That which I do not have,
Or for you to receive from me what you do not have,
That would demand separation. Do you see?
And what is the fundamental message I bring to you?
THERE IS NO SEPARATION.
Separation is your only and fundamental problem,
The basic misperception that allows
All of this illusion to seem to be.
And thus I have said to you,
The gift of union is the only gift I came to give.

I would speak with you this day about sacrifice.
I would speak with you about being
Host to God, or hostage to the ego.
I would speak with you about your great illusion,
That you can be host to the ego, or hostage to God.
And I would speak with you about your belief
That your only choices here, in this world of illusion, are those.
Shall I be host to the ego, or shall I be hostage to God?

Do you see that in your belief in separation,
In your belief in beings with wills different from your own,
Be it your brother's will, or God's Will—
Do you see that in that belief system

It seems that there are those who give, and those who receive.
And I have told you that the fundamental nature of guilt
Is based upon the notion of separation itself.
But more than that, it is based upon the belief
That someone else, your brother, or God, if you will,
Determines who and what you are.
And this makes you seem to be the victim.

There is another way to say that,
That you believe yourself to be victim.
And it is that you believe yourself to be hostage.
And I have told you that you believe
It is possible to be hostage to God,
And that that is one of your basic choices—
Shall I be host to the ego, or hostage to God?
And I would tell you now, in clear words,
One of the fundamental beliefs
Of the thought system of the ego—
If there is a host, there MUST BE a hostage.
If God is host to you, then your belief demands
That you are the hostage of God.
If you are host to the ego, then your thought system demands
That the ego be hostage to you.

Well, what does it means to be host, and hostage?
What if God IS host to you?
When you are host to another being,
That being, as you think of it, stays with you, lives with you,
Relies on you for sustenance,
And indeed, in a sense, for existence itself.
And that is your understanding of what it means to be host.
If God is host to you, then you, literally,
Depend upon God for your existence.

Ah, what if you are host to the ego?
Then that means that the ego, its existence, depends upon you.
And without you, the ego could not exist.
What if you take that notion of host
And blend it with your belief in separation?
If God is host to you, then you are hostage to God.
And what does that mean?
That means that you look upon God
To and for your very existence.

And that you believe, do you not?
That somehow God could,
In the twinkling of an eye, obliterate you.
For such is the infinite power of God.
If you are host to the ego, and the ego is hostage to you,
Then the ego depends upon you for its existence.
And in this world of perceived guilt,
I have already told you that you believe that God,
Your brother, your sister, beings outside of yourself,
Give you the gifts that determine who and what you are.
So do you see?
You have ascribed to God, to your brothers,
To those outside of you, the role of host.
And thus you become hostage.

And so, in your belief in separation,
You see yourself as hostage to God,
As hostage to your brother
Who seems to be separate from you.
And if you would be host to the ego,
What does that seem to be to you?
That seems to be to you that you have, from within yourself,
The power to make your own existence.
And this you desire to believe, of course.
You desire to believe that you are free,
That you are in control of your own life.
And if you believe that you are host to ego,
And see yourself as ego, then you, in some sense,
Can believe yourself to be free.

But within that context you are bound
To look outside yourself to discern who you are.
Do you see the conflict?
Do you see the insanity of this scenario?
Your belief in separation, your guilt,
Demands that your brother can tell you who you are.
And yet your belief that you can be host to the ego
Causes you to believe that YOU can determine who you are.
And is it not true, that in your world
Of space and time and separation, this world of illusion,
You have mixed feelings, feelings that say—
I do not need the rest of the world.
I am the captain of my own soul.

I determine my own existence.
And yet, at the same time, you realize how much,
How desperately, you need relationship,
How much you need to be loved.

And thus you seek for relationships which seem to reflect to you
That which you want to believe about yourself.
You look for relationships which will be but a mirror
To show you an image of who you are,
Which image you already hold.
You choose relationships which simply confirm
What you believe to be your own choice of who you are—
When in truth, it does not work that way at all.

And these, in one sense,
Are the relationships which I call special.
Well, what of these relationships
Which seem to tell you who you are?
You find yourself needing a gift from your brother.
And the gift you would receive
Is simply the CONFIRMATION of who you are,
Which ultimately represents for you your existence itself.
And so you look outside yourself at your brother,
And ask HIM to give YOU the gift of YOUR OWN life.
And your brother does the same for you.
And in your special relationships,
You try to choose those brothers
Who will tell you what you want to hear,
So you can believe of yourself
What you so desperately wish to believe—
And that is that you are loved,
AND that you are free.

And now comes the scenario of giving
Within the world of the ego.
For what you do is believe that you give love,
When what you are really doing is offering to your brother
What you believe he needs to hear in exchange, if you will,
For his giving back to you your life itself,
Which is represented by what you wish to hear.
And what you do, whether you know it or not,
Is give to your brothers, give to God,
For the PURPOSE OF RECEIVING.

I have spoken to you about sacrifice.
And I told you the Time of Christ is the end of sacrifice.
Do you know what sacrifice is?
In simple definition, A SACRIFICE IS A GIFT
WHICH YOU GIVE FOR THE PURPOSE OF RECEIVING.
A sacrifice is a gift you give, which you BELIEVE to be love,
But which you give for the purpose of BEING loved,
For the purpose of receiving love.

And in your scenario of space and time and separation,
You believe that if there is host, there must be hostage.
And the hostage depends upon another for his existence.
And the hostage is therefore BOUND to offer gifts,
To offer sacrifices—do you see—to the host,
In order to receive what he believes to be love.
But really he gives in order to receive his ego, his self-image,
His EXISTENCE itself as he understands it.

You believe it must be so that
If there is host, there must be hostage.
If there is one who gives, there must be one who receives.
And the giver loses something,
Which the receiver then takes unto himself.
And you see, once again,
Even as you play out your struggle for love—
You but foster your belief in separation.
Thus I have told you that sacrifice speaks of separation.
And sacrifice literally decries love.
Do you see now what I mean?

There are only love and fear, two emotions.
But fear is not real, and does not exist.
And what does love do? Love extends.
Love gives, and gives, and gives . . .
Always the flow is in one direction, outward,
Arising from the infinite fullness of what one is.
And this is what I call extension.

Love gives.
Sacrifice PRETENDS to give,
Out of a sense of desperate need.
Sacrifice pretends to love for the purpose
Of being allowed to exist.

You believe yourself, within this world,
To be hostage to your brothers.
For you believe your brothers make you what you are,
That they form your self-image, your ego,
This false collection of thoughts you have about what you are.
And it seems if your brother would betray you,
That, in some sense, part of you dies.
And you all know that experience so well,
In the playing out of your special relationships
Of which I have spoken,
And of which I will speak much more in the future.

You believe that God IS perfect Love.
But yet you believe there must be a hostage,
When God is host.
And you believe if God is your creator,
Then God is YOUR host.
And you are the hostage.
And if you would give a gift to God,
If you would give a gift to perfect Love
For the purpose of receiving that perfect Love,
Then what must be the gift that would warrant
The return of infinite Love, of everything?
The gift must be EVERYTHING.
And do you see, once again,
The struggle and the insanity with which you live?

You want so desperately to exist, and to feel free,
To feel that you are the creator of your own existence.
And yet, if you would be loved by God,
You must COMPLETELY give yourself to God.
And thus you feel that you must somehow cease to exist,
In order to keep existing.
Do you sense the conflict with which you live?
And so you speak in words, and say—
"I give my life to God.
I dedicate my every waking moment,
My every thought, to God.
I will be the perfect servant of God for all of my life."
And why do you say those words?
For the purpose of allowing yourself to believe
That you then become worthy of your host.
You allow yourself to believe

That you have given the ultimate sacrifice,
In order to receive the ultimate Love.

And what if God, in a whim, chooses not to love you?
All of you have struggled with that thought.
And thus you seem to tremble in the presence of God,
As you wonder if your sacrifice of yourself to God
Will be, or can be, enough to warrant His Love.

And I have come to tell you about the Time of Christ.
I have come to tell you about
My Christmas gift to you, if you will,
The gift I came to this world to bring you.
I told you I have come to bring you the gift of union—
And that the Time of Christ, the holy instant, is a time
In which the Son of God becomes aware of his perfect freedom.

What does it require for you to understand the Time of Christ?
What does it require for you to be able
To celebrate my birth into the world?
It takes this awareness—
It takes your understanding of this truth—
In the Kingdom of God, in the universe of reality,
THERE ARE NO HOSTAGES.

I have told you that I cannot receive from you
A gift which I have not already given.
If it were not so, we would not be One.
And the gift of union, of Oneness, is what I came to give.
And so, God gives infinite Love, which IS Himself,
Out of a fullness that leaves no room
For needing anything in return.
It is not possible for God, or for me,
Or for anyone who understands Love, to sacrifice.
For there is nothing to receive. Do you see?

So God IS host to you.
God IS host to me.
But, I am host to God.
And I am host to you.
Just as you are host to me.
And we are host to all brothers and sisters
Who have ever walked this sojourn through space and time.

For all that there is, is the fullness of life,
Which does not, and can not, need anything.

And if you would SACRIFICE,
If you would give to God the gift of your very life,
For the purpose of receiving God's Love,
YOU MUST BE ATTACKING GOD.
You must be calling Him incomplete and afraid,
Just as you perceive yourself to be,
But which God is not. Do you see?
God is not capable of receiving sacrifice.
And sacrifice is not love at all.
SACRIFICE IS ATTACK. Do you see?

And so if you would celebrate my birth into the world,
Open your heart to the realization of this simple truth—
Within the Kingdom of God there is only host,
And there are no hostages.
What does it take for you to realize that there are no hostages?
What it takes is for you to realize, in simplest truth,
That you are not a body.
For you believe, do you not,
If you perceive yourself to be a body, that you need . . .
Does it matter what you need? Of course not.
You need shelter. You need food.
You need money. You need warmth. You need clothing.
You need love. You need love. You need love,
All of which you need to allow yourself to believe
That you are a being separate from others,
But somehow still in control of your own life.
As long as you would perceive yourself to be a body,
You MUST believe in sacrifice,
And you CAN NOT, hear me well, understand Love.

When you take the step beyond that belief—
When you realize that your body
Is but a figment of imagination—
Then you realize that your reality is mind itself,
That minds are joined, that minds communicate,
Because there is no other option.
When you realize that minds are joined,
Then you realize that every thought,
Every gift of existence given by mind,

Blesses and enriches all beings.
And you realize that you, the giver of the gift,
Are enriched as well.
For that IS extension.

And so what it takes to realize that Love is extension
Is simply the realization that you are not a body.
And so if you would celebrate the Time of Christ,
If you would celebrate Christmas,
If you would celebrate my birth into the world,
Then be aware of the gift I came to give,
Which is the simple gift of Love.
I came to bring you the gift of Love which extends unto you
Perfect union, perfect communication, and perfect freedom,
Without exception, without any need or demand of any kind.
Were either of those present, it would no longer be Love.
It would have become sacrifice.

And what I brought to this world was
The Love of God to human form.
And that is the gift that I give to you.
That is my Christmas present to you—
A perfect Love which brings with it
No expectations, and no demands,
Nothing but perfect freedom.
And all that you have to do in order to understand,
And to receive that gift I have brought to you,
Is give it to your brothers
In exactly the same measure in which I give it to you.

And then we can truly celebrate my birth into the world.
We can truly celebrate the Time of Christ.
Because in the giving of this Love,
Without demand or expectation of any kind—
In the giving of this Love, one to another,
We realize that indeed, we are all One,
And that all of us are host to all of Life.
And we realize that all of us are One with,
And shall always remain, God.

My blessings upon you all. That is all.

APPENDIX I

Listing of the Chapters of the Text of *A Course in Miracles* which correspond to the Chapters of *The Other Voice*.

APPENDIX II

REFERENCES FROM A COURSE IN MIRACLES

References from *A Course in Miracles* are made using notation developed for use with the Second Edition of the Course. This will be explained using an example from both the Text and the Workbook. Using the same format, a student who owns the First Edition should be able to readily find the passage being referenced.

From the Text, the notation T-21.II. 3.4 refers to the Text, Chapter 21, Section II, Paragraph 3, Sentence 4: "No accident nor chance is possible within the universe as God created it, outside of which is nothing." From the Workbook, the notation W-pI.189. 7.5 refers to the Workbook, Part I, Lesson 189, Paragraph 7, Sentence 5: "Forget this world, forget this course, and come with wholly empty hands unto your God."

I am grateful to the Foundation for Inner Peace for allowing these references.

1.... W-pI.4 Heading
2.... W-pI.4. 2.3-3.1
3.... W-pI.10. 1.1-2
4.... W-pI.45. 1.1-5
5.... W-pI.15. 1.1-6
6.... T-3.IV. 2.1-2
7.... C.1. 7.1-5
8.... W-pI.131. 10.3
9.... T-21.II. 3.2-4
10.... Intro 1.1
11.... T-3.IV. 6.2
12.... T-9.I. 10.5
13.... W-pI.189. 7.1-5
14.... Other voice T-5.II.3.6
15.... T-2.VI. 7.5-8
16.... T-26.VII. 4.7
17.... Intro 2.3
18.... T-6.V.A. Heading
19.... T-6.V.B. Heading
20.... T-6.V.C. Heading
21.... T-9.VII 8.2
22.... T-11.IV. 4.1
23.... T-11.V. 13.1
24.... T-12.III. 2.6-7